Global Norms and Local Action

OXFORD STUDIES IN GENDER AND INTERNATIONAL RELATIONS

Series editors: J. Ann Tickner, American University, and Laura Sjoberg, University of Florida

Windows of Opportunity: How Women Seize Peace Negotiations for Political Change
Miriam J. Anderson

Women as Foreign Policy Leaders: National Security and Gender Politics in Superpower America
Sylvia Bashevkin

Gendered Citizenship: Understanding Gendered Violence in Democratic India
Natasha Behl

Enlisting Masculinity: The Construction of Gender in U.S. Military Recruiting Advertising during the All-Volunteer Force
Melissa T. Brown

The Politics of Gender Justice at the International Criminal Court: Legacies and Legitimacy
Louise Chappell

Cosmopolitan Sex Workers: Women and Migration in a Global City
Christine B. N. Chin

Intelligent Compassion: Feminist Critical Methodology in the Women's International League for Peace and Freedom
Catia Cecilia Confortini

Complicit Sisters: Gender and Women's Issues across North-South Divides
Sara de Jong

Gender and Private Security in Global Politics
Maya Eichler

This American Moment: A Feminist Christian Realist Intervention
Caron E. Gentry

Troubling Motherhood: Maternality in Global Politics
Lucy B. Hall, Anna L. Weissman, and Laura J. Shepherd

Breaking the Binaries in Security Studies: A Gendered Analysis of Women in Combat
Ayelet Harel-Shalev and Shir Daphna-Tekoah

Scandalous Economics: Gender and the Politics of Financial Crises
Aida A. Hozić and Jacqui True

Rewriting the Victim: Dramatization as Research in Thailand's Anti-Trafficking Movement
Erin M. Kamler

Equal Opportunity Peacekeeping: Women, Peace, and Security in Post-Conflict States
Sabrina Karim and Kyle Beardsley

Gender, Sex, and the Postnational Defense: Militarism and Peacekeeping
Annica Kronsell

The Beauty Trade: Youth, Gender, and Fashion Globalization
Angela B. V. McCracken

Rape Loot Pillage: The Political Economy of Sexual Violence in Armed Conflict
Sara Meger

From Global to Grassroots: The European Union, Transnational Advocacy, and Combating Violence against Women
Celeste Montoya

Who Is Worthy of Protection? Gender-Based Asylum and US Immigration Politics
Meghana Nayak

Revisiting Gendered States: Feminist Imaginings of the State in International Relations
Swati Parashar, J. Ann Tickner, and Jacqui True

Out of Time: The Queer Politics of Postcoloniality
Rahul Rao

Gender, UN Peacebuilding, and the Politics of Space: Locating Legitimacy
Laura J. Shepherd

A Feminist Voyage through International Relations
J. Ann Tickner

The Political Economy of Violence against Women
Jacqui True

Queer International Relations: Sovereignty, Sexuality and the Will to Knowledge
Cynthia Weber

Bodies of Violence: Theorizing Embodied Subjects in International Relations
Lauren B. Wilcox

Global Norms and Local Action

The Campaigns to End Violence against Women in Africa

PEACE A. MEDIE

OXFORD
UNIVERSITY PRESS

OXFORD
UNIVERSITY PRESS

Oxford University Press is a department of the University of Oxford. It furthers the University's objective of excellence in research, scholarship, and education by publishing worldwide. Oxford is a registered trade mark of Oxford University Press in the UK and certain other countries.

Published in the United States of America by Oxford University Press
198 Madison Avenue, New York, NY 10016, United States of America.

© Oxford University Press 2020

All rights reserved. No part of this publication may be reproduced, stored in a retrieval system, or transmitted, in any form or by any means, without the prior permission in writing of Oxford University Press, or as expressly permitted by law, by license, or under terms agreed with the appropriate reproduction rights organization. Inquiries concerning reproduction outside the scope of the above should be sent to the Rights Department, Oxford University Press, at the address above.

You must not circulate this work in any other form
and you must impose this same condition on any acquirer.

Library of Congress Control Number: 2019053082
ISBN 978-0-19-092296-2

1 3 5 7 9 8 6 4 2

Printed by Integrated Books International, United States of America

For Madam Mary L. Mills, my grandmother

Contents

List of Figures and Tables   ix
List of Abbreviations   xi
Acknowledgments   xiii

Introduction: How and Why Do States Implement International Women's Rights Norms?   1

PART I: THE DOMESTIC IMPLEMENTATION OF INTERNATIONAL NORMS

1. Violence against Women and Law Enforcement in Africa   17
2. The Domestic Implementation of International Women's Rights Norms   41

PART II: VIOLENCE AGAINST WOMEN IN LIBERIA AND CÔTE D'IVOIRE

3. Violence against Women in Liberia   53
4. The Response to Violence against Women in Liberia   73
5. Violence against Women in Côte d'Ivoire   89
6. The Response to Violence against Women in Côte d'Ivoire   109

PART III: NATIONAL AND STREET-LEVEL IMPLEMENTATION OF THE INTERNATIONAL WOMEN'S JUSTICE NORM

7. Establishment of the Specialized Units in Liberia and Côte d'Ivoire   123
8. Street-Level Implementation in Liberia and Côte d'Ivoire   163

Conclusion: Specialized Mechanisms and the Campaigns to End Violence against Women in Africa   192

Appendix 201
Notes 205
References 209
Index 227

Figures and Tables

Figures

I.1. The relationship between international norms and practices.   2

2.1. International pressure and the domestic implementation of international norms.   47

Tables

1.1. Specialized Criminal Justice Sector Mechanisms in Africa   35

7.1. Creation of Specialized Units   125

7.2. Institutionalization of Specialized Units   147

List of Abbreviations

AFELL	Association of Female Lawyers of Liberia
AFJCI	Association of Female Lawyers of Cote d'Ivoire
AFI	Association of Ivorian Women
AIDF	Ivorian Association for the Defence of Women's Rights
AU	African Union
CEDAW	Convention on the Elimination of all forms of Discrimination against Women
DANIDA	Danish International Development Agency
ECOWAS	Economic Community of West African States
GBV	Gender-Based Violence
IO	International Organization
IR	International Relations
IRC	International Rescue Committee
LNP	Liberia National Police
MoJ	Ministry of Justice
MoGD	Ministry of Gender and Development
MFFAS	Ministry of Family, Women, and Social Affairs
MSFFE	Ministry of Solidarity, Family, Women, and Children
NGO	Nongovernmental Organization
NTGL	National Transitional Government of Liberia
NTLA	National Transitional Legislative Assembly
ONEF	Organization for Children, Women, and Family
PDCI	Democratic Party of Côte d'Ivoire
UN	United Nations
UNICEF	United Nations Children Fund
UNMIL	United Nations Mission in Liberia
UNOCI	United Nations Mission in Côte d'Ivoire
UNPOL	United Nations Police
UNSC	United Nations Security Council
VAW	Violence against Women
WACPS	Women and Children Protection Section

Acknowledgments

This book has grown with me over many years. I began thinking about the themes of armed conflict, women, and violence when I was a teenager, after having lived in Liberia in the early stages of the civil war. This interest motivated me to pursue a PhD and to focus my research on violence against women. I am grateful to the many people who have helped me bring this project to fruition.

This book began as my doctoral dissertation at the University of Pittsburgh. I offer my deepest thanks to the members of my dissertation committee. Taylor Seybolt, the chair of the committee, gave me thoughtful comments and guidance. Lisa Brush provided invaluable feedback and was a voice of encouragement throughout. Müge Finkel gave me constructive comments, and Harvey White's input was very helpful and is deeply appreciated. I am also indebted to Charli Carpenter for her support when I began my doctoral training.

The Oxford-Princeton Global Leaders Fellowship afforded me the time to think and write and introduced me to a community of scholars who helped me to improve the manuscript and supported me along the way. I greatly benefited from conversations with and feedback on the manuscript from Ngaire Woods, Robert Keohane, Nic Cheeseman, Thomas Hale, and Emily Jones. I am also indebted to Ngaire Woods for helping me navigate the publication process. In addition, I appreciate the thoughtful and insightful feedback received from participants in the Global Leaders Fellows Colloquiums, including Jonny Steinberg, Jennifer Widner, John Ikenberry, and Global Leader Fellows.

I presented parts of this project at the International Studies Association and African Studies Association annual conferences, in addition to presenting chapters at seminars at the University of Ghana, University of the Free State, University of Oxford, University of Birmingham, University of Cambridge, Coventry University, University of Exeter, University of Delaware, Georgetown University, University of Ottawa, University College London, Princeton University, and University of Massachusetts-Boston. I would like to thank the participants in these forums for their helpful feedback.

Furthermore, I am indebted to Alice Kang, Faith Okpotor, and Susanne Zwingel, who generously read sections of the book manuscript and gave me thoughtful and incisive feedback that greatly improved the work. Martin Williams was incredibly generous with his time. Conversations with him, as well as his comments on the manuscript, helped me to sharpen my ideas. I would like to offer him my sincerest gratitude. I would also like to thank the anonymous reviewers at Oxford University Press for their incisive feedback on the manuscript.

Thanks are also due to my editor, Angela Chnapko, who was supportive from the beginning and patiently worked with me throughout the publication process. In addition, I would like to thank the team at OUP for their work on the book.

I received several research grants and fellowships for this project. I am grateful for institutional grants from the University of Pittsburgh that funded my dissertation fieldwork in Liberia. The African and African Diaspora Studies Dissertation Fellowship at Boston College also afforded me the time to write the dissertation. Grants from the Harry Frank Guggenheim Foundation and the African Peacebuilding Network of the Social Science Research Council enabled me to conduct fieldwork in Côte d'Ivoire, and a Book Manuscript Completion Grant from the African Peacebuilding Network supported my writing.

An array of people in Liberia and Côte d'Ivoire supported my fieldwork. Particular thanks are owed to Davidetta Browne-Lansanah in Liberia, who made key introductions. Vivian Dixon opened her home to me and embraced me into her family; I am eternally grateful to her. In Côte d'Ivoire, Josiane Kouassi not only provided excellent research assistance on two trips but was also a good friend who made me feel welcome. I would also like to thank Joel Kouassi for research assistance during my third trip to Côte d'Ivoire and Robtel Pailey, who hosted me. There are so many other kind and generous people who facilitated my work, some of whom I cannot name, and I would like to offer them my deepest thanks.

Finally, I am grateful to my parents, who have supported me every step of the way. Thanks to my mother, Rose, who has been a source of encouragement. I am grateful to my stepmother, Jimi, and my father, Eric, who helped to facilitate my fieldwork in Liberia. My father has been unwavering in his support and has been a source of inspiration. Thank you to my sisters, Madia, Erica, Vanessa, and Adobia, who have been there for me in diverse ways since I began this project as a doctoral student. I am deeply appreciative.

Above all, so many people in Liberia and Côte d'Ivoire took time out of their busy days to speak with me. This book would have been impossible without them and I am deeply grateful for their kindness and generosity. I have been inspired by the work that is being done by so many people to help survivors of violence—work that often goes unnoticed and unacknowledged. I would like to thank them for their incredible service, generosity, and commitment. Particular gratitude is owed to the many survivors of violence and their families who opened up to me to speak of difficult issues. They are at the heart of this book and I will remain eternally grateful to them.

This book is dedicated to Madam Mary L. Mills, my beloved grandmother, whom we lost in the Liberian civil war.

Introduction

How and Why Do States Implement International Women's Rights Norms?

In Africa and across the globe, states have adopted progressive women's rights laws, policies, and practices. These laws, policies, and practices (often termed "best practices") originate from and reflect changing international norms. In other words, they are products of international women's rights norms, and their adoption is a demonstration of the diffusion of these norms. Women's movements and international organizations (IOs) such as the United Nations (UN) have played a critical role in persuading states to adopt these measures to address problems such as violence against women (VAW), a scourge that plagues the life of girls and women globally. However, the role that women's movements and IOs play in the implementation of these measures is less clear. Thus, while their influence on states' adoption of laws, policies, and practices has been theorized, their influence on implementation, particularly implementation in Africa and at the street level, is less clearly understood.[1] This book contributes to the literature by describing and theorizing the domestic implementation of a practice: the establishment of specialized police and gendarmerie units. It also analyzes how these units change the performance of law enforcement officers.

Specialized police and gendarmerie units form part of specialized criminal justice mechanisms that have been established to address VAW. This "best practice" is a product of an international women's justice norm for VAW, which is a type of women's rights norm. This international women's justice norm has emphasized formal accountability for perpetrators of VAW, and gender-based violence (GBV) more broadly, and sensitivity toward survivors of this violence. The mechanisms promoted by this norm include specialized police units, prosecution units, and courts that are mandated to respond to VAW, and sometimes, also to gendered violence against boys and men. They have proliferated across Africa since the first decade of the 2000s, though states have differed in the institutional models

Global Norms and Local Action. Peace A. Medie, Oxford University Press (2020). © Oxford University Press.
DOI: 10.1093/oso/9780190922962.001.0001

2 GLOBAL NORMS AND LOCAL ACTION

adopted and in how these units have been established.[2] Indeed, a close look at specialized mechanisms in Africa reveals that they have been unevenly established and that they have been increasingly introduced in post-conflict countries (Figure I.1). While some countries have dedicated officials and institutional structures in place, others do not. Liberia and Côte d'Ivoire are two post-conflict countries that illustrate this difference.

Liberia's specialized police unit, the Women and Children Protection Section (WACPS), was created in 2005, about two years after the end of the country's 14-year conflict. Within a few months, the section had a central directorate, and officers worked exclusively on cases of GBV and on cases involving children. Three years after its creation, there was a WACPS in each of Liberia's 15 counties. Côte d'Ivoire differed in how it established its specialized unit, the gender desk, which was renamed Bureau d'Accueil Genre in 2017. The unit was created in the police force and gendarmerie in 2014, about three years after the end of the country's 11-year conflict. However, in 2017, more than three years after its creation, there was no central directorate for the gender desk in the police force or gendarmerie. Officers were not assigned exclusively to the gender desk and the unit had not been installed in all regions of the country. The differences between these countries is a puzzle that is illustrative not only of how specialized mechanisms have been

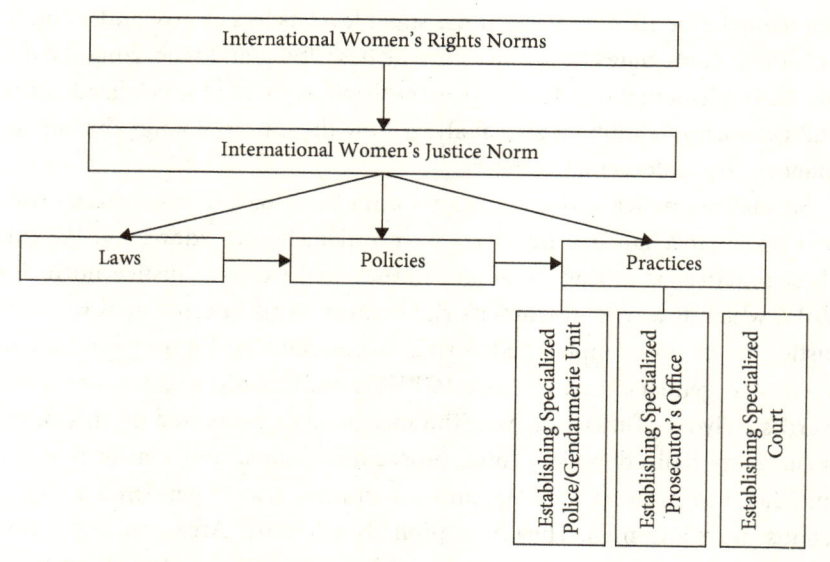

Figure I.1. The relationship between international norms and practices.

established across Africa, but also of how international women's rights norms are implemented on the continent, and globally. What explains how and why post-conflict countries in Africa implement the international women's justice norm? What accounts for the variation in the establishment of specialized mechanisms, and thus in the implementation of the international women's justice norm? What roles do IOs and the women's movement play in states' establishment of these specialized mechanisms? How do specialized mechanisms change street-level implementation? Furthermore, how does the degree of institutionalization of a specialized mechanism affect street-level implementation and women's access to justice? The contrast between both countries provides insight into the implementation of an international best practice, and thus into the implementation of a progressive international norm, and raises several important questions that have implications for the international relations (IR), gender and politics, and African studies literatures.

While the role of IOs and social movements in states' adoption of progressive laws, policies, and practices has received scholarly attention, their influence on implementation, particularly in Africa and at the street level, has been less studied. In this book, I describe and theorize how and why post-conflict states in Africa have established specialized police and gendarmerie units, and how and why they have implemented the international women's justice norm. I argue that implementation occurs in stages, and therefore probe how the UN and women's movements shape three stages of the implementation process: creation, institutionalization, and street-level implementation. The stages often overlap, such that institutionalization and street-level implementation sometimes occur simultaneously. Creation is operationalized as a written statement by the government or the UN, announcing that the government has decided or agreed to establish a specialized unit. Institutionalization describes the formalization of the unit as a section of the police force or gendarmerie. It includes the setting up of a central directorate, the installation of units across the country, and the assignment of officers dedicated exclusively to VAW or GBV to work in these units. Street-level implementation describes police officers' and gendarmes' attitudes in terms of the re-victimization of survivors and the referral of rape and domestic violence cases to the prosecutor.

First, the book identifies the international women's justice norm and describes its emergence. This norm is an important development in the efforts to end VAW globally. Second, it theorizes the creation of specialized criminal justice sector mechanisms in Africa. I explain the creation of the WACPS in Liberia and the gender desk in Côte d'Ivoire with a focus on the roles of the UN and the women's movements in this process. Third, the book theorizes the institutionalization of these mechanisms. Specifically, I analyze the variation in Liberia's and Côte d'Ivoire's institutionalization of their specialized units and the impact that domestic factors had on this variation. Fourth, because implementation does not end with the creation and institutionalization of specialized mechanisms, I examine how these institutional changes affected street-level implementation in both countries. I analyze how the degree of institutionalization of the specialized unit affected the treatment that survivors of rape and domestic violence received from police officers and gendarmes, and their access to justice. I draw on over 300 interviews conducted in both countries—Monrovia and Gbarnga in Liberia and Abidjan and Bouaké in Côte d'Ivoire—to achieve these objectives.

This book is, therefore, an examination of the domestic implementation of a type of women's rights norm—the international women's justice norm. It is also a study of the implementation of a practice, which originates from the norm. The book theorizes norm implementation at multiple stages (creation, institutionalization, and street-level) with a focus on the roles and influence of the UN and women's movements. This systematic analysis of international norm implementation at multiple stages in Africa enables a novel contribution to the IR, gender and politics, and African studies literatures.

Central Argument in Brief

I argue that a high level of international pressure from the UN was important for the *creation* of specialized units to combat VAW in both countries, but that in addition to high international pressure, high domestic pressure from the women's movement and favorable political and institutional conditions were essential for rapid *institutionalization* of the units, and thus for the rapid implementation of the international women's justice norm. In Liberia, high international pressure from the UN combined with high domestic pressure from the women's movement and favorable political and institutional conditions to spur not just the creation of the WACPS, but also its relatively rapid institutionalization. But while international pressure was high and political and institutional conditions moderately favorable in Côte d'Ivoire, domestic pressure was low. While these dynamics did not prevent the creation of the gender desk, they slowed its institutionalization.

I also argue that the degree of institutionalization affected street-level performance. While performance improved in both countries, the international women's justice norm was more salient in Liberia than in Côte d'Ivoire as a result of the degree to which it was institutionalized in the former. Police officers in Liberia were more likely to recognize that rape cases should be referred to the prosecutor than police officers and gendarmes in Côte d'Ivoire. While there were significant deficiencies in the specialized units in both countries that undermined gender-responsive policing and women's access to justice, the comparison revealed that the greater degree of institutionalization in Liberia served to more firmly entrench the international women's justice norm.

These findings are significant for several areas of scholarship. They contribute to the IR literature on norm diffusion by specifying the stage of implementation at which IOs can have a disproportionate impact and the pathways and mechanisms through which they influence implementation. Scholars have argued that the effect of pressure from IOs on implementation is mediated by domestic political dynamics (Avdeyeya, 2015; Betts and Orchard, 2014; Deere, 2009; Montoya, 2013). I build on this literature by showing that international pressure played a larger role at the creation stage. Thus, even when domestic pressure was low and domestic conditions moderately favorable in Côte d'Ivoire, creation occurred, and the gap in the pace of creation between the countries was narrow. However, domestic actors and conditions became more important at the institutionalization stage. Thus, while pressure from the UN was enough to get each country to agree to nominally create a specialized unit, domestic actors and conditions were key to how quickly these units were institutionalized (formalized and installed across the country). This finding speaks to the IR literature on the localization of norms and on the importance of domestic dynamics to norm diffusion (Acharya, 2004; Engwicht, 2018; Zimmerman, 2016; Zimmerman, 2017; Zwingel, 2011).

This finding is also important for the gender and politics literature, which has shown that activism by women's movements is essential for policy adoption (Adomako Ampofo, 2008; Anyidoho, Crawford, & Medie, 2020; Crawford & Anyidoho, 2013; Htun & Weldon, 2010; Kang, 2015; Kang & Tripp, 2018; Medie, 2013; Tripp, Casimiro, Kwesiga, & Mungwa, 2009; Tsikata, 2009). I build on this literature by demonstrating that strong women's movements can also play a key role in the implementation of an international practice, and thus a norm, although they appear to be more essential at the institutionalization stage. This specification of the conditions for and patterns of institutional change also contributes to the African studies literature. The literature on the police in Africa has shown that international actors are often limited in their ability to transform this institution (Medie 2018). This study has demonstrated that a degree of institutional transformation can occur with the involvement of certain domestic actors and under specific conditions. Furthermore, the effect of institutionalization on the salience of the international women's justice norm at the street level demonstrates the importance of IOs and social movements in street-level implementation. However, the persistent deficiencies in street-level implementation in both countries underline the strength of competing domestic norms and the challenge of sustaining specialized mechanisms.

What We Know about Norm Implementation

In Africa and globally, countries have adopted progressive laws, policies, and practices on domestic violence, rape, and other forms of VAW. Yet, in many of these countries, victims of violence are usually unable to get justice from the formal criminal justice system. Many rely on informal justice mechanisms, which include customary courts, to adjudicate this violence. Indeed, for many victims, the laws and policies on paper have no direct impact on their lives. Thus, many girls and women live in countries with laws and policies that entitle them to protection and services, but struggle to access these protections and services when they are victimized. This points to a major implementation gap and also raises questions about the role that women's rights defenders play in implementation and in reducing this gap.

Women's movements and IOs have paid increasing attention to VAW, particularly to VAW in conflict-affected states. This attention resulted in the adoption of several UN resolutions, including United Nations Security Council (UNSC) Resolution 1325 on Women, Peace, and Security, which, among other things, calls for an end to impunity for sexual violence. Persistent sexual and physical violence after the official end of conflicts underscored the problem of VAW and the challenges of addressing the issue. Thus, both women's movements and IOs such as the UN have emphasized a victim-friendly approach in the criminal justice sector and have urged post-conflict states to prosecute perpetrators, particularly perpetrators of sexual violence, and thus to end impunity for this violence. Impunity describes the failure of law enforcement officers to investigate, arrest, and refer offenders for prosecution, and the failure of the formal courts to prosecute these offenders. In essence, women's movements and the UN have promoted an international women's justice norm for sexual violence, and to a lesser extent, for other forms of VAW. One international women's justice measure that has been promoted by the UN in Africa is the establishment of specialized criminal justice sector mechanisms: specialized police units, prosecution units, and courts (United Nations Division for the Advancement of Women, 1997; United Nations Office on Drugs and Crime, 2010). Outside of Europe and North America, specialized police stations were first introduced in Brazil in the 1980s and have since spread to other countries in the region. In Brazil, they took the form of women's police stations, staffed entirely by women, to receive cases of VAW (Santos, 2005). Other Latin American countries adopted variations of this model, and since the late 1990s, the UN has promoted these specialized mechanisms as a best practice for addressing the ineffectiveness, abuse, and discrimination that typically characterize police interaction with survivors of domestic violence, rape, and other forms of VAW (United Nations Office on Drugs and Crime, 2010; United Nations Division for the Advancement of Women, 1997). It has also been argued that the personnel of specialized mechanisms are more likely to implement the international women's justice norm by investigating, arresting, and prosecuting offenders (UN Women, 2012).

However, despite the importance of these specialized mechanisms, they have not received much attention in the IR, gender and politics, or African studies literatures. Therefore, we do not know much about how and why they have been adopted across the continent, and the literature is mostly silent on how their personnel perform. However, research in Latin America has offered some insight into these specialized mechanisms by showing that international cooperation agencies and the women's movement played a key role in their establishment and that they led to some improvements in policing (Medie & Walsh, 2019; Walsh, 2015). These findings echo the literature on international norms, which has shown that international pressure and domestic actors and conditions affect the domestic implementation of international norms (Avdeyeya, 2015; Betts and Orchard, 2014; Deere, 2009; Grimm and Weiffen, 2018; Montoya, 2013). This book identifies the international women's justice norm and brings the discussion of its implementation to Africa. I ask why specialized units have been established, how they have been established, and how they have changed street-level performance and women's access to justice.

Scope of the Argument

My objective is to explain how international and domestic actors and domestic conditions interact to shape how a norm is implemented at three stages of the implementation process. I have, therefore, developed a framework, showing how the interplay of international and domestic factors lead to varied outcomes. The framework and arguments presented here are necessarily bounded, because the implementation process and its outcomes are shaped by a multiplicity of factors, which are themselves dependent on the context and policy issue area. This study focuses on two post-conflict countries with UN peacekeeping missions. Furthermore, both countries experienced high international pressure, mainly from the UN, paired with varying levels of domestic pressure. Therefore, the argument presented here is more likely to apply to countries that have experienced high international pressure paired with low/high domestic pressure and favourable/unfavourable political and institutional conditions. More research is needed to understand how a low level of international pressure impacts the implementation of the international women's justice norm.

Nonetheless, this framework and the arguments may be useful in explaining norm implementation in other post-conflict as well as non-conflict-affected settings. While a heavy peacekeeping presence in Liberia and Côte d'Ivoire was key to the UN exerting high international pressure, international pressure to establish specialized mechanisms can even occur in countries that have not experienced conflict and do not have a peacekeeping mission (see Anyidoho, Crawford, & Medie, 2020). And depending on the prevalence of the problem, this international pressure could be high. Indeed, the IR literature has underlined the influence of external actors on norm diffusion not only in Africa, but also in other areas of the developing world and in non conflict-affected countries (Avdeyeva, 2015; Deere, 2009; Montoya, 2013; Risse, Ropp, & Sikkink, 2013). Thus, the relationships and mechanisms observed in these cases might be relevant in countries without a peacekeeping mission. Furthermore, while the discussion in this book is limited to the international women's justice norm, international and domestic factors interact to affect implementation in a range of issue areas. Therefore, the interplay of factors and the observed outcomes could offer insights into the implementation of other international human rights norms that are promoted by external actors.

Methods and Sources

This book is a qualitative study of international norm implementation at the domestic level. I employ the method of structured-focused comparison to analyze two case studies that have different outcomes (George and Bennett, 2005). To develop theory, I used both within-case and cross-case techniques (Mahoney, 2007). They were critical for identifying causal mechanisms and pathways, testing observable implications, and assessing the conditions for implementation. The book draws on extensive fieldwork conducted in Liberia and Côte d'Ivoire between 2010 and 2017. I comparatively studied and analyzed how both countries responded to rape and domestic violence. I collected data in Liberia in 2010 and 2011 and in Côte d'Ivoire in 2014, 2015, and 2017 with the objective of understanding the decisions and actions of key politicians and of high-level and street-level bureaucrats. Data were collected through interviews, focus group discussions, the observation of key actors, and reviews of newspapers and background documents. I collected crime statistics from law enforcement agencies and the UN as well as documents produced by other government agencies, local and international NGOs, and bilateral and multilateral agencies.

In Liberia, data were collected in Monrovia in Montserrado County and Gbarnga in Bong County. I interviewed about 150 people in Liberia from June to October 2010 and May to June 2011. Interviewees were survivors of rape and intimate partner violence, police officers, officials in the Ministry of Gender and Development, Ministry of Justice, and Ministry of Interior, United Nations personnel, personnel of other international organizations, staff of local NGOs, and staff of women's rights NGOs. I conducted about 180 interviews in order to understand the implementation of the international women's justice norm in Côte d'Ivoire. In-country interviews were conducted in Abidjan and Bouaké and interviewees were lawmakers; officials in the Ministry of Interior and Security and the Ministry of Women, Family, and Children; staff of key UN agencies and of related IOs; staff of NGOs;

police officers and gendarmes; and survivors of domestic violence and rape. I also conducted five focus group discussions.

Data collection in both countries was intensive and comprehensive and has afforded me insight into the decision-making processes at multiple levels.

Definition of Key Terms

This is a study of violence against women (VAW). I define VAW as "any act of gender-based violence that results in, or is likely to result in, physical, sexual, or mental harm or suffering to women, including threats of such acts, coercion or arbitrary deprivation of liberty, whether occurring in public or in private life" (UN Declaration on the Elimination of Violence against Women, 1993). The victims of VAW are girls and women. The term "gender-based violence" emphasizes the role of gender in causing this violence and the gendered impacts of the violence. While this study focuses on violence against women and girls, who tend to be disproportionately affected by GBV, it recognizes that boys and men are also victims of GBV.[3] Throughout the book, I use VAW when referring only to girls and women and use GBV when discussing gendered violence against girls, boys, women, and men. I also use GBV when it is the term used in policy documents, in the literature, and by interviewees.

Chapter 2 provides an overview of VAW in Africa, but the analyses in the book focus on rape and domestic violence. Rape is a form of sexual violence. The law in Liberia and Côte d'Ivoire define the term "rape." Thus, I am guided by the law in my analysis of its enforcement in each country. Domestic violence in this book refers to intimate partner violence (IPV) and describes physical or sexual violence against a girl or woman by a current or former intimate partner.[4] It includes partner-perpetrated sexual violence. I have adopted the term "domestic violence" instead of IPV because the former is used by the police in Liberia and features heavily in policy documents. I employ IPV when discussing a document that uses this term.

This book is a study of the implementation of a practice: the establishment of specialized criminal justice sector mechanisms. I use the term "practice" to mean a technique for operationalizing a norm.[5] This is a technique that norm promotors have identified as an effective or the most effective means of locally enacting a norm. Often, a collection of practices, termed "best practices," are widely recognized by norm promotors. Examples of practices that operationalize the international women's rights norms are the establishment of specialized mechanisms, the establishment of shelters for survivors of domestic violence, and the introduction of skills program for survivors of GBV. Practices are sometimes outlined in policy documents, which are themselves sometimes informed by national laws.

This book is also a study of the implementation of a norm, from which this practice emanates. A norm may be defined as "intersubjective understandings that constitute actors' interests and identities, and create expectations as well as prescribe what appropriate behaviour ought to be" (Björkdahl, 2002, p. 21). The norm that is being studied is the international women's justice norm, a type of women's rights norm. It is an international women's rights norm because it has been promoted by international human rights organizations, domestic women's rights advocates, and also by transnational advocates who have sought to advance women's rights. This norm encompasses a variety of laws, policies, and practices. The laws include those criminalizing marital rape, domestic violence, and female genital mutilation. Some measures are not put into laws but constitute national policy documents. They include the National Action Plans that countries have adopted to implement UNSC Resolution 1325 and national gender policies that have been developed by many African countries.

I use the term "war" to describe a period when there was a minimum of 1,000 battle deaths in a year, in accordance with the Correlates of War data set. Thus, I write about the First Liberian Civil War (1989–1997), the Second Liberian Civil War (1999–2003), the First Ivoirian Civil War (2002–2004), and the Second Ivoirian Civil War (2011). There were periods of ceasefire and reduced violence that separated the wars in each country; in Côte d'Ivoire, this period has been described as "neither war nor peace" and lasted from 2004 to 2010. When specifically discussing these four episodes of violence in each country, I use the term "war." Therefore, when discussing the First Liberian Civil War, I use the term "war." However, when discussing one or both of the civil wars in either country, and the lull in the violence, I use the term "conflict." Therefore, when discussing the Ivoirian civil wars and the six-year period of "neither war nor peace," I use the term "conflict." Thus, "conflict" describes the entirety of the violence, and "post-conflict" describes the end of the war as well as the end of the period of "neither war nor peace."

Organization of the Book

This introduction is followed by Part I: *The Domestic Implementation of International Norms*, which provides an overview of the topic and lays out the theoretical framework. Chapter 1 builds on several themes in the introduction by providing an overview of VAW in Africa and a background on the creation of specialized criminal justice sector mechanisms. Because of the diversity across countries, I do not aim to tell a single story about VAW in Africa or of states' responses. Instead, I identify commonalities in the types of violence experienced in most countries and in the causes of this violence, as well as in what states have done in response. I highlight the role of patriarchal gender norms in causing this violence and in shaping the criminal justice sector's response. This is also where I identify the international women's justice norm and show how it has constituted and has been constituted by various international instruments. I discuss the emergence of specialized criminal justice mechanisms and draw on secondary sources to develop a typology of these mechanisms and to document their spread across the continent. I explicate the study's theoretical framework in Chapter 2. I draw on the IR, gender and politics, public administration, and African studies literatures to develop a framework that explains implementation at the national and street-levels. I show that an interplay of external and domestic factors shape implementation but specify that domestic actors and conditions become more essential at the institutionalization stage.

Part II of the book is titled *Violence against Women in Liberia and Côte d'Ivoire* and is a historical overview of VAW in both countries and of how the state and society has responded to the problem. Chapter 3 traces the problem of VAW in Liberia and explains how the conflict exacerbated the problem and rendered women vulnerable in its aftermath. I explain that patriarchal gender norms were always at the core of this violence and contributed to Liberians' reluctance to report rape and domestic violence to the police or to support the prosecution of offenders. However, widespread sexual violence during the conflict and post-conflict campaigns by the state and non-state actors led to shifting attitudes and to increased reporting of these crimes. Chapter 4 covers how the government and women's organizations responded to this violence. I explain that prior to the conflict, VAW was largely absent from the agenda of governments and women's organizations. I describe how the 14-year conflict changed this and generated strong international and domestic pressures on post-conflict governments to strengthen the criminal justice sector response to VAW, particularly sexual violence, and to establish specialized criminal justice sector mechanisms. Throughout this analysis, I focus on the roles of the UN and the women's movement and outline the relationship between these two actors and how it transformed the state's response to VAW.

I present the Ivoirian case in Chapters 5 and 6. In Chapter 5, I mirror the Liberian case by tracing the problem of VAW in Côte d'Ivoire and the effect of the country's 11-year conflict on this violence. Similar to Liberia, patriarchal gender norms were at the root of this violence and contributed to Ivoirian's reluctance to turn to the state for help. I, however, explain that while the Liberian conflict led to widespread sexual violence, the dynamics of the Ivoirian conflict resulted in sexual violence that was less widespread and was more concentrated in certain regions of the country. Nonetheless, this violence led to shifting attitudes, such that the reporting of domestic violence and rape increased after the conflict. I cover the government, women's movement, and international actors' responses to this violence, before and after the conflict, in Chapter 6. I explain that unlike Liberia, there was some government and civil society attention to VAW before the conflict. The UN's attention to sexual violence during the Ivoirian conflict increased after the second civil war and generated pressure on the government to create the gender desks.

This exposition is followed by Part III, *National and Street-Level Implementation of the International Women's Justice Norm*, in which I comparatively analyze the establishment of the specialized units and the performance of street-level officers in Liberia and Côte d'Ivoire. In Chapter 7, I show how pressure from the UN shaped the creation of the specialized unit in both countries. I demonstrate how this international pressure interacted with domestic pressure and conditions to produce varied implementation outcomes. In Chapter 8, I draw on interviews with police officers and gendarmes to show how the greater degree of institutionalization led to a deeper salience of the international women's justice norm in Liberia. I conclude the book with a discussion of how specialized mechanisms can serve to increase girls' and women's access to justice in Africa, but only if embedded within a holistic framework.

PART I
THE DOMESTIC IMPLEMENTATION OF INTERNATIONAL NORMS

1
Violence against Women and Law Enforcement in Africa

The majority of girls and women who experience gender-based violence (GBV) do not seek help from the formal criminal justice system due to sociocultural norms and financial constraints. Unethical practices, gender bias, and capacity gaps in the criminal justice system also deter reporting and render formal justice inaccessible to many. This violence, along with the accompanying impunity and lack of support for victims, has received considerable attention in Africa since the 1980s.[1] Women's rights activists and organizations have initiated and led campaigns for international, regional, and subregional organizations to adopt instruments that spell out how states should address various forms of VAW and to require them to implement the norms and accompanying practices that are promoted in these instruments. The targeted organizations, including the UN and the African Union (AU), have responded by adopting international consensus documents which recognize that some forms of VAW are criminal offenses, condemn these offenses, and urge states to prosecute perpetrators of these acts. Thus, they have promoted a collection of VAW norms, including an international women's justice norm. Some of these documents also specify that states should establish specialized criminal justice sector mechanisms to deal with VAW. Specialized mechanisms typically consist of personnel who are specially trained to investigate and prosecute crimes categorized as VAW or GBV and are responsible for handling incidents of such cases that are reported to their respective agencies. These personnel work in agencies that are dedicated (sometimes exclusively) to responding to VAW or GBV more broadly. International and regional organizations argue that these specialized mechanisms are "more responsive and effective in dealing with VAW" (UN Women, 2012, p. 16). However, they can lead to the marginalization of VAW in the criminal justice system and can be ineffective when personnel are not adequately trained and resourced (Morrison, Elsberg, & Bott, 2007). Nonetheless, in recommending them as a best practice, proponents have

Global Norms and Local Action. Peace A. Medie, Oxford University Press (2020). © Oxford University Press.
DOI: 10.1093/oso/9780190922962.001.0001

promoted institutional change in the form of specialized criminal justice sector mechanisms to deal with VAW.

The promotion of these mechanisms has coincided with their diffusion in Africa. Forty-one countries have created at least one specialized police, prosecutorial, or court mechanism since 2000. Also notable is that post-conflict countries have made progress in creating specialized mechanisms, although some have made more progress than others. For example, while Angola has only one specialized mechanism, Liberia has four. Furthermore, the models adopted and degree of institutionalization vary widely across countries. On one hand, reports suggest that these specialized mechanisms have led to improvements in survivors' interactions with the criminal justice system in Africa, and in their access to justice (UNPOL, 2015). On the other hand, personnel in specialized agencies have been found to exhibit some of the negative behaviors that have characterized non-specialized personnel in regular criminal justice sector agencies in Africa (Medie, 2018). Despite these weaknesses, specialized mechanisms are a major initiative in the bid to reduce impunity for VAW and to ensure that girls and women are treated with sensitivity, instead of being further victimized by personnel of the criminal justice system.

However, despite their importance, we do not understand variation in their creation or institutionalization in African countries. Furthermore, with the exception of reports produced by government agencies and IOs, there are few systematically conducted studies of specialized agencies and personnel in Africa. This book addresses these gaps in the literature, and this chapter provides an overview of VAW in Africa and states' responses to the problem, including their creation of specialized mechanisms. I explain that in addition to passing and amending laws, states have established specialized criminal justice sector mechanisms, mostly after the year 2000. I distinguish between two main types of specialized mechanisms—independent units and embedded units. I show that post-conflict states are more likely to establish specialized police and court mechanisms, and I discuss the implications for women's access to justice and law enforcement in Africa.

Violence against Women in Africa

Violence against women in Africa takes many forms and includes domestic violence, non-partner rape, human trafficking, female genital mutilation

(FGM), and forced marriage (Medie, 2019). While some forms, such as domestic violence and rape, are ubiquitous, others such as FGM and forced marriage are typically confined to specific countries or to regions within countries. There is also within-country variation in the prevalence of VAW. For example, while Liberia's 2008 Demographic and Health Survey does not reveal a rural-urban divide in the prevalence of non-partner sexual violence, it shows that women in River Cess, Sinoe, and Grand Gedeh counties were more likely to have experienced this form of violence (24 percent) than women in Rivergee, Grand Kru, and Maryland counties (8 percent). There is also variation across countries.

In fact, domestic violence is the most common form of violence experienced by girls and women on the continent. While both men and women are victims of this act, women are disproportionately affected. Perpetrators often seek to dominate and control their victims by curtailing their freedom of movement, association, speech, and their freedom to make basic life choices (Barnett & Maticka-Tyndale, 2016; Nwabunike & Tenkorang, 2017). Despite evolving norms, many survivors and their communities perceive this violence as a private dispute that does not require the state's intervention (Umubyeyi et al., 2016). Sexual violence, including rape, is another form of violence to which girls and women are disproportionately subjected. Studies show that the majority of non-partner rapes are committed by individuals whom the victims know, for example male relatives, teachers, friends, and neighbors (Muganyizi, Kilewo, & Moshiro, 2004). Survivors, both children and adults, are also often subjected to secondary victimization from relatives and their community. Although societies generally disapprove of rape, there is a tendency to blame victims for causing the act by their style of dress or behavior (Jewkes, Penn-Kekana, & Rose-Junius, 2005). Communities also sometimes stigmatize survivors, causing them to feel ashamed to speak about and seek help for their victimization. In some communities, even children are not spared the stigma that is attached to survivors of rape (Boakye, 2009).[2] Survivors in some communities are perceived as "damaged goods" and therefore no longer desirable as partners (UC Berkeley School of Law 2015, p. 29). This stigmatization and blaming exacerbate the trauma experienced by survivors and contribute to their reluctance to report rape to law enforcement officers.

Similar to other global regions, gender inequality is at the root of VAW in Africa (Jewkes, 2002; Kposowa & Ezzat, 2016). Globally and in Africa, societies have given more power to boys and men while assigning subordinate roles and positions to girls and women. In addition to fostering exaggerated versions of masculinity that are characterized by violence toward others, this gender inequality has caused and legitimized violence against girls and women (Adjei, 2016b; Kposowa & Ezzat, 2016). This is because the belief in male superiority—which is often couched in and bolstered by political, religious, and cultural texts, discourses, and practices—requires, among other things, that girls and women submit to boys' and men's authority within and outside of the domestic sphere. It also requires girls and women to be available for boys' and men's sexual pleasure while simultaneously denying their own sexual desires (Muhanguzi, 2011). Violence—psychological, physical, and sexual—is a tool that is used not only to signify, impose, and reinforce this male power, but also to control and punish women who refuse to quietly occupy the space that society has hollowed out for them (Adjei, 2016a; Adomako Ampofo & Boateng, 2007; Mathews, Jewkes, & Abrahams, 2014; Moffett, 2006). It is used to ensure women's submission by preventing them from "rebelling" and by forcing them back in line when they are perceived to have "rebelled." Consequently, women who defy gender norms by failing to do housework, staying out late, speaking up, wearing clothing that is deemed suggestive, among others acts, are at risk of domestic violence. Some of these actions also put women at risk of non-partner sexual violence. The practice of "corrective rape" in South Africa, where boys and men have raped lesbians, with the intention of punishing them and "correcting" their sexual preference, illustrates how this violence is used to force girls and women to perform socially sanctioned roles (Msibi, 2009).

Although this violence is global, the relative prevalence of physical and sexual violence against women in Africa demonstrates that the gender norms that undergird VAW are particularly salient across the continent. A World Health Organization (WHO) study found that the estimated lifetime prevalence of non-partner sexual violence in Africa was 11.9 percent (2013). This was the highest out of the five global regions for which data were available. Levels of domestic violence are also high. A study found that women in Africa were most at risk of being killed by their partners, at a rate of 1.7 per one-hundred thousand female population (UNODC, 2018). According to the study, "More than two thirds of all women (69 percent) killed in Africa in 2017 were killed by intimate partners or family members" (UNODC, 2018, p. 11).

The high level of acceptance of domestic violence among some sections of women illustrates the salience of patriarchal gender norms (Doku &

Oppong-Asante, 2015). For example, 58 percent of women surveyed in Uganda agreed that there are conditions under which it is acceptable for a man to beat his partner (Ministry of Health and ICF International, 2012). The specified conditions are burning food, going out without telling a partner, arguing with or refusing to have sex with him, and neglecting the children. The results from Liberia, Côte d'Ivoire, Sierra Leone, and Angola are equally troubling. The salience of patriarchal gender norms is also demonstrated by the tendency to blame and stigmatize rape survivors. The effects of these norms are exacerbated by risk factors that increase the likelihood of the occurrence of VAW.

While the findings have been ambiguous, certain factors, in addition to gender inequality, have been found to generally increase the likelihood that a girl or women will be subjected to certain forms of GBV. Alcohol use and poverty are factors that increase women's vulnerability to both domestic violence and rape (Jewkes, 2002). The normalization of violence in a society also puts girls and women at risk of violence (Jewkes, 2002); that is, girls and women are particularly vulnerable when they live in a society that is accepting of violence. Armed conflicts, where violence is usually highly normalized, therefore, pose a heightened level of threat to them. Indeed, reports reveal that armed groups and state forces have subjected girls and women to sexual violence in many conflicts in Africa (Cohen & Nordas, 2014; Turshen & Twagiramariya, 1998). Boys and men have also been victims of this violence.

However, the role that gender inequality plays in causing wartime rape is debated by scholars. Some have argued that gender inequality does not explain variation in the use of rape by armed groups. Instead, wartime rape has been attributed to conflict recruitment mechanisms—armed groups that recruit combatants by force use sexual violence to build unit cohesion (Cohen, 2013). In a study to explain the relative absence of wartime rape by the Liberation Tigers of Tamil Eelam of Sri Lanka, Woods (2009) argued that the banning of sexual violence and the enforcement of this decision by the organization prevented its use by combatants. Others have, however, argued that there is a need to further examine the role of gender in wartime sexual violence. Among other things, this would require scholars to interrogate why sexual, as opposed to other forms of violence, has been used to achieve the goals of armed groups (Davies & True, 2015; Prügl & Tickner, 2018). While this debate is beyond the scope of this book, the fact that armed conflict heightens women's vulnerability to non-partner rape is supported by empirical evidence. Furthermore, the weak (and often absent) rule of law in armed conflicts ensures that most survivors do not have recourse to formal justice, and engenders a culture of impunity.

But while much of the focus has been on non-partner sexual violence, domestic violence, which includes partner-perpetrated sexual violence, is also widespread during armed conflicts. The rampant impunity and broken social support structures, which characterize conflicts, aggravate the problem (Annan & Brier, 2010). Furthermore, the normalization of violence that pertains during conflicts does not cease with the signing of peace agreements. Consequently, girls and women in post-conflict countries are likely to be more vulnerable to domestic violence and rape than they were before the outbreak of conflict. Some boys and men come to perceive domestic violence as a normal way of dealing with challenges and frustrations (Horn et al., 2014). Increased poverty and drug and alcohol abuse further heighten the risk of VAW (Carlson, 2005; Horn et al., 2014). The continued weaknesses in the rule of law and in the criminal justice system that characterize post-conflict countries make formal justice inaccessible to most survivors.

While much of the focus has been on causes operating at the regional, national, and subnational levels, the global political and economic order also has an effect on the occurrence of some forms of VAW (Medie & Kang, 2018). Indeed, studies of the colonial period showed that colonial officials and the troops under their command raped women (Andersen & Weis, 2018). Thus, VAW in Africa cannot be separated from colonialism. More recently, sexual violence in the Democratic Republic of Congo (DRC) has been partly attributed to neoliberal globalization (Meger, 2016). Men who have been marginalized by globalization adopt "militarized forms of masculinity" in order to shift their status (Meger, 2016, p. 43). This violence, regardless of when it occurs, has several negative implications for survivors, their families, and their communities.

The effects of domestic violence, rape, and other forms of VAW are far-reaching and often extend beyond the lives of victims to affect their relatives and communities. Both forms of violence can result in injuries that sometimes incapacitate temporarily or permanently. Studies have found a strong relationship between domestic violence and negative reproductive health outcomes such as unwanted pregnancies (Kaye et al., 2006), terminated pregnancies, miscarriages, and infant mortality (Bola, 2016; Emenike, Lawoko, & Dalal, 2008; Okenwa, Lawoko, & Jansson, 2011). Women in abusive relationships also face an increased likelihood of HIV infection (Dunkle et al., 2004; Durevall & Lindskog, 2015). Rape survivors are also at risk of contracting HIV and other sexually transmitted diseases (Mills et al., 2006). In the most extreme but not uncommon instances, both domestic violence and rape result in death (Adinkrah, 2014; Mathews, Jewkes, & Abrahams, 2014). In South Africa, a country that has experienced a crisis of VAW, most murders of women are at the hands of a partner (Abrahams et al., 2009). But the effects of VAW are not always physical. Survivors often suffer psychological trauma that can lead to a host of emotional problems (Vinck & Pham, 2013). In the case of rape survivors, this trauma is aggravated by the victim-blaming and stigmatization that follow the act. Both the visible and invisible injuries significantly affect girls' and women's well-being. They derail education and employment, disrupt relationships, and limit survivors' ability to freely socialize and participate in community activities.

The community is very important in the lives of girls and women, such that the adjudication of domestic violence and rape cases generally occurs within this space. Survivors have mostly relied on informal mechanisms when seeking help after experiencing domestic violence and rape. Domestic violence is largely perceived as a problem to be resolved within the family, and survivors who do otherwise may face severe physical and socioeconomic repercussions. Therefore, girls and women are more likely to disclose to relatives and friends than to law enforcement agencies. Furthermore, when they do report to these agencies, they often do not seek the prosecution of their abuser, but rather want an intervention that can bring an end to the violence without rupturing the relationship with the abuser (Medie, 2015). Rape is more likely to be reported to law enforcement agencies than is domestic violence; however, in a reflection of the global trend, rape is highly underreported (Berkeley Human Rights Center, 2015; Fisher et al., 2003; Muganyizi, Kilewo, & Moshiro, 2004). Social pressures, including the stigmatization of survivors, is a major reason for girls' and women's reluctance to report this offense (Medie, 2017). Relatives discourage reporting not only to avoid bringing shame upon the family, but also because in some communities, the prosecutorial process and the incarceration of offenders are perceived as too divisive, harsh, and inadequate (Berkeley Human Rights Center, 2015; Medie, 2017; Porter, 2015). The fear of retaliation is another deterrent. Communities, therefore, tend to prefer customary and other informal approaches to justice that typically prioritize reconciliation and community cohesion over individual rights and punishment, and offer restitution, a practice that is usually absent from the formal criminal justice process.

Distrust of the criminal justice system is another reason for not reporting and not pursuing prosecution. Across Africa, the police and courts are rated as the most corrupt public institutions (Armah-Attoh et al., 2007). Citizens' assessment is supported by studies of the police and courts in many countries. The police force in most African countries has been described as corrupt, ineffective, and in some cases, abusive toward those seeking justice (Alemika, 2009; Hills, 2016; Ivković & Sauerman, 2015; Mayamba, 2013; Tankebe, 2008; Tankebe, 2013). These problems in the police have been attributed to the lack of training, infrastructure, and equipment; low pay; and politicization; and they have negatively affected how women experience the criminal justice system. Although there have been improvements, the police and courts have generally not treated VAW cases seriously and have often re-victimized survivors who seek help. In fact, survivors' challenges with the criminal justice system often begin before they even enter a police post. The police often do not come when they are called, and this is sometimes because they do not have vehicles and fuel to visit crime scenes (Human Rights Watch, 2013). They frustrate women who try to file complaints and sometimes refuse to record complaints. They have been accused of discouraging girls and women from filing complaints and in some instances of compelling them to withdraw complaints (Amnesty International, 2010; UN Women, 2011). Even when police are willing to help, police stations and courts are sometimes inaccessible. They are either too far away to access or so far away that survivors have to travel long distances, sometimes on precarious roads and on motorbikes, to reach them. This is particularly prohibitive for the poor. For girls and women who have recently undergone physical and sexual abuse, the journey is an ordeal that exacerbates the physical pain and suffering. Furthermore, prosecuting a case requires repeated visits to the police station and courts; these visits take a physical, emotional, and financial toll on survivors. For girls and women on the margins, taking multiple days off from work is a loss in income that they cannot afford, particularly in places where the state does not provide the necessary socioeconomic support and assistance. However, research has shown that despite social pressures and the lack of trust in the institution, girls and women report rape to the police when they have the support of their relatives and friends (Medie, 2017). Unfortunately, this support is not always offered.

Domestic violence and rape are, therefore, pressing problems that require attention from policymakers and implementers in Africa. Over the last two decades, countries have responded to these problems by passing laws, formulating policies, and establishing institutions. While some of these initiatives are aimed at addressing the health and socioeconomic dimensions of domestic violence and rape—for example, the establishment of shelters for battered women—many focus on the criminal justice sector. This focus on the criminal justice sector is in line with international norms which frame some forms of VAW as crimes, encourage the prosecution of perpetrators, and recommend the establishment of specialized criminal justice sector mechanisms to facilitate and enhance arrest, investigation, and prosecution. These norms have been promulgated by IOs through various international policy documents.

International Instruments and the International Women's Justice Norm

Transnational activism by women's organizations, including organizations based in Africa, placed VAW on the agenda of major IOs and regional organizations such as the UN and the AU, and has led these organizations to urge member states to address the problem. These instruments task states with implementing preventive, protective, and punitive measures and with providing health services and socioeconomic support for survivors. In fact, the enactment and enforcement of laws are core recommendations of most international instruments, and African countries are party to them. With the exception of Sudan and Somalia, they have signed and ratified or acceded to the Convention on the Elimination of all Forms of Discrimination against Women (CEDAW), the cornerstone of global women's rights policymaking. When it was adopted in 1979, CEDAW included articles on several women's rights issue areas, including health, education, and employment, but did not mention VAW. This omission was rectified by General Recommendation 19, adopted in 1992. This recommendation calls on state parties to put in place legal, social, economic, and health measures to prevent VAW and to assist survivors. It urges states to enforce penal sanctions but leaves room for alternative forms of adjudication and punishment, including civil remedies:

Article 16
  (r) Measures that are necessary to overcome family violence should include:

(i) Criminal penalties where necessary and civil remedies in cases of domestic violence;

...

(t) That States parties should take all legal and other measures that are necessary to provide effective protection of women against gender-based violence, including, inter alia:

(i) Effective legal measures, including penal sanctions, civil remedies and compensatory provisions to protect women against all kinds of violence, including inter alia violence and abuse in the family, sexual assault and sexual harassment in the workplace (CEDAW, 1992).

The convention requires states to submit a report every four years that details their progress in reaching these goals, but most state parties have failed to regularly honor this commitment (United Nations Economic Commission for Africa, n.d.). Furthermore, nine countries, four of them in North Africa, have entered reservations to the convention. Nonetheless, it remains the foundational and guiding global policy document for action on VAW at the international and national levels (Bond, 2014; Tamale, 2001). Its adoption has been followed by several other global and regional policy documents, all of which charge states to enact and enforce VAW laws.

The 1993 UN Declaration on the Elimination of Violence against Women (DEVAW) was the first global consensus document to focus exclusively on VAW. It defines the problem, affirms that it is a violation of women's rights and freedoms, and similar to General Recommendation 19, provides a framework for action at the international and national levels. It, however, explicitly objects to tradition taking precedence over women's rights, an issue that is only recognized as a problem in General Recommendation 19. According to DEVAW:

States should condemn violence against women and should not invoke any custom, tradition or religious consideration to avoid their obligations with respect to its elimination (United Nations General Assembly, 1993).

Another seminal international document that urges states to end impunity for VAW is UN Security Council Resolution 1325 (2000) on Women, Peace, and Security. Similar to CEDAW, African women played a key role in the adoption of this resolution. Advocacy by activists and civil society organizations on the continent and elsewhere in the Global South was instrumental to its passage (Cohn, 2003; Basu, 2016). Furthermore, the resolution was sponsored by Namibia, which held the presidency of the Security Council when it was adopted. The resolution:

> 11. Emphasizes the responsibility of all States to put an end to impunity and to prosecute those responsible for genocide, crimes against humanity, and war crimes including those relating to sexual and other violence against women and girls, and in this regard stresses the need to exclude these crimes, where feasible from amnesty provisions (United Nations Security Council, 2000).

Côte d'Ivoire was the first country to launch a national action plan to implement Resolution 1325. As of December 2019, 23 other African countries, many of them recovering from war or political instability or still in political turmoil, had launched national action plans to localize the resolution.

Regional organizations in Africa have also identified women's rights, which include protection from VAW, as a policy priority. This has been reflected in instruments developed by these organizations. The AU's Protocol to the African Charter on Human and People's Rights on the Rights of Women in Africa (Maputo Protocol), adopted in 2003, is a progressive instrument. Activism by women's organizations led the AU to place women's rights on its agenda and to the drafting of the protocol (Banda, 2006). The protocol builds on CEDAW and other international instruments, but addresses some of the gaps that have been identified therein (Gawaya & Mukasa, 2005). It is the first international instrument to call on states to legally prohibit harmful traditional practices such as FGM. It also does not explicitly leave room for states to adopt civil remedies in domestic violence cases.

The Maputo Protocol requires state parties to commit the necessary budgetary allocation and other resources for its full implementation and for monitoring performance. It also requires countries to submit a progress report every two years that shows the legal and other measures taken to realize the objectives therein. Unlike General Recommendation 19, the protocol is legally binding and as of December 2018 had been signed and ratified by 33 state and signed but not ratified by 15. Both Liberia and Côte d'Ivoire have signed and ratified the protocol. Three states—Botswana, Egypt, and Tunisia—had not signed or ratified the protocol as of December 2018. Six states have entered reservations since its adoption, and as of September 2018, only nine states had submitted all of their progress reports in accordance with Article 26 of the protocol.

The Economic Community of West African States (ECOWAS), the East African Community (EAC), and the Southern African Development Community (SADC) have also adopted subregional instruments that require member states to prevent and punish VAW. SADC's 2008 Protocol on Gender and Development goes beyond calling on states to enact and enforce laws to urging them to create specialized mechanisms. According to the protocol, "State Parties shall establish special counselling services, legal and police units to provide dedicated and sensitive services to survivors of gender based violence." This protocol is the first international instrument that calls for the creation of specialized mechanisms in the criminal justice sector. It is, however, not the only international document to do this. The UN, through international handbooks, training manuals, and reports, has recommended that countries, particularly post-conflict countries, establish specialized criminal justice sector mechanisms to investigate and prosecute VAW. UN Women has urged states to create gender desks, focal points, and units within security sector agencies (UN Women, 2011). In addition to calling for adequate gender-sensitivity training for police and criminal justice professionals and standards of behavior that promote equality and justice for women, the UN's 1997 Model Strategies and Practical Measures on the Elimination of Violence against Women in the Field of Crime Prevention and Criminal Justice urges states to establish specialized units staffed by personnel who are trained to "deal with the complexities and victim sensitivities involved in cases of violence against women" (p. 8). The UN Office on Drug and Crime's (UNODC) Handbook on Effective Responses to Violence against Women also promotes specialized expertise and units as best practices (2010). The UN's promotion of specialized mechanisms has not been limited to international policy documents. UN agencies have advised African governments to establish these mechanisms and have funded their establishment in many post-conflict countries, including Liberia, Côte d'Ivoire, and Rwanda.[3]

The UN and other international organizations have promoted specialized mechanisms partly based on their assessment of how these agencies have performed in other regions. They gained international attention when Brazil began creating police stations, staffed exclusively by female police officers, who were tasked with receiving and investigating cases of VAW. The first such police station was established in Sao Paolo in 1985 and was a product of feminist activism for an improved response to VAW, progressive politics ushered in by re-democratization, and political opportunism (Nelson, 1996; Roggeband, 2016; Santos, 2004). The expectation was that these women's police stations would ameliorate the mostly inadequate and sometimes abusive and discriminatory response to VAW that prevailed in the traditional police force in Brazil. According to Nelson, "Police, almost always men, routinely ignored and rarely prosecuted cases of physical and sexual abuse of women and often blamed and harassed the victim" (1996, p. 131). The establishment of these women's police stations led to a significant increase in the number of cases reported to the police (Santos, 2004). In Brazil and Nicaragua, they also improved how police responded to VAW (Medie & Walsh, 2019; Santos, 2005; Walsh, 2015). Reports from post-conflict countries in Africa—Rwanda, Sudan, Sierra Leone, and Liberia—also suggest that specialized mechanisms have led to improved police performance. In fact, the UN has lauded Rwanda's One-Stop Centre in Kigali, where trained police officers coordinate with the health service to provide a more comprehensive response to VAW, as a best practice (UNPOL, 2015). The UN Police, which lists the establishment of specialized mechanisms as a best practice in peace-building, has identified several benefits to having them. They include increased confidence to report and pursue justice, better quality of services provided by trained personnel, and decreased re-victimization of survivors (UNPOL, 2015). According to UNIFEM, "Women's Police Stations and dedicated gender units help to counter the under-reporting of crimes against women that is ubiquitous in patriarchal societies as well as in their police services. By allocating specific resources to deal with gender-based violence, a strong message is sent to the population about the end of the impunity for these crimes" (2007, p. 6).

The recognition of some forms of VAW as crimes by major international bodies and the emphasis on the prosecution of perpetrators of these crimes and on the creation of specialized criminal justice sector mechanisms are three major developments in the campaigns to end VAW. I say *some forms of VAW* because some documents, including General Recommendation 19, do not classify harmful practices such as FGM and forced marriage as crimes. They, however, recognize that neither domestic violence nor rape is a private dispute to be resolved within the family or community; rather, they are offenses that should be resolved by the state. And by making this recognition and promoting the establishment of specialized mechanisms, they have set the standard for how countries should deal with VAW. However, states vary in how they address each form of VAW. Most states have not harmonized some or all of their domestic laws with international policy documents, and in some cases, have not passed the necessary laws. There is also extensive evidence that implementation is weak or nonexistent in many countries, including those that have passed progressive laws (Olonisakin & Hendricks, 2013; UN Women, 2015). In other words, the laws on paper often do not benefit women on the ground. Relatedly, not all states have established specialized legal and police mechanisms, and there is variation in the types of mechanisms adopted by states, the resources invested in them, and their performance. Indeed, it is evident that international instruments and policy documents and the norms they generate are not sufficient to cause states to enact and enforce laws, to establish specialized mechanisms, or to set and enforce standards of behavior within these mechanisms. While the literature is mostly silent on law enforcement and on the establishment and performance of specialized mechanisms in Africa, scholars have identified factors that influence states to pass VAW laws. Their findings are relevant for understanding the establishment of specialized mechanisms and the performance of personnel within them.

The Domestic Adoption of International Policies

The state's role as an entity that prevents and protects against VAW in Africa is a paradoxical one. This is because the state, represented by the police, gendarmerie, border patrol agents, the military, and other security sector agencies, has perpetrated physical and sexual violence against women not only during wars, but also in periods of relative peace (Adomako Ampofo & Prah, 2009). Furthermore, most countries have had, and continue to have, discriminatory laws on the books, many of them dating from the colonial period, that legitimize gender inequality and VAW. For example, the marital rape exemption in effect in many African countries is a remnant of British colonial law (Stafford, 2007). Nonetheless, it is impossible to prevent VAW and to assist survivors in the absence of the state. It is for this reason that the enactment and the enforcement of laws are important; and research shows that African countries are making progress on the first front. Indeed, there has been a revolution in their legal response to VAW over the last two decades; many of them have passed and amended rape and domestic violence laws during this period. All 54 countries have passed a rape law. Of this number, 20 had amended the rape law at least once as of December 2018, and 15 of these amendments were passed after the year 2000.[4] The amendments have typically strengthened the law by expanding the definition of rape, institutionalizing harsher punishment, and in seven cases, criminalizing marital rape. However, some of these laws are inadequate for several reasons, one being that they do not touch upon the issue of consent. Furthermore, only 23 countries have criminalized marital rape.[5]

Some attempts by women's organizations (including in Liberia) to introduce marital rape clauses have been met with resistance from lawmakers and groups within society, including some women's groups (Adomako Ampofo & Prah, 2009). This resistance is due to the reluctance to take away men's rights over their partners' bodies, a product of patriarchal gender norms and structures. Patriarchal gender norms also partly explain the resistance to the enactment of domestic violence laws in some countries. As of December 2019, 17 countries, including Côte d'Ivoire, did not have a domestic violence law, so the act was prosecuted under other articles of the penal code such as assault and battery. The absence of a domestic violence law signifies a failure on the part of policymakers to recognize the gravity of the offense.

Post-conflict states have led the way in the passage of women's rights laws. Scholars attribute the enactment of laws in both post-conflict and non-post-conflict states to activism by women's movements (Adomako Ampofo, 2008; Tripp et al., 2009; Tsikata, 2009). Strong women's organizations, working collectively, have not only placed VAW on the international agenda and pressured states to sign international instruments, but also lobbied them to pass and amend domestic legislation. Their efforts have been facilitated by evolving international norms which have given way to increased attention to and funding for VAW initiatives, particularly those that focus on sexual violence. Tripp (2015) argues that disruptions caused by conflict have also led to changes in gender power relations and thus have increased the passage of laws in post-conflict countries.

These laws have been complemented by various national policies that seek to prevent VAW, and to assist survivors in accessing justice and care. States have introduced policies dedicated to specific forms of VAW, including domestic violence and rape, and others that target all forms of VAW. In some of these policies, VAW is included as one of many women's rights issue areas, in addition to areas such as health, education, and employment. These polices spell out countries' plans for combating VAW, and where a form of violence has been criminalized, these policies also include plans to enhance law enforcement. They, therefore, outline steps to improve various criminal justice sector agencies' responses to domestic violence, rape, and other forms of VAW.

However, as explained earlier, there is an enforcement deficit in many African countries. Consequently, most survivors in countries with very progressive domestic violence and rape laws are unable to receive justice from the formal criminal justice system. For the majority of survivors, the laws on paper have not made any difference in their lives. Even more troubling is that some of these problems have been identified within newly created specialized mechanisms. Reports suggest that although specialized mechanisms can improve performance in the criminal justice sector, they exhibit some of the weaknesses found in non-specialized agencies (Medie & Walsh, 2019). Women's police stations in Brazil continued many of the negligent practices found in the regular male-run police stations (Nelson, 1996). Specialized police units in Africa have been subjected to similar criticism. Activists have criticized these units for the low rate of prosecution of cases and the continued high level of impunity (Medie, 2012). Reports of unethical practices, re-victimization of survivors, and failure to investigate complaints and effect arrests have emerged in post-conflict countries such as Liberia and Sierra Leone. These reports clearly demonstrate that the establishment of specialized mechanisms is not sufficient to correct all of the problems in the criminal justice system. However, reports suggest that even though these mechanisms are not a panacea, they have led to some improvements in women's access to justice. For example, Sierra Leone's Saturday Courts, which were created to clear a backlog of 700 VAW cases, accelerated the hearing of cases and significantly increased conviction rates (IRIN, 2013). It is this improvement that this book seeks to trace and explain in Liberia and Côte d'Ivoire, in addition to how specialized police and gendarmerie mechanisms came to be established.

Specialized Criminal Justice Sector Mechanisms

A major development in how African states respond to VAW has been the establishment of specialized police, prosecutorial, and court mechanisms to address one or multiple forms of VAW or GBV. Forty-one African states have created at least one specialized mechanism in the criminal justice sector to address VAW or sometimes GBV, such that boys and men are also served by the mechanism. With a few exceptions, these mechanisms were established after the year 2000. They have been structured in two ways: (1) specialized independent units and (2) specialized embedded units. The former describes specialized units of the police force, gendarmerie, prosecutor, or court, established to investigate or prosecute one or more forms of VAW or GBV. Personnel of independent units typically work exclusively on VAW or GBV cases. They receive specialized training and although they sometimes share office space with other personnel (who are not mandated to work on VAW or GBV), they are set apart by the fact that they form part of a distinct sub-institution. They are also set apart by their training and mandate. They receive specialized GBV training and exercise jurisdiction over one, several, or all forms of VAW or GBV. Examples of these independent units are Liberia's Women and Children Protection Section (WACPS) of the police force, created in 2005; Liberia's Criminal Court E, created in 2008 to prosecute sex crimes; and Sierra Leone's Family Support Unit of the police, created in 2001 to receive and investigate cases of violence against women and children. Another example of an independent unit is the Saturday Court in Sierra Leone that was held in the capital, Freetown, and in Makeni, the largest city in the north of the country. It consisted of two magisterial courts and one high court that exclusively heard VAW cases and others that fell under the Devolution of Estates Act and the Registration of Customary Marriage and Divorce Act, on Saturdays. The independence here does not mean that these are autonomous units. In fact, they generally work closely with various branches of the criminal justice system and the health sector. Rather, the independence of these units derives from the fact that they are an entity set apart from generalized and other specialized units by their structure, mandate, rules, and expertise. Indeed, there are other units that deal with VAW in the police force, gendarmerie, and justice sector but are integrated into generalized units. I refer to these as specialized embedded units.

Specialized embedded units describe personnel (or sometimes one person) within the police force, gendarmerie, prosecutor's office, or court that have been assigned (formally or informally) the task of handling VAW or GBV in their respective posts. They include gender focal persons in these institutions. Typically, officials in embedded units have received some specialized training in how to investigate and/or prosecute cases of VAW or GBV. They, however, differ from specialized independent units in two ways. The first difference is that independent units are sub-institutions within the criminal justice system, while embedded units consist of individuals (formally or informally) stationed in generalized police or gendarmerie units, prosecutorial offices, or courts. For example, although Liberia's WACPS falls under the Criminal Investigations Division, it is not a part of another section within the police force. Conversely, most gender focal points in Côte d'Ivoire in the initial post-conflict period were not stationed in a gender desk. Personnel of embedded units operate within the boundaries, mandate, and rules of the generalized unit in which they are stationed. A second difference between independent units and embedded units is that while personnel of the former usually deal exclusively with VAW, GBV, and sometimes violence against children, the latter sometimes handle unrelated cases.

It is clear that the establishment of independent units necessitates major changes in a criminal justice sector agency. It requires the state to transfer jurisdiction over one or more offenses from an existing unit to a new one. It also involves the recruitment and training of a new crop of officials or the posting of existing personnel to the specialized unit and their training. The creation of these independent units also requires separate infrastructure such as buildings, as well as equipment such as vehicles, to ensure that investigation and prosecution meet the standards that have been defined in international consensus documents. However, it is important to note that not all independent units meet these standards. For example, many of Liberia's WACPS units were under-resourced (Medie, 2015). Consequently, they often had insufficient office space and lacked vehicles and other basic tools and equipment needed to enforce the law. I will explain in Chapter 8 that this often proved a challenge to enforcing the law in accordance with international standards. Embedded units also face these challenges. However, the introduction of embedded units generally requires less transformation within traditional security sector agencies. This is because these units are often inserted into traditional agencies without much change to institutional structure, rules, and norms. While I have been able to identify two types of specialized mechanisms, it is a challenge to identify the type of mechanism in each country without having access to detailed secondary description or having visited these units. Therefore, Table 1.1 does not distinguish between types of unit. It is also possible that some countries have informal arrangements that have not been written about and are therefore not captured in this table.

Table 1.1 shows that the majority of specialized mechanisms have been created within the police force, followed by the prosecutorial/legal services. Overall, 35 police and 27 prosecutorial mechanisms have been created across

Table 1.1 Specialized Criminal Justice Sector Mechanisms in Africa

Country	Specialized Police	Specialized Prosecutor/Legal Services	Specialized Court
Algeria	No	No	No
Angola	No	Free Legal Assistance	No
Benin	Office Centrale de la Protection des Mineurs, de la Famille et de la Répression de la Traite des Etres Humains (OCPMRTEH)	One Stop Care Centres	No
Botswana	Botswana Police Service GBV Focal Points	Legal Aid Services	No
Burkina Faso	Brigade for Moral and Juvenile Affairs	No	No
Burundi	The Brigade for the Protection of Women and Children	HUMURA	No
Cabo Verde	The Police Support Offices for Victims of GBV	Care Network Initiatives	No
Cameroon	Special Morals Brigade	No	No
Central African Republic	No	No	No
Chad	Women and Children Protection Units Gender desk in the Integrated Security Detachment (DIS) Unit	Centre d'Ecoute	No
Comoros	No	No	No
Congo	No	No	No
Côte d'Ivoire	Gender Desks and Gender Focal Points	No	No
Democratic Republic of Congo	Police Special Protection of Children and Women Unit	No	Mobile Courts[a]

Continued

Table 1.1 *Continued*

Country	Specialized Police	Specialized Prosecutor/Legal Services	Specialized Court
Djibouti	No	La Cellule d'Ecoute, d'Information et d'Orientation (CEIO)	No
Egypt	The Violence Against Women Unit	The Ombudsman Office at NCW	No
Equatorial Guinea	No	No	Family Court
Eritrea	No	No	No
Ethiopia	Child and Women Protection Units	No	
Gabon	No	No	No
Gambia	No	No	No
Ghana	Domestic Violence Victims Support Unit (DoVVSU)[b]	Free Legal Aid Service	Gender-Based Violence Courts
Guinea	Office for Gender and Children Protection of Police (OPROGEM)	No	No
Guinea-Bissau	No	Access to Justice Center (CAJ)	No
Kenya	The Spider Squad Gender Desk	National Legal Aid Scheme, One-Stop Shop, Office of the Director of Public Prosecutions	No
Lesotho	Child and Gender Protection Unit	No	No
Liberia	Women and Children Protection Section (WACPS)	Sexual and Gender-Based Crimes Unit and Gender-Based Violence Unit	Criminal Court E
Libya	No	No	No
Madagascar	No	Centers for Listening and Legal Advice Centers	No
Malawi	Victim Support Units (VSUs)	One-Stop Centers	No

Table 1.1 Continued

Country	Specialized Police	Specialized Prosecutor/Legal Services	Specialized Court
Mali	The Brigade of Moral and Youth Affairs	Advisory Committee for Gender Issues	No
Mauritania	No	No	No
Mauritius	Police Family Protection Unit	Legal Aid Act and Family Support Bureau	No
Morocco	No	Specialized Protection Cells and Tamkine	No
Mozambique	Special Women's and Children's Units (Gabinetes de Atendimento)	IPAJ Legal Aid	No
Namibia	Women and Child Protection Units (WACPUs) and Gender-Based Violence Investigation Unit (GBVIU)	Specialized Unit for Prosecution	Specialized Unit for prosecution of sexual offenses and domestic violence
Niger	No	No	No
Nigeria	Juvenile Welfare Centre, Anti-Human Trafficking Unit and Gender Unit	Legal Aid	No
Rwanda	Gender Desk/Gender-Based Violence Focal Points	Isange One Stop Centre	No
Sao Tome and Principe	No	No	No
Senegal	The Brigade of Moral Affairs	No	No
Seychelles	The Family Squad	The Family Violence Act	The Family Tribunal
Sierra Leone	Family Support Units[c]	No	Saturday Court
Somalia	Office of Public Relations and Women and Children Desks		No

Continued

Table 1.1 Continued

Country	Specialized Police	Specialized Prosecutor/Legal Services	Specialized Court
South Africa	SAPS' Family Violence, Child Protection and Sexual Offences Investigations Unit	One Stop Centers	Sexual-Offense Courts
South Sudan	Special Protection Units	No	Specialized Women's and Children's Court
Sudan	The Family and Child Protection Unit	Unit for the Suppression of Violence against Women and Children	No
Swaziland	Domestic Violence, Child Protection and Sexual Offences Unit (DCS)	One Stop Centers	Child Friendly and Victim Friendly benches within the Federal First Instance Court
Tanzania	Gender and Children Desks	No	No
Togo	No	No	No
Tunisia	No	No	No
Uganda	The Child and Family Protection Unit (CFPU) and the Criminal Investigations Directorate (CID): Gender Based Department	No	No
Zambia	Victim Support Unit and Sex Crimes Unit	One-Stop Centre/ Coordinated Multisectoral Response Centres (CRCs)	Fast track court for Gender Based Violence (GBV)
Zimbabwe	Victim Friendly Unit (VFU)	Legal Aid Directorate	Victim Friendly System "Courts"

[a] These courts are often temporarily set up in remote villages to conduct military and civilian rape trials.

[b] Previously known as the Women and Juvenile Unit (WAJU), established in 1998.

[c] Previously known as the Domestic Violence Unit (DVU), established in 1999.

Source: UN Women's Global Database on Violence against Women, review of newspapers, and policy documents. Data collected from 2016–2018.

the continent. Specialized courts are the least common form of specialized mechanisms with 12 been created as of December 2018.

Another interesting trend in states' responses is that post-conflict states have created proportionately more specialized police and court mechanisms than non-post-conflict states.[6] Indeed, research has shown that post-conflict states have more rapidly adopted women's rights reforms (Tripp, 2015). Eighty-four and 23 percent of post-conflict states have created specialized police mechanisms and courts, respectively, in comparison to 58 and 9 percent of non-post-conflict states. Conversely, 51 percent of non-post-conflict states have created prosecutorial mechanisms, in comparison to 46 percent of post-conflict states. A further analysis of the table raises another question about variation within post-conflict states; some have made more changes than others. Liberia, with four mechanisms, is at the head of the pack. Somewhere in the middle is Côte d'Ivoire with two. Angola is one of the countries lower on the list, with one unit, and a country at the bottom is Eritrea, which has not created a specialized mechanism in the criminal justice sector.

Although I do not have the date of creation of all mechanisms listed in the table, in countries with available dates, only seven had created a specialized unit before the year 2000.[7] The explosion in the creation of specialized mechanisms, therefore, coincided with the international promotion of the practice, particularly by the UN, which began to do so heavily in the mid- to late 1990s. It also coincides with the end of several armed conflicts in Africa and the deployment of UN peacekeeping missions. Therefore, I seek to understand the influence that the UN, which has promoted specialized mechanisms, has had on their establishment in Africa. How have women's organizations, which have been key to the adoption of VAW laws, policies, and practices, influenced the establishment of specialized mechanisms? Furthermore, how do international organizations and the women's movement influence the performance of personnel within these specialized mechanisms? These questions animate this book, and I seek to answer them by analyzing the establishment of specialized mechanisms in the police and gendarmerie in Côte d'Ivoire and in the police in Liberia, and the performance of personnel in these specialized units.

Conclusion

The last two decades have witnessed increased attention to VAW, especially sexual violence. This increased attention has been as a result of women's movements that have pressured states and international organizations to address the problem. International organizations such as the UN have responded with international instruments and manuals that have promoted an international women's justice norm for VAW, particularly sexual violence, and have urged states to create specialized criminal justice sector mechanisms. In accordance with these international documents, states have adopted VAW laws and policies. They have created specialized criminal justice sector mechanisms. Evidence from Latin America and countries in Africa where these mechanisms have been studied suggests that they have the potential to increase women's access to justice and to improve how they are treated by the criminal justice sector. In other words, they could mitigate some of the problems that plague non-specialized criminal justice sector agencies in Africa. Indeed, the progress that has been made in some countries, particularly post-conflict countries such as Rwanda, suggest that an improved access to justice for women is more likely when these specialized mechanisms are in place. However, these mechanisms can suffer from many of the problems that plague regular non-specialized criminal justice agencies. Therefore, there is a need to better understand them. While the literature has theorized how laws and policies come to be adopted, it has yet to systematically examine the establishment of specialized mechanisms and the performance of their personnel in Africa. This has limited our understanding of the issue and stymied efforts to end violence against girls and women. In the next chapter, I present the study's theory and explain how it advances the literature on IR, gender and politics, and African studies.

2
The Domestic Implementation of International Women's Rights Norms

What explains why and how post-conflict states in Africa implement international women's rights norms? More specifically, what explains why and how post-conflict states in Africa implement the international women's justice norm? What accounts for the variation in the establishment of specialized mechanisms, and thus in the implementation of the international women's justice norm? What roles do external and domestic actors play in states' establishment of these specialized mechanisms? How do specialized mechanisms change street-level implementation? Furthermore, how does the degree of institutionalization affect street-level implementation and women's access to justice? These questions frame this book's investigation into implementation at the domestic level of the international women's justice norm through its associated best practice of establishing specialized mechanisms for addressing violence against women (VAW). I operationalize implementation as three actions: (1) the creation of a specialized police and gendarmerie unit (through a declaratory statement); (2) the institutionalization of this unit (creating a central directorate, assigning officers to work exclusively on VAW, installing units in all administrative regions of the country); and (3) the performance of officers in this unit (referring cases to the prosecutor and treating victims with sensitivity).

The literature on the domestic implementation of international norms points to an interplay of international and domestic factors that explain how and why implementation happens. However, there are actors and relationships that need to be further examined. Is an IO like the UN equally influential across all stages of the implementation process? Are domestic actors and conditions equally important at all stages of the implementation process? How does implementation at the national level affect street-level implementation? This chapter presents a theoretical framework for addressing these questions.

Global Norms and Local Action. Peace A. Medie, Oxford University Press (2020). © Oxford University Press.
DOI: 10.1093/oso/9780190922962.001.0001

It shows that a combination of international pressure, domestic pressure, and domestic political and institutional conditions explains the establishment of specialized units in post-conflict states in Africa. I argue that a high level of international pressure, mainly from the UN, exerted by raising awareness of VAW, lobbying decision-makers in the state, naming and shaming state perpetrators of violence, and capacity building, is key to the creation of specialized mechanisms. Domestic pressure from the women's movement and favorable domestic political and institutional conditions also facilitate rapid creation. However, domestic pressure and conditions become more important at the institutionalization stage. Thus, when domestic pressure is low and domestic political and institutional conditions unfavorable, the pace of institutionalization is significantly slower. This outcome of implementation at the national level affects street-level implementation. Consequently, the international women's justice norm is likely to be more salient with a greater degree of institutionalization of a specialized mechanism.

In this chapter, I draw on literature in international relations (IR), gender and politics, public administration, and African studies to isolate the mechanisms that connect international and domestic factors to institutional change and to street-level performance. I also draw on these bodies of work to delineate the pathways through which change occurs.

A Theory of Norm Implementation

Implementation is an incredibly complex process that involves a multiplicity of actors and conditions that are contextually dependent and constantly changing; theories of implementation that apply to all policies and scenarios are thus inevitably limited in their scope of application. Since my primary objective is to explain how and why implementation of the international women's justice norm occurred in my empirical cases, which are post-conflict countries in Africa that both experienced a high level of international pressure, I focus on the theoretical aspects of implementation that are most relevant for my purposes, and necessarily place other aspects in the background. While this theoretical framework can be employed in studying implementation in other political and geographic settings and policy issue areas, it will inevitably be more relevant for some contexts than others.

Theorizing Implementation: A Confluence of the International and the Domestic

Most international norms cannot be put into practice without implementation by domestic actors. However, despite the centrality of implementation to the norm cycle and to domestic-level change, the IR literature has mostly sought to explain the manifestation of norms by studying compliance, a concept that is related but not identical to implementation. In a positive development, a new wave of norm scholarship has sought to conceptualize implementation and to systematically identify the variables and causal mechanisms that explain how states implement norms at the domestic level (Avdeyeva, 2015; Betts & Orchard, 2014; Deere, 2009; Huelss, 2017; Montoya, 2013). Raustiala and Slaughter (2002) define implementation as the "process of putting international norms into practice" (p. 539). Compliance—states' behavior and practices that conform to international norms/rules (Buchanan & Keohane, 2006; Risse & Ropp, 2013)—is an outcome of the implementation process. Importantly, implementation is neither necessary nor sufficient for compliance, because states can comply with international rules without taking any action prescribed by the international norm (Raustiala, 2000; Raustiala & Slaughter, 2002; Treib, 2014). Raustiala and Slaughter (2002) propose three components of international norm implementation: "the passage of legislation, creation of institutions (both domestic and international) and enforcement of rules" (p. 539). This book examines and explains the second and third components of the implementation process (the establishment of institutions and street-level enforcement) in Liberia and Côte d'Ivoire.

While this study is grounded in the IR and gender and politics literatures, it also draws on the African studies literature. This is because IR scholars have recognized that the domestic political context delimits the influence of international actors who seek to promote an international norm (Acharya, 2004; Betts, 2014; Cardenas, 2007; Cortell & Davis, 2000; Deere, 2009; Simmons, 2009; Zwingel, 2011). The institutional structure of implementing agencies also affects if and how a norm is implemented (Betts & Orchard, 2014; Deere, 2009). It is, therefore, impossible to explain domestic implementation without an analysis of domestic political and institutional dynamics.

In fact, scholars have concluded that norm implementation is influenced by an interplay of factors at the international and domestic levels (Avdeyeya, 2015; Engwicht 2018; Deere, 2009; Montoya, 2013; Walsh, 2015; Zwingel,

2011). At the international level, actors such as powerful states, multilateral organizations, and transnational advocacy networks influence implementation by exerting pressure on states with the goal of getting them to act and/or to ensure that their actions conform with international expectations (Keck & Sikkink, 1998). International actors have a variety of tools at their disposal that they use to pressure states, particularly developing and conflict-affected states such as Liberia and Côte d'Ivoire. Risse and Ropp (2013) identify four such mechanisms that induce states' compliance with international human rights norms: (1) coercion (use of force and legal enforcement), (2) changing incentives (sanctions and rewards), (3) persuasion and discourse, and (4) capacity building (p. 15). Due to the overlap between compliance and implementation, some of these mechanisms are also used by international (and in some instances domestic) actors to compel states to implement. In her study of the implementation of the Trade-Related Aspects of Intellectual Property Rights (TRIPS), Deere (2009) found that developed countries used their economic power to influence implementation by linking economic rewards to the progress that developing countries made in TRIPS reform. The tools used to exert this economic power, and thus to incentivize developing countries, included bilateral trade and investment deals, the threat of sanctions, and trade sanctions. Deere (2009) also found that powerful players used ideas to persuade developing countries to implement TRIPS. They sought to influence expertise, know-how, and institutional capacity, and employed such strategies as framing debates and building a sympathetic community of experts. Walsh (2015) also found that IOs, which formed part of transnational advocacy networks operating in Nicaragua and Guatemala, influenced the establishment of women's policing units by providing funds to build and modify institutions and by disseminating information on institutional models at regional and sub-regional meetings. Montoya (2009), in her study of the European Union's efforts to combat VAW in member states, also found that the organization employed resources and information to help states implement policies and argues that these steps can improve the prospects for domestic implementation. However, despite international and transnational actors' use of this repertoire of strategies to pressure states to implement international norms, studies show that their impact is filtered through and mediated by the domestic political and institutional contexts in which they seek to effect change.

Therefore, international pressure does not independently explain how states implement international norms or the variation in implementation.

Instead, domestic actors and conditions delimit the effect that international pressure has on the implementation process. Domestic actors can serve as gatekeepers and, depending on their numbers, can stall action (Busby, 2007; Tseblis, 2002). These gatekeepers include policymakers, legislators, judges, and civil society organizations (Ayeni, 2016). Among other things, civil society organizations can serve as intermediaries who "appropriate, translate, and remake transnational discourses" for a local audience (Merry, 2006, p. 3). Their actions, combined with political and institutional conditions, such as political stability, state capacity, and citizens' participation in governance, influence domestic implementation.

Although capacity often emerges as a key predictor of implementation in most studies, the actors and conditions that matter can differ according to the state and the policy issue area. In a comparative study of internally displaced people's policies, Orchard (2014) found that a capacity gap in the Nepalese and Ugandan governments, coupled with political infighting in Nepal and widespread confusion about implementation across sectors in Uganda, stalled implementation. Deere (2009) attributes variation in countries' implementation of TRIPS to "the interplay of global IP [intellectual property] debates, international power pressures, and political dynamics within developing countries" (p. 17). She concludes that government capacity, public engagement, and government coordination shaped developing countries' ability to filter and manage international pressures to implement TRIPS.

Research on specialized police stations in Latin America have contextualized the relationship between international and domestic factors. This scholarship identifies three main factors that have influenced the establishment of specialized police units: (1) mobilization by women's movements, (2) funding and information from IOs, and (3) the process of democratization, which created a favorable political opportunity structure (Hautzinger, 2002; Santos, 2004; Walsh, 2015). This literature shines a light on the important role that women's movements and their constituent organizations play in the domestic implementation of international norms. In Nicaragua, women's rights advocates spearheaded efforts to create specialized policing for women (Medie & Walsh, 2019). This finding is in line with scholarship on women's movements that has shown that they are critical to the adoption of progressive women's rights policies. Weldon (2002), in her study of how democratic states address VAW, argued that governments' responsiveness is driven by "the presence of a strong, autonomous women's movement that draws on and reinforces state institutions designed to promote the status of women" (p. 5).

The importance of autonomous women's movements resonates in Africa (Tripp, 2001), where authoritarian governments have sometimes co-opted women's activism to serve the interests of the ruling elite. Overall, the literature demonstrates that domestic implementation of international norms cannot be explained without understanding both international and domestic factors and dynamics. While this scholarship has mostly not disaggregated the stages of the implementation process, focused on Africa, or systematically examined street-level performance, it provides key insight into how and why implementation occurs. Thus, the central thesis of this book originates in this literature.

I argue that international pressure is key to the creation of specialized mechanisms. Where domestic pressure is high/strong and domestic political and institutional conditions favorable, the process of creation is slightly accelerated. However, domestic actors and conditions have a larger impact at the institutionalization stage. This is in line with the IR literature that has underlined the centrality of domestic actors and conditions (Acharya, 2004; Avdeyeya, 2015; Betts & Orchard, 2014; Brown, 2014; Deere, 2009; Montoya, 2013; Tholens & Groß, 2015; Zwingel 2011). Thus, as shown in Figure 2.1, where domestic pressure is low/weak and political and institutional conditions unfavorable, institutionalization of a specialized mechanism is slow, even when international pressure is high. Furthermore, the findings of studies of women's movements suggest that even if a low level of domestic pressure is paired with a high level of international pressure and favorable political and institutional conditions, it is more likely to result in a slow pace of institutionalization of the specialized mechanism. This is because these movements, when strong and autonomous (and thus able to exert a high level of pressure), have been shown to take advantage of political and institutional conditions to enact change. Thus, strong and autonomous movements are needed to exploit the favorable political and institutional conditions in order to generate rapid change. High international pressure might be sufficient to get a state to agree to implement a norm (e.g., in a policy document), but the actual day-to-day work of comprehensively translating this agreement into action would likely be stymied by low domestic pressure and unfavorable domestic conditions.

This framework parses out the implementation process to explain when international and domestic actors are most influential, and domestic conditions most impactful on implementation. I demonstrate this relationship between international and domestic actors and conditions in the case studies of Liberia and Côte d'Ivoire.

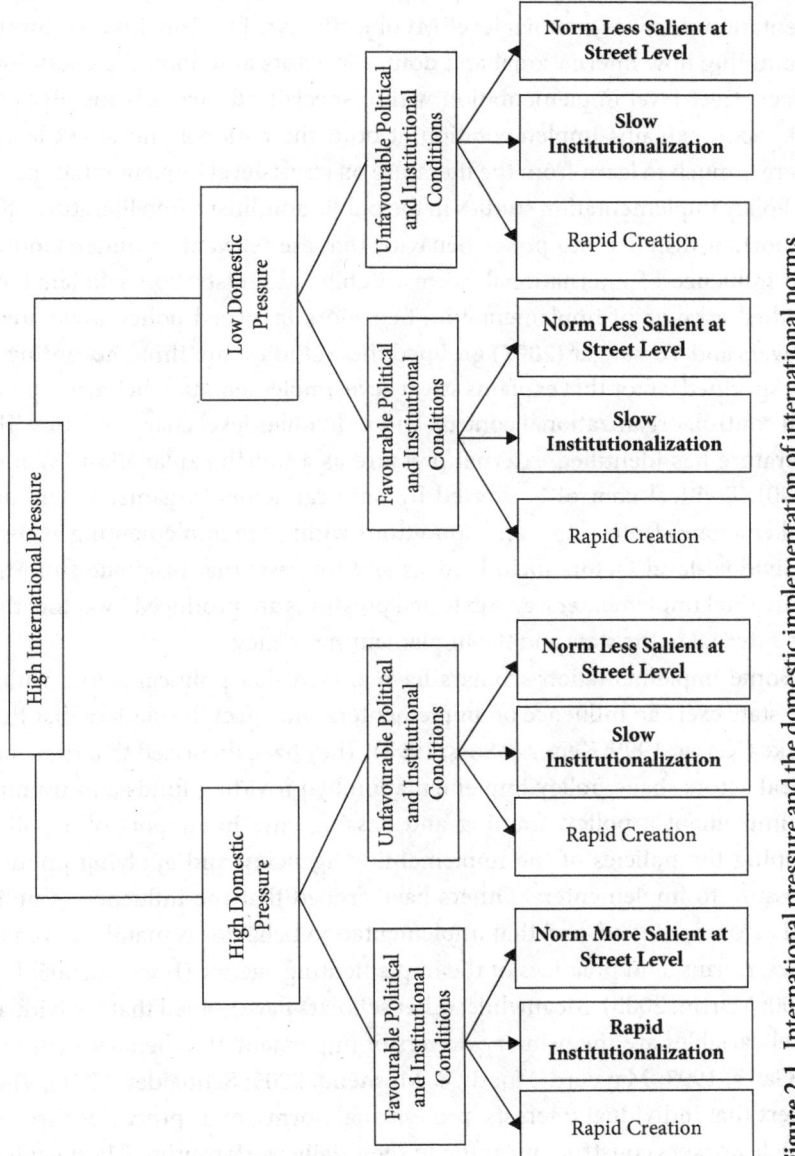

Figure 2.1 International pressure and the domestic implementation of international norms.

Street-Level Implementation

The literature on street-level implementation provides insights into implementation at a more granular level. My objective is to build on this literature by examining how international and domestic actors and domestic conditions affect street-level implementation within specialized mechanisms. Because this book explains implementation at both the national and street levels, there is much to learn from the literature on street-level implementation.

Policy implementation studies in the public administration literature offer important insights into police behavior that are relevant to understanding the influence of international norms. Public administration scholars have studied a range of implementation behaviors in varied policy issue areas. Meyers and Vorsanger (2007) grouped these studies into three, according to the specified factor that explains street-level implementation behavior: political control, organizational control, and individual-level characteristics. The literature has identified external pressure as a fourth explanation (Winter, 1990). Political control is exerted by political actors; organizational control emanates from actors and conditions within the implementing agency; individual-level factors include ideas and interests that originate from the individual implementers; and external pressures are produced by actors that are external to the state and the implementing agency.

Some implementation scholars have argued that political actors within the state exert an influence on implementers and affect the choices that they make (Keiser, 1999; Keiser & Soss, 1998). They have theorized that these political actors shape policy implementation by providing funds and training to implement a policy, framing and passing laws in support of a policy, shaping the policies of the implementing agencies, and applying political pressure to implementers. Others have argued that the influence of political actors is limited, and that implementation behavior is mainly driven by rules, norms, and practices of the implementing agency (Brewer, 2005; Lin, 2000; Martin, 2005). Meanwhile, other scholars have argued that individual-level variables are the primary drivers of implementation behavior (Brehm & Gates, 1997; Maynard-Moody & Musheno, 2003; Schneider, 1991). They assert that individual interests, professional norms, and "processes through which workers construct meaning in their daily work routines" best explain the street-level behavior (Meyers & Vorsanger, 2007, p. 156). This argument is particularly important for our understanding of women's rights policies as gender norms within society have affected the criminal justice response to women, and have led to poor treatment of victims of gendered violence (UN Women, 2012). Finally, external actors also impact street-level behavior. Søren Winter (1990) theorized that policy implementation is conditional upon the willingness of the policy's target group to cooperate with its implementation. Non-state actors also influence the enforcement of women's rights laws. In the United States, the women's movement advocated for rape and domestic violence to be placed on the public agenda and then sued the police forces in several states when they continued to refuse to intervene in incidents of intimate partner violence (Bevacqua, 2000; Boneparth & Stoper, 1988; Schneider, 1991). Religious organizations in countries across the world have actively lobbied against the implementation of women's rights policies that they view as threats to their doctrine (Joachim, 2007). These non-state actors use both material and normative power to achieve their goals.

The literature underlines four intersecting factors that determine street-level implementation: political control, organizational control, individual-level characteristics, and external pressure. Actors such as the UN and women's organizations can, therefore, influence street-level behavior by exerting pressure on political actors. Through this pressure, they also can play a role in directly shaping the organizational structure. Indeed, the degree of institutionalization determines how the organizational structure and culture are reshaped, and thus impacts street-level behavior. We should, therefore, expect a greater degree of institutionalization to lead to a greater salience of the international women's justice norm.

In summary, the literature shows that international actors matter for implementation. They employ a variety of strategies to get states to implement international norms. However, their influence is affected by domestic actors, including social movements, and is mediated by domestic conditions. Furthermore, implementation at the national level has implications for street-level implementation.

Conclusion

The UN has promoted the establishment of specialized mechanisms in the criminal justice sector as a best practice for addressing VAW. These mechanisms have spread across Africa, with police and court mechanisms being more common in post-conflict states. This study seeks to explain how and why post-conflict states are establishing these mechanisms. It also seeks to explain why the institutionalization of these mechanisms has not occurred uniformly across states. The literature reviewed in this chapter offers some direction in understanding the variation in norm implementation. The IR literature shows that international pressure matters, but its impact depends heavily on domestic actors and conditions (Avdeyeva, 2015; Betts & Orchard, 2014; Deere, 2009; Montoya, 2013; Zwingel, 2011). This literature emphasizes the importance of taking the domestic context seriously. The gender and politics literature confirms the importance of the domestic context by demonstrating the critical role that women's movements play in pushing for women's rights domestically (Adomako Ampofo, 2008; Anyidoho, Crawford & Medie, 2020; Crawford & Anyidoho, 2013; Htun & Weldon, 2010; Kang, 2015; Kang & Tripp, 2018; Medie & Walsh, 2019; Tripp, Casimiro, Kwesiga & Mungwa, 2009; Tsikata, 2009). Strong and autonomous movements would exert strong pressure and are more likely to be able to use favorable political and institutional conditions to advance their cause. And even where the political conditions are not favorable, women's movements can fight to change them, by, for example, lobbying for the creation of a women's ministry, as happened in Liberia during Charles Taylor's presidency. A woman's ministry can serve as an ally to the women's movement. We should therefore expect that when paired with a high level of international pressure, a high level of domestic pressure is more likely to positively impact both the creation and institutionalization of a specialized mechanism and that this will ultimately transform how law enforcement officers treat survivors of violence. The literature on street-level implementation reveals that political, organizational, individual, and external factors affect street-level behavior, and that strategies adopted by international and domestic actors, including naming and shaming and capacity building, can impact all of these factors. This framework enhances our understanding of norm implementation as it tells us which combination of factors is more likely to result in the rapid institutionalization of a specialized mechanism and when we are more likely to see change at the national level affect the street-level implementation of an international norm. In the next section of the book, I study the problem of VAW and how it was dealt with in Liberia and Côte d'Ivoire.

PART II
VIOLENCE AGAINST WOMEN IN LIBERIA AND CÔTE D'IVOIRE

PART II

VIOLENCE AGAINST WOMEN: LIBERIA AND CÔTE D'IVOIRE

3
Violence against Women in Liberia

In this chapter, I sketch the problem of VAW in Liberia, with a focus on domestic violence and sexual violence.[1] Widespread sexual violence was one of the most notorious features of the country's 14-year conflict. It rendered Liberia one of the most discussed cases of sexual violence in conflict in the academic literature and the policy arena. However, sexual violence predates the civil war and is only one of several forms of GBV that disproportionately affect women in the country. This chapter draws on interviews, anthropological studies, news reports, policy documents, and police records to discuss the occurrence of domestic violence and sexual violence, as well as communities' attitudes toward these acts, particularly in relation to the criminal justice system. These sources allow for an analysis of the occurrence of both forms of violence and for a more nuanced discussion of beliefs and practices surrounding them.

I explain that before, during, and after the conflict, factors such as patriarchal gender norms rendered women vulnerable to both forms of violence. All warring factions perpetrated sexual violence during the conflict, heightening the risk and brutality that girls and women faced during this time.[2] The risk of VAW was also heightened by the social and economic conditions that were produced by the country's 14-year conflict and persisted even after the 2003 Comprehensive Peace Agreement was signed. The conflict also brought national and international attention to sexual violence in the country, such that the discussion of this problem was no longer restricted to the private sphere. This chapter identifies the linkages in the causes of domestic violence and non-partner sexual violence over three distinct political periods in Liberia (pre-conflict, conflict, and post-conflict) and discusses how communities have responded to these problems.

Global Norms and Local Action. Peace A. Medie, Oxford University Press (2020). © Oxford University Press.
DOI: 10.1093/oso/9780190922962.001.0001

Legal Systems and Legal Authority in Liberia

Liberia is located in West Africa, with a 2017 estimated population of 4.732 million people. It is bordered on the south by the Atlantic Ocean, on the west by Sierra Leone, on the north by Guinea, and on the east by Côte d'Ivoire. The country was created in 1822 when freed blacks and manumitted slaves, under the auspices of the American Colonization Society, began settling in the territory. The territory was already occupied by about 16 indigenous ethnic groups, some of whom resisted the efforts of Americo-Liberian governments to establish their authority. Despite this resistance, political power became centralized among the Americo-Liberian elite in the nineteenth century. This Americo-Liberian domination of politics continued until 1980 when Master Sergeant Samuel Doe, a Krahn, seized power in a violent coup. It also paved the way for the 14-year armed conflict that began in December 1989 when Charles Taylor and his rebel group, the National Patriotic Front of Liberia (NPFL), launched their attack on Doe's government.

This political divide between Americo-Liberians and indigenous groups contributed to the institutionalization of a dual legal system. Thus, Liberia has statutory law that applies to Americo-Liberians and indigenous people, and customary law that applies almost exclusively to the latter. Rural-urban migration, which intensified in the early twentieth century, blurred the distinction between Americo-Liberians and indigenous groups. This migration, combined with governments' efforts to curb the influence of chiefs and other traditional leaders, extended the reach of statutory law. Nonetheless, customary courts and other informal justice mechanisms remained central to the adjudication of civil and criminal cases, including domestic violence and rape, even after the conflict. In fact, Liberia has two main types of customary law. There is state-sponsored customary law, as laid out in the Revised Laws and Administrative Regulations for Governing the Hinterland 1949, which was most recently revised in 2000. There are also customary law systems that have operated mostly outside the purview of the state since the introduction of state-sponsored customary law (International Crisis Group [ICG], 2006). These include family palavers, where members of an extended family meet to resolve disputes, and in the powerful Poro and Sande secret societies.

The adoption of the 1949 hinterland laws was the state's attempt to regulate the actions of chiefs, whose appointment they controlled. It gave paramount chiefs jurisdiction over "Criminal Cases subject to punishment by a fine not to exceed $10.00 or imprisonment for a period not to exceed three months" (Republic of Liberia, 1949, p. 27). Both rape and aggravated assault were, therefore, outside of chiefs' jurisdiction. However, the state placed cases connected to marriage and divorce under the jurisdiction of clan chiefs, such that aggravated assault in marriage was within their remit. Indeed, chiefs and other traditional leaders adjudicated these cases among members of their ethnic groups. Among these groups, customary law typically commanded more respect than statutory law in certain issue areas, particularly in marriage and other matters concerning the family.[3]

The outbreak of the conflict in 1989 ruptured both legal systems. The warring factions destroyed the criminal justice infrastructure of the state, and lawmakers and enforcers fled the violence, and in some cases, participated in the carnage. Customary authority—inclusive of chiefs, elders, and secret societies—in many communities was weakened as leaders fled and those who stayed mostly saw their authority usurped by combatants, most of them young men. Yet both the formal and customary systems functioned in a limited capacity. The end of the conflict paved the way for the restoration of customary authority and the rebuilding of the communities that support it. Thus, even in post-conflict Monrovia, customary law, which is not static and has evolved, was used by representatives of ethnic groups to solve disputes (ICG, 2006, p. 7). These representatives operated alongside Christian and Muslim leaders who also adjudicated the claims of members of their respective religious groups, as well as other community-level dispute resolution mechanisms. This restoration occurred alongside the reform of the criminal justice system by the state and the international community.

Violence against Women before the Liberian Conflict (Pre-1989)

Although it was not until the conflict that scholars began to systematically study VAW, with a focus on rape, there are historical accounts of both domestic violence and non-partner rape (McAllister, 1896; Schwab & Harley, 1947). Domestic violence was normalized in many communities. Describing attitudes in the 1970s and 1980s, E. J., a staff member of a women's NGO, explained that "... domestic violence for people was not much [of an] issue, it was part of the love relationship. The woman must be beaten, some of them would even boast, way back, if your husband beats you it means he loves you, it means he really cares" (interview, Gbarnga, June 25, 2011).

Despite the normalization of this violence, a woman's relatives would usually object to repeated beatings or to domestic violence they perceived as excessive. Relatives and neighbors would also intervene to stop such beatings, and some women left violent relationships with the encouragement and support of relatives. However, women rarely reported this violence to the police or to other formal actors such as magistrates. Instead, both Americo-Liberian and indigenous women dealt with it in informal forums such as family meetings. When these forums failed to resolve the problem, members of indigenous groups could elevate cases to customary courts.

While the adjudicators, relatives, and others present in these forums generally disapproved of domestic violence they perceived as excessive, they did not challenge the norm of male superiority in which it was rooted and nurtured. Indeed, in a reflection of societies across the world, women were mostly subject to men in Liberian society. This does not mean that Liberian women lacked authority within the home or in the public sphere. Among some ethnic groups, women controlled the activities of the household (Schwab & Harley, 1947; Stewart, 1886). Women also held leadership positions in customary and national institutions (Pailey, 2014). At the customary level, they were either incorporated into the ruling male hierarchy or exercised power in complementary women-only institutions. There were, therefore, female paramount and clan chiefs among some ethnic groups, as well as female traditional councils (Moran, 1990; Schwab & Harley, 1947). Female customary leaders sometimes gained legendary status. Queen Suakoko, an "infinitely feared and respected" Kpelle chief and also the first female paramount chief in Bong County, mediated a war between Americo-Liberians and indigenous peoples (Mills, 1926, p. 67; Steady, 2011). The Sande secret society of the Kpelle was another locus of power for a few women (Bledsoe, 1984). The leaders of these societies, the Zoes, initiated girls into womanhood (including through FGM) and commanded respect from women and men.

Furthermore, laws contained clauses that granted rights to women, and women were represented in formal institutions. The 1949 Revised Laws and Administrative Regulations for Governing the Hinterland forbade husbands from beating wives on suspicion of committing adultery (Republic of Liberia, 1949). An 1824 Act of the legislature gave Americo-Liberian women who emigrated without their family "a town lot, or two acres of plantation lands on their own account, and one acre on account of each of their children"

(Commonwealth of Liberia, 1824). From the nineteenth century, Americo-Liberian women could buy and sell land, enter into contracts, and initiate divorces, making them some of the most progressive in the world during this period (Fuest, 2008b, p. 207). Beginning in 1946, when Ellen Mills Scarborough assumed the position of secretary of education, women were appointed to ministerial positions (Tripp, 2015). Liberia extended suffrage to Americo-Liberian women in 1946, making it one of the first African countries to grant women the right to vote. Indigenous women were granted suffrage in 1951. Liberia is also the first African country to have a female president of a national university, and Cuttington College, the second largest institution of higher education, had a female enrollment rate of more than 30 percent by 1975, which, by international standards, was high (Henries, 1974).

Nonetheless, leadership positions in customary and state institutions were limited to a minority of women, and their rank and authority rarely surpassed that of male leaders. Furthermore, despite their representation in formal and informal institutions, they were still subject to the rules of a patriarchal society—rules that were sometimes enforced by other women (Bledsoe, 1976). This was the case of Zoes, who trained initiates into the Sande society to submit to male authority and circumcised them in order to control their sexuality (Bledsoe, 1984). The entrenchment of male power contributed to fostering an environment in which boys' and men's use of violence to compel girls and women to submit to male authority and perform their gender-assigned roles was tolerated and sometimes accepted. This violence was also used to punish those who defied gender norms in the private and public spheres. Therefore, women who failed to perform household chores or refused to have sex with their partners (among other actions) were at risk of physical and sexual violence from their partners. These gender norms also rendered women vulnerable to non-partner rape.

Liberians mostly perceived this type of rape as an attack on a woman's dignity and a blight upon her family. This contributed to the stigmatizing and blaming of survivors, causing most survivors and their family to conceal the offense. The secrecy surrounding rape is evidenced by the near absence of the act in historical accounts of crime and justice in Liberia. Nonetheless, communities generally disapproved of rape and the act was first recognized as a crime by the supreme court in *Coleman v. Republic of Liberia* (1898).[4] In this ruling, the court described rape as a "heinous crime" and "among the lowest and most debased crimes one can be guilty of ".[5] However, it was rarely disclosed, and was more likely to be adjudicated in informal forums.

Bennetta Holder Warner, head of the LNPs' Women and Children Protection Section, summarized pre-conflict attitudes toward the reporting of domestic violence and rape:

> Now, before the war, we know that there were rape cases going on, there were domestic violence cases but these cases were not reported and around that time, they were not aware or educated to the extent that they might have a case, I can go and take my complaint to this particular area for proper redress and like I said before, most times the perpetrators are either within the family or within the community, in the church and so take for example, if my, if I had a case where my sister or some relative was sexually abused by her stepfather and that is my husband, and my daughter was abused by him, because that's not his daughter, now before the war, it was not where I could come out openly and complain, saying my husband sexually abused my daughter or my daughter won't come and say, my father sexually abused me, because if she had gone to report, she was not going to be allowed to go back home again and she will be more vulnerable than before. (interview, Monrovia, July 10, 2010)

However, communities were more likely to view cases involving child victims as serious and to involve the police in them. Out of the eight stories of rape that were published in the *Daily Observer* between October 1981 and March 1990, six concerned children.[6] Adult rape was the subject in two cases: one that was committed in the course of a murder and the other of a man raping his mother. Yet, reporting to the police was not guaranteed even when the victim was a child because of the fear of stigmatization and retaliation, distrust of the police, and pressure to maintain social harmony. The director of a woman's NGO explained that a "strong" father, willing to fight for justice, was needed for the rape of a girl to be reported to the police and followed through to court (interview A.S., Gbarnga, May 25, 2011). Data on rape cases reported to the LNP and included in the Ministry of Justice's annual reports show the low levels of reporting. The ministry recorded only three reports of rape between October 1964 and September 1965 and two between January and December 1971.

The low level of reporting does not indicate a low level of sexual violence; instead, it shows that both Americo-Liberians and indigenous peoples mostly settled rape and domestic violence cases outside of the criminal justice system. A lack of trust in the system, born out of abusive and corrupt practices of personnel, and its emphasis on assigning blame and punishment, instead of reconciliation, made the police and courts unattractive options to many Liberians. Beginning with the Liberian Frontier Force, state representatives had exploited and abused Liberians, particularly of indigenous groups, and had proven ineffective at addressing their concerns (Akpan, 1973; Anderson, 1952; Strong, 1930). There was also a clash between the formal and informal approaches to justice.

Despite differences within and across groups, the emphasis in informal forums—customary courts, family palavers, Poro and Sande societies, and so on—was on restitution and reconciliation, with the goal of maintaining social harmony. Trial procedures and judgment rarely sought to assign blame and punish, but rather to discourage nonconformity to societal norms, appease offended parties, and in the case of marital disputes, to reconcile husband and wife or grant a divorce where reconciliation was impossible (Sibley & Westermann, 1928). Among some groups, punishment was typically meted out only in the most extreme cases or when dealing with a repeat offender. Most communities viewed the retributive approach as detrimental to cohesion, particularly in areas where people's lives were closely connected and discord between families could have severe socioeconomic, religious, and political consequences. Indeed, marital disputes, including incidents of domestic violence, brought before customary courts were not considered to be between two individuals, but between two families. Consequently, judgments that were viewed as excessively punitive, such as those handed down by formal courts, would lead to discord between the families, and within the community concerned. The reliance on informal forums was also bolstered by the efforts of customary leaders to maintain their customs and their position of power in society. Indeed, both women and men, especially the elderly, tried to preserve the customary dispute-resolution systems (Gibbs, 1960). Their efforts were, however, derailed by the outbreak of the conflict.

Violence against Women during the Conflict (1989-2003)

Rape and other forms of sexual violence were perpetrated by rebel and government forces during the conflict, but this was not the first time that armed forces had committed mass rapes. Soldiers of the Liberian Frontier Force had raped indigenous women with impunity (Akpan, 1973) and the military under Doe used rape to terrorize the president's perceived opponents (Gifford, 1993; Wills, 1986). Armed groups perpetrated this violence on a larger scale and with more brutality during the war, with Charles Taylor's forces torturing, raping, and murdering girls and women when he was a rebel leader and during his presidency (Fleischman, 1993; Paye-Layleh, 2002; Zavis, 1993). Forty-nine percent of women surveyed in Montserrado County reported having experienced one act of physical or sexual violence at the hands of combatants between 1989 and 1994 (Swiss et al., 1998). Of this figure, 17 percent of respondents reported that they had been beaten, tied up, or detained; 32 percent were strip searched on one or more occasions; and 15 percent were raped, subjected to attempted rapes, or were sexually coerced. Combatants also kidnapped girls and women and forced them to serve as porters, cooks, and fighters.[7]

As explained in Chapter 1, the causes of wartime rape continue to be debated. While this book cannot speak to the dynamics of wartime rape in Liberia, the post-rape experiences of survivors highlight the centrality of gender norms. Even during the conflict, survivors faced stigmatization, which discouraged them from seeking medical care. Ruth Caesar, who co-established the Abused Women and Girls Project in Monrovia in 1993, explained that many women were reluctant to visit the facility to receive gynecological care and HIV/AIDS testing for fear that community members might identify them as rape victims (interview, Monrovia, June 11, 2011). Therefore, even though the conflict had ruptured communities, women and girls could not escape the shaming that often followed the act of rape.

The presence of domestic violence during the war also demonstrates the salience of patriarchal gender norms. Although this violence during the conflict has not received as much attention as rape, the prevalence of domestic violence in other conflict-affected settings suggests that women in Liberia were at risk during the conflict. Research in displacement camps in Uganda revealed "significant" domestic violence (Okello & Hovil 2007). Fourteen percent of married women surveyed reported having experienced physical abuse from their partners in the preceding two months (p. 6). In Côte d'Ivoire, 14.9 percent of ever-partnered women surveyed reported forced sex by a partner during and after the country's first civil war (Hossain et al., 2014). Some of the risk factors for the perpetration of domestic violence are exacerbated by violent conflict. They include heightened poverty, alcohol and drug abuse, unemployment, the disruption of families, and the weakening of women's support network (Annan & Brier, 2010). Women's assumption of roles traditionally held by men could also precipitate violence. Many Liberian women became the primary breadwinner during the war, because of the death of their partner, the lack of jobs, and because of the risk men faced outside of the home (Tripp, 2015). Women also became politically active during this period (Pailey, 2014). These new roles, which bucked the gender status quo, combined with men's inability to financially support their family, could fuel frustration and heightened the risk of domestic violence. However, while the conflict pushed many women into non-traditional roles, it does not appear to have shifted expectations about women's place in society. Indeed, even after the election of a female president, beliefs about the superiority of men prevailed. These beliefs sustained the environment in which VAW was sometimes tolerated.

Violence against Women after the Conflict (Post-2003)

Despite women's activism for peace during the conflict and the election of a female president in two consecutive elections (2005 and 2011), Liberia remained a patriarchal society after the conflict (Pailey, 2014). Nonetheless, for the first time, the state, through various laws, policies, institutions, and programs, recognized VAW as a policy priority and placed it on the national agenda (Ministry of Gender and Development [MoGD], 2009b).[8] Gyude Bryant, the chairman of the National Transitional Government of Liberia (NTGL), his successor, President Ellen Johnson Sirleaf, senior government officials, and street-level bureaucrats in various sectors spoke about VAW, particularly rape, and how to address it. Some of these senior officials and street-level bureaucrats, as well as women's rights advocates interviewed for this study, argued that in comparison to the 1980s, the incidence of domestic violence and rape had increased across the country. They also asserted that the proportion of cases reported to the police was higher than what pertained in the years before the conflict. Others argued that it was awareness of rape, as opposed to the occurrence, that had changed. The absence of pre-conflict data makes it impossible to compare the prevalence of either offense over time. Police records, however, support the assertion that the reporting of rape increased in Liberia; 344 cases of rape were reported to the police between January and December 2009, and 152 of these cases were transferred to court. The reports produced by the Ministry of Justice before the conflict show that this was a sharp increase. Furthermore, studies conducted since the conflict provide a picture of girls' and women's vulnerability to violence.

Domestic Violence

After the conflict, domestic violence was the most prevalent form of VAW and was also the most-reported offense to the police. In the country's 2008 Demographic and Health Survey, 33 percent of women reported that they had experienced spousal violence sometimes or often in the past 12 months (LISGIS et al., 2008). Thirty percent of respondents reported slapping as the most common act; followed by pushing, shaking, and having something thrown at them (17 percent); kicking, dragging, beating (16 percent); and forced sex (9 percent). Thirty-one percent of respondents reported being insulted and demeaned by their partners. Women in their twenties had the highest rate of physical and emotional violence, while sexual violence was highest among ever-married girls and women between the ages of 15 and 19.

The factors that render women vulnerable to this violence were amplified in the aftermath of the conflict. High levels of poverty and unemployment created tensions within relationships as men resented their inability to perform their socially assigned role of provider. This resentment was often compounded when women began to carry more of the financial burden at home or assumed the position of primary breadwinner (Kumar, 2001). Indeed, Liberian women began to play a more prominent economic role, and in the process, disturbed the gender status quo where the man is the primary breadwinner, a role that legitimizes his position as the head of the home (Fuest, 2008b). Although women's financial independence did not always result in violence, it was a risk factor (Horn et al., 2014).

It has also been argued that the experience of war increased the use of violence by men in Liberia (Horn et al., 2014). According to respondents in a focus group, men "... had come to see violence as a normal way of responding to challenges or frustrations and as an appropriate way of getting what they wanted" (2014, p. 7). Indeed, there is a strong relationship between the normalization of violence in a community and the occurrence of domestic violence (World Health Organization [WHO], 2009). A 2010 study of Liberia found a significant association between exposure to traumatic war-related events and domestic violence as a victim or perpetrator. "Among men, exposure to crimes, direct experience of war-related potentially traumatic events, coercion, witnessing war-related violence, and taking part in the conflict were all associated with higher odds of beating a spouse or partner" (Vinck & Pham, 2013, p. 45). Attitudes toward this violence also underline the salience of the problem.

A large proportion of respondents justified domestic violence. Almost 6 in 10 women (59 percent) agreed that husbands were justified in beating their wives under certain conditions (LISGIS et al., 2008). Forty-five percent believed that beating is justified when she neglects the children, when she argues with him (43 percent), when she goes out without telling him (42 percent), when she refuses to have sex with him (22 percent), or when she burns the food (14). In comparison, only 30 percent of men agreed to at least one of these scenarios. Certain groups of women were more likely to justify this violence: rural women, women with no education, women in the lower wealth quintiles, and women in the North Central and North Western regions (LISGIS et al., 2008, p. 215).

There are several implications of this justification of domestic violence. An analysis of Ghana's Demographic and Health Survey showed that the odds of physical and sexual violence were higher among women who justified beatings (Tenkorang & Owusu, 2013). A study of 17 countries, including Liberia, found that women's justification of domestic violence, in comparison to men, decreased with a country's economic status, gender development index, and human development index (Uthman, Lawoko, & Moradi, 2010). These findings demonstrate how the economy, gender inequality, and VAW are connected. The high level of justification of domestic violence among women in Liberia signals the degree to which the practice was normalized and partly explains the low level of reporting. Indeed, it makes sense that women are less likely to report violence they view as justified. They are also more likely to discourage other women from reporting the offense.

Domestic violence after the conflict remained a problem that often went undisclosed, and when it was disclosed, it was to actors within the informal sphere—relatives, religious leaders, community leaders, and chiefs. A 2008–2009 survey of 2,500 households in five counties showed that 53 percent of domestic violence cases were not taken to any dispute-resolution forum, 46 percent were sent to an informal forum, and only one percent went before a formal authority such as the police (Isser et al., 2009). Horn et al. (2014) identified five factors that determined the decision that women made after they experienced domestic violence in Liberia: structural factors, cultural factors, resources available, emotional factors, and severity of the violence.

Structural factors refer to the gaps in the criminal justice system. Regarding cultural factors, the authors stated that "[g]enerally, both culture and religion in Sierra Leone and Liberia value the woman remaining in an abusive relationship and suppressing her needs in favor of the needs of her children" (2015, p. 9). "Resources available" refers to women's financial dependence on their abusers, which compelled them to stay in abusive relationships, as did the lack of support from relatives. The love a woman feels for her partner is another factor that affects her willingness to report this offense. Furthermore, some women still interpret the domineering behavior of their partners and the accompanying violence as a sign of love and, therefore, do not want to be separated from them. This belief was so pervasive that it was parodied into a hit song titled *That Is Love* in 2011 (Crafty, 2011). However, women were more likely to seek help when the violence was severe.

Women's overwhelming reliance on informal mechanisms illustrates the strength of the informal justice system. According to Isser et al. (2009), Liberians preferred a restorative approach to justice as opposed to the retributive approach of the criminal justice system. They state:

> In summary, appropriate "punishment" in the Liberian social context is not primarily about inflicting pain on a guilty party, whether through removing social freedom or causing physical or economic harm. Rather, to most Liberians "punishment/redress" is viewed as most sensible when it is primarily a matter of providing compensation to victims, restoring social relations between parties, and providing public signs of atonement that signal a perpetrator's renewed commitment to the social mores of the community. (2009, p. 49)

This preference reflects the pre-conflict period. However, women's preference for the informal over the formal system in domestic violence cases is not unique to Liberia (Amoakohene, 2004). A study conducted in Sierra Leone and Liberia found that stopping the violence was the immediate response of most women (Horn et al., 2015). This usually involved neighbors who were present during the assault. After the attack had been stopped, women preferred to report it to relatives, hers and her partner's, for mediation.

> For both families, the priority is usually to keep the couple together, especially if they have children. If the man continues to beat the woman, the woman's family may take her back to their home for her protection. This

may be a temporary solution, while discussions with the husband and his family take place, or, in more serious cases, a permanent arrangement. Some of the women we spoke to said that families will not always accept a woman back, perhaps because they feel she has created the problem by staying with an abusive man for too long, or because they cannot afford to support the woman and her children. Sometimes they may become tired of a situation that goes on for a long time and withdraw their involvement or advise the woman to report the case to the police. (Horn et al. 2015, p. 113)

It was when women failed to get the necessary support from their families, or when their families were absent, that they elevated the complaint to community leaders, who, like relatives, advised the couple and tried to mediate a settlement (Horn et al., 2015). However, unlike relatives, chiefs also imposed fines on the offending party. The authors found that chiefs would often elevate the most serious cases to the police or an NGO. It is, however, important to note that not all women preferred the customary system.

A few NGOs provided temporary shelter to women, in addition to financial assistance. They also mediated these disputes. My interviews revealed that most of them encouraged women to report domestic violence that resulted in injuries that were judged to be serious to the police. However, they typically did not compel women to file complaints. Members of staff of NGOs, many of them activists, understood the socioeconomic factors that shaped women's reporting choices and recognized that pressuring them to report domestic violence could cause more harm—physical, social, and economic. Women who reported domestic violence to the police were at risk of retaliatory violence from their partners. Those who were financially dependent on their partners also risked losing this support. In the absence of a safety net provided by the state, and with high levels of poverty that restricted the financial support that relatives could provide, separation from their partners could mean destitution. However, when women agreed to report domestic violence to the police, NGO staff members sometimes accompanied them to the police station to file a complaint and supported them in following up on the complaint.[9]

However, even when women reported domestic violence to the police, they generally did not seek the prosecution of their partner. Instead, the objective was often for the police to advise the partner to stop the beating, and in cases where the man was uncooperative, to frighten him into doing so. Between January and December 2009, police received 994 simple assault cases and

189 aggravated assault cases. I will explain in Chapter 8 that while police officers generally mediated simple assault cases, they sometimes sought to compel women to pursue prosecution in cases of aggravated assault. The police often required the accused to cover the victim's medical expenses, sometimes while he was detained, before either mediating the dispute or preparing the case file for transfer to the prosecutor. Some women were satisfied with police mediation and a promise from the accused not to repeat the act (Horn et al., 2015). However, reporting to the police was seen as a risky strategy because it could rupture the relationship (Horn et al., 2015). Indeed, this fear led most women to resist police attempts to refer aggravated assault cases to court. Women's financial dependence on their partners and pressure from relatives also prevented them from lodging complaints and led to the withdrawal of complaints. According to CB, a female officer,

> Some of them are saying it [that they want to settle domestic violence cases] out of fear, that when the case is carried forward the men will leave them. Some of them due to their traditional practice which says that one is not supposed to carry one's husband's complaint to the law and some feel that the person is all to them, they are their life, without that person they can't live their living; the person is feeding them, doing everything for them. How will they eat, who will do things for them? Some of them, family pressure: "let's carry the case home, I am your man." "When you leave here and the man goes to jail, you will see how you will eat, you will see who will pay your house rent, you will see how you will survive." Based on that they get weak and some of them start to get afraid and come to tell us that they want to carry the case home. Then if you insist that the case should go to court, you won't see them coming back to send them to court and when there is no complainant, there is no case. (interview, Monrovia, September 29, 2010)

Police officers' insistence on prosecution often caused complainants to stop cooperating with them. F.L., a senior officer, explained:

> Almost every day we receive a case of domestic violence, where the husband severely beat his wife, we have not received any case where the wife beat the husband. . . . But the problem we face is that the woman will always come out with a compromise at the end of the day, she will always say I don't want to go to court, I don't want you to put my husband in jail, in fact, I regret why I even came to the police. So the victim in domestic violence cases,

most of the time, is not willing to go for prosecution. (interview, male, Monrovia, July 12, 2010)

Police officers reported that some women initially agreed to proceed to court but often reversed this decision after speaking to relatives or community leaders. These pressures also affected girls' and women's decision to support the prosecution of rapists. These accounts are not intended to blame women for not cooperating with the police; rather, they are meant to show the challenges that women face in pursuing formal justice.

Sexual Violence

Sexual violence in Liberia is a scourge that negatively impacts the lives of survivors in diverse ways. A study showed that post-traumatic stress disorder was higher among the segment of the adult population that had experienced sexual violence (69 percent) than those who had not (38 percent) (Johnson et al., 2008). The prevalence of this violence underlines the challenges that confront girls and women in the country.

Data show that women were vulnerable to rape, which was mostly perpetrated by their partners, and to a lesser extent, by strangers. In a 2007 study, 24.3 percent of respondents in Montserrado County and 33.8 percent in Nimba County reported that they had experienced rape or attempted rape outside of marriage (Stark et al., 2013). The figures, however, show that the threat to girls and women came from those closest to them. In Montserrado County, 91.6 percent of rapes were committed by a husband or boyfriend, and in Nimba County, the figure was 94.1 percent (Stark et al., 2013). In the country's 2008 Demographic and Health Survey, 31.9 percent of women who had ever experienced sexual violence stated that their current husband or partner was the perpetrator, and 10.2 percent said it was a current or former boyfriend (LISGIS et al, 2008). Eight percent were abused by police or soldiers, former husband and partner (5.2 percent), friend and acquaintance (4.6 percent), strangers (3.8 percent), and family friend (3.5 percent) (LISGIS, 2008, p. 231). Minors were not only highly victimized but were also perpetrators. Attitudes toward rape provide some insight into the prevalence of the problem.

Although women were increasingly recognizing that forced sex within a relationship constitutes rape, marital rape was generally not perceived as a crime. This was partly because of gender norms that dictate that women should be sexually available to their partners at all times (Zannettino, 2012). Discussing attitudes toward martial rape in Ghana, Adinkrah (2011) underlined the idea within communities that "traditional notions of marriage confer on husbands an inalienable right to have sexual intercourse with their wives on demand" (p. 16). These ideas also prevailed in Liberia and fostered the problem, in addition to silencing women. However, attitudes toward non-partner rape differ. Fuest (2009) explained that some Liberians viewed rape as a source of shame because "in the traditional rural context, rape tends to be perceived as a violation of property (of the family or the husband), which is shameful in principle and is therefore glossed over, particularly if the perpetrator is a relative" (p. 133). While the offense is largely viewed as a serious crime, girls and women who disclosed rape were often accused of lying, were blamed for their victimization, and were stigmatized (KAICT, 2011; Isser et al., 2009; United Nations Mission in Liberia [UNMIL], 2008). UNMIL explored attitudes toward rape in a survey of 1,000 households in all 15 counties and found that many of the pre-conflict attitudes persisted. Communities blamed girls and women for causing rape by their style of dress and their behavior, and thought that sanctions in such cases should be restorative instead of punitive (Isser et al., 2009, p. 6). Sixty-nine percent of respondents agreed that "women contribute to rape by flirting with men," and 61.9 percent agreed that "women contribute to rape by being alone with a man in a room" (2009, p. 41). Survivors were also viewed as "damaged goods," "leftovers," unfit for marriage, and incapable of bearing children (KAICT, 2011; UNMIL, 2008). This blaming and shaming of survivors is extremely harmful not only for their psychological well-being, but also for bringing perpetrators to account. Eighteen percent of survivors pointed to a fear of stigmatization as the reason for not reporting rape (UNMIL, 2008). Meanwhile, communities appeared not to similarly stigmatize rapists, particularly those who were relatively wealthy and of high social standing (UNMIL, 2008). Self-blame and familial ties to the attacker also discouraged disclosure to a third party. The study showed that this victim blaming did not exist in the case of young children, but even then, parents of minors who had been victimized faced pressure to settle cases informally, instead of involving the police.

Indeed, in a survey of five counties, 50 percent of sexual abuse cases were not reported to a third party, 28 percent went to an informal forum, and 21 percent to a formal forum (Isser et al., 2009). A study conducted by UNMIL (2008) found that 65 percent of survivors disclosed their rape to someone. They were most likely to disclose to parents (50 percent) and friends (22 percent). A smaller proportion reported to the police (12.5 percent). Survivors in urban areas were more likely to report their attacks to the police (68 percent) than those in rural areas (34 percent) (UNMIL, 2008). A 2012 survey of 1,100 girls and boys underscored the extent to which survivors relied on informal forums, but also showed that an increasing number of people were turning to the criminal justice system for help (Postmus et al., 2014). Therefore, while 65.8 percent said that they disclosed sexual violation to friends, 34.2 percent said they reported to the police/legal person.[10] Activists as well as the police argued that the awareness-raising that followed the war encouraged reporting. Nonetheless, there continued to be a tension in survivors' decision-making, such that informal forums remained important.

In addition to stigmatization and other social pressures, the criminal justice system itself deterred reporting. Indeed, the lack of trust in this system was another reason why survivors failed to report rape (Isser at al., 2009; UNMIL, 2008). Communities pointed out that law enforcement officers have raped women and colluded with perpetrators for financial gain (Isser at al., 2009, p. 6). The police and courts were two of the least trusted institutions in the country (Wambua, 2015). The lack of trust in the police, which was a product of their historical and ongoing ineffectiveness and their abusive and corrupt practices, was, therefore, a deterrent to reporting. Indeed, survivors and their families were deterred by the costs that came with navigating the criminal justice system. Some accused the police and courts of demanding money for transportation, phone air time, filing documents, and so forth, and of soliciting bribes. Furthermore, the perceived divisiveness of the system and its failure to provide compensation to complainants were also problems (Isser et al., 2009). A female police officer explained that "... people do not really like the police, even though when there is a crime they come to us, when they have a problem they come to us to solve it, but they don't love the police, they consider us their enemy" (interview C.S., Monrovia, October 13, 2010). While this statement might be extreme in some regard, it reflects the state of the criminal justice sector–community relations since the end of the conflict.

It follows that most survivors and their family turned to the informal system (family meetings and religious and customary forums) for the adjudication of rape cases. Survivors, including adults, usually made their decision in concert with relatives. It was common for survivors and their relatives to accept monetary payment from perpetrators in exchange for not reporting to the police or for withdrawing after filing a report. While this practice can be attributed to widespread poverty, the fact that many poor girls and women and their relatives reported rape demonstrates that poverty was only one of many factors that led to the acceptance of money in exchange for not reporting rape. Indeed, the fear of retaliation, the lack of support from family and friends, and the weaknesses of the formal system rendered a monetary settlement the only option for some survivors. Similar to the pre-conflict period, these informal forums appeared to privilege a non-retributive approach in all but the most extreme cases. Indeed, traditional and religious leaders have been known to exert pressure on survivors and their relatives, in order to prevent them from filing complaints with the police, and to get them to withdraw cases after they have been filed. Police in some rural areas have also reported threats of "spiritual" and physical attacks from traditional leaders and community members. These threats have been used to discourage case investigation and referral. A senior officer explained that "in the interior, in the leeward, where we have the chiefs and then the older people, the police officer himself is not secured because they are afraid for their life first, second, they are afraid that they will get affected by some other means if they want to enforce the law. When a town chief marries a 17- or 16-year-old girl, they will be very skeptical in dealing with such cases because of self-preservation" (interview, male, Monrovia, July 12, 2010).

This interference in investigations occurred despite the state's issuance of a directive, which prohibited traditional leaders from interfering in rape cases. Isser et al. (2009) stated that "the majority of rural Liberians, including chiefs, are generally well aware that rape is an issue that the state justice system has reserved for its exclusive jurisdiction" (p. 66). Women's organizations reinforced the directive by raising awareness and reporting chiefs' interference in rape cases. While this deterred some traditional leaders from adjudicating rape cases, others continued to intervene. Furthermore, community and religious leaders, both Christian and Muslim, in urban and rural areas, also interfered in rape cases and adjudicated them.

Yet, even though some Liberians viewed the customary system as an alternative to a corrupt, ineffective, and divisive criminal justice system, traditional leaders were accused of exhibiting some of the characteristics of the police officers, magistrates, prosecutors, and judges that Liberians have criticized. For example, they were accused of collecting bribes to rule in favor of guilty parties (Isser et al., 2009). They also tended to pronounce judgment without regard for women's rights or well-being. In fact, the prioritization of the preservation of the family unit and of harmony within the community rendered survivors' preferences and needs an afterthought, if anything at all. The same problem could be found when Christian and Muslim leaders adjudicated domestic violence and rape cases.

Indeed, there was some overlap in the experiences of domestic violence and rape. For survivors of both crimes, the inability to physically access police stations and courts was another reason for not reporting or following through to prosecution. This was particularly the case for survivors who lived in rural areas and, therefore, had to travel long distances for services. A lack of understanding of the criminal justice process by some also led to frustration and to complainants abandoning cases. Police officers explained that complainants usually expected the police to arrest and detain a suspect until a case was called to trial. Consequently, delays caused by the gathering of evidence, or police failure to detain a suspect indefinitely, despite insufficient evidence, led to accusations of police corruption, frustrated complainants, and caused them to turn away from the criminal justice system. These concerns also led to withdrawals after rape cases were reported. However, I will explain in Chapter 8 that rape cases were less likely to be withdrawn than domestic violence cases. Police officers explained that this was because in comparison to survivors of domestic violence, rape survivors were more likely to pursue prosecution, sometimes after being encouraged to do so by police officers, but also because the police were more likely to deny complainants' requests to withdraw rape cases. Consequently, the referral of rape cases to court increased after the conflict. However, there was no guarantee that a referred case would end in a guilty verdict. In fact, the extremely slow pace of prosecution, particularly by Criminal Court E, the specialized rape court, meant that many survivors had to wait for a very long time for formal justice. Furthermore, formal justice is only one step, as survivors need socioeconomic support, which was often lacking. Overall, the aftermath of the conflict was characterized by women's vulnerability to GBV but also by a tension between formal and informal criminal justice systems.

Conclusion

Although VAW in Liberia only began to receive international humanitarian and scholarly attention during the conflict, girls and women in the country have always been vulnerable to this gendered violence. As is the case globally, it has touched all areas of their lives and has had devastating consequences. In this chapter, I have drawn on primary and secondary sources to explain how patriarchal gender norms interacted with political and socioeconomic conditions to place girls and women at risk of sexual and domestic violence before, during, and after Liberia's conflict. Expectations about appropriate female behavior and male entitlement contributed to boys and men committing acts of psychical and sexual violence against girls and women. The conflict exacerbated girls' and women's vulnerability to this violence and weakened formal and informal institutions that had traditionally addressed the problem. However, girls and women overwhelmingly relied on informal dispute-resolution mechanisms such as family palavers and customary courts, even as the number of reports to the police increased after the conflict ended in 2003. This reliance on informal dispute-resolution mechanisms was closely tied to deficiencies in the criminal justice system that had existed since its creation. It was also a product of the emphasis on reconciliatory instead of retributive justice in many Liberian communities. Girls' and women's vulnerability to gendered violence and the reliance on informal justice mechanisms in Liberia reflect the situation in many other African countries where patriarchal gender norms are salient and both formal and informal justice forums do not prioritize the preferences and well-being of women. In the next chapter I discuss how the state's response to sexual and domestic violence evolved over the pre-conflict, conflict, and post-conflict time periods and how international and domestic actors and conditions shaped this response.

4
The Response to Violence against Women in Liberia

Since the end of its conflict, Liberia has led the way in the creation of specialized mechanisms in the criminal justice sector. These mechanisms were created with the primary objective of arresting and prosecuting perpetrators of rape and other forms of sexual violence and of reducing impunity for such crimes. One of these mechanisms is the Women and Children Protection Section (WACPS) of the Liberia National Police (LNP). This specialized mechanism was created in 2005; by 2008, every county in Liberia had one WACPS unit. However, the Liberian state has not always prioritized the creation of specialized mechanisms to address VAW. In this chapter, I describe the state's response to VAW before and after the civil war. I begin by describing how the criminal justice sector addressed VAW before Liberia's 1989–2003 conflict. I show that VAW was mostly absent from the public agenda and was unrecognized as a category of crime. Consequently, the LNP lacked policies and specialized mechanisms to address the problems. Survivors of domestic violence and rape were vulnerable to secondary victimization, and prosecution was only prioritized in the most extreme cases. After this, I focus on the conflict and explain that widespread sexual violence committed by all warring factions partly led to the mobilization of the women's movement, which contributed to drawing domestic and international attention to the problem. I then describe the specialized mechanisms created since the end of the conflict and conclude with a discussion of how Liberia's response to VAW changed over time.

The Response to Violence against Women before the Conflict (Pre-1989)

Prior to the outbreak of the conflict in December 1989, VAW was largely absent from the public agenda, and this was reflected in the country's policies

Global Norms and Local Action. Peace A. Medie, Oxford University Press (2020). © Oxford University Press.
DOI: 10.1093/oso/9780190922962.001.0001

and institutions. With the exception of the rape statute in the penal code, Liberia lacked policies and institutions to address domestic violence, rape, and other forms of VAW. Rape was first recognized as a crime by the supreme court in 1898, and was classified as a felony by the criminal code.[1] The country did not have a domestic violence law and prosecuted the offense as common assault and battery, assault and battery with intent to do grievous bodily harm, assault and battery with intent to commit a felony, and assault and battery with intent to kill. Thus, with the exception of the rape law, there were no other specific laws or policies on VAW. The lack of VAW policies is at odds with Liberia's involvement in international women's rights advocacy during this time.

In 1975, Liberia sent a delegation to the first UN Conference on Women in Mexico City. VAW was one of the issues discussed at the conference, although not extensively. The Liberian government was also represented at the Third World Conference on Women held in Nairobi in 1985. VAW, including domestic violence and rape, was one of the focal points of this conference (UN, 1986). In fact, the Liberian government delegation participated in the discussion of these issues. It co-sponsored a draft resolution on Sexual Violence against Women and Children. The co-sponsors of this resolution noted that women and children were frequently abused sexually and called upon "governments to take appropriate steps to protect, in an effective manner, women and children from any form of violence" (UN 1986, p. 216). They made several progressive proposals for addressing the problem, including the introduction of laws that would not criminalize survivors or re-victimize them. Liberia also co-sponsored a draft resolution on Domestic Violence against Women at the Nairobi Conference. The prevalence of domestic violence across all racial, social, and economic cleavages was recognized in this resolution. Government agencies were urged to "pay special attention to violence against women and to treat such behavior as criminal, and to provide services to assist battered women and their children" (UN, 1986, p. 254). However, the delegates' participation at the international level did not translate into action at the domestic level.

Upon their return, they "promulgated a comprehensive population policy which significantly endorsed the Nairobi recommendations as they pertain, particularly, to the role and status of women" ("Women Urged to Fight Discrimination," 1989, p. 1). This 1988 National Policy on Population for Social and Economic Development focused on the need to reduce the high rate of population growth and emphasized the economic empowerment of women and the enhancement of their contribution to agriculture and other areas of national development. VAW (or a term referring to the problem) was not mentioned in the document. The policy did not reflect the relatively extensive and progressive proposals that the Liberian delegation to the Nairobi conference had co-sponsored in the draft resolutions on sexual and domestic violence. The absence of VAW in the women's health and social status sections of the 1986 Demographic and Health Survey further demonstrates the absence of the issue from the policy agenda. VAW was similarly absent at the institutional level.

Prior to the conflict, Liberia did not have a state bureau that was responsible for women's affairs. One of the proposals made in the 1988 population policy was for the establishment of an apolitical bureau of Women's Affairs (National Population Council, 1988, p. 15). This proposal was discussed at a three-day national workshop on the "Improvement of the Role and Status of Women in Liberia" that was attended by state and women's organizations' representatives in Monrovia in 1989, but was not acted upon until 1994 when a women's desk was created in the Ministry of Planning ("Women Urged to Fight Discrimination," 1989, p. 1). The state did not establish a permanent ministry until 2002, when women's organizations, with the support of the United Nations Development Programme (UNDP), lobbied the government of Charles Taylor to create the Ministry of Gender and Development (MoGD) in 2001 (Morris, 2005). Therefore, the benefits that could result from having a centralized women's rights machinery within the state apparatus, which have been identified in the women and politics literature (Green, 1999; Tripp, 2010; Waylen, 2007; Weldon, 2002), were largely absent in Liberia.

The Ministry of Justice (MoJ), inclusive of the LNP, did not have specialized mechanisms to address VAW. In fact, the MoJ had not officially recognized VAW as a category of crime, as a priority area, or as an issue that required specialized procedures. The near-absence of VAW from the MoJ's annual reports underscores this point.[2] Rape was the only form of VAW documented in the reports and only to list the number of cases reported to some police stations and included in court records. Assault figures in the reports were not disaggregated by the sex of the accused and the victim, or detailed enough to determine which cases were incidents of domestic violence. Furthermore, police officers and officials of the MoJ did not receive specialized training in the handling of VAW cases. Consequently, cases of domestic violence and rape were handled by personnel who lacked specialized training and worked in institutions that lacked mechanisms dedicated to VAW.

The absence of specialized training and agencies shaped law enforcement at the street level. Secondary victimization of survivors was normalized in the police and courts. The investigation of domestic violence and rape cases was handled by the Detective Division of the LNP, a unit that had not received specialized training in how to handle such cases so as to prevent the re-victimization of survivors and to ensure successful evidence gathering and case prosecution. Thus, the few women who reported these offenses and sought prosecution often faced an uphill battle to formal justice. Police officers generally recognized that rape was a crime but did not always view it as an offense that should be prosecuted. Reflecting the societal norm, they perceived the rape of an adult as less serious than the rape of minors, and thus as less deserving of prosecution and incarceration. The belief that women and girls held some blame for rape prevailed in the force and also contributed to the perception that some instances of rape should not be prosecuted. Therefore, it was common for the police and judges to blame survivors for their victimization, to side with the perpetrators, and to agree to or even encourage the withdrawal of cases for extrajudicial adjudication. According to Deddeh Kwekwe, head of the Sexual and Gender-Based Violence Unit at the Ministry of Gender and Development (MoGD), "The police didn't know how to handle sexual and gender-based violence. If someone came to report domestic violence, the police would say, 'It's your fault you were beaten.' If a woman reported rape, the police would suggest she had caused it. They would make it worse, and women would be traumatized" (quoted in Bacon, 2012, p. 3). A police officer explained that they rarely withdrew cases of statutory rape but withdrew cases of "common rape"—the rape of adult women—with the approval of their supervisors (telephone interview, officer #49, male, April 22, 2012). This blaming of women deterred survivors from reporting and increased the likelihood that cases would be poorly investigated or would not be investigated at all.[3]

The support for extrajudicial adjudication was even more salient in domestic violence cases. Police viewed most domestic violence cases—except the most grievous—as private disputes to be settled by the family or the community. In the absence of training and organizational rules that emphasized prosecution, and of any signal from the government or the LNP to indicate that the prosecution of these offenses was a priority, officers were under no pressure to investigate and refer them to court. An officer who served on the force in the 1980s explained that the police rarely referred domestic violence cases to the courts (interview, female, Monrovia, September 19, 2010). An investigator who served on the force during the same period stated that "much emphasis was not placed on abuse against women" (telephone interview, officer #42, male, August 18, 2011). He explained that the norm in the police force was to view the domestic abuse of women as an acceptable form of discipline except where it resulted in grievous injury or death. During this period, the government, inclusive of street-level officers, did not face significant domestic or international pressure in the area of VAW.

Domestic Pressure

The police did not face strong domestic pressure to address domestic violence, rape, and other forms of VAW. There was no national or subnational campaign, launched by women's organizations, to address VAW. There is no indication that VAW was on the agenda of women's organizations. Women's organizations established in the 1950s, including the Federation of Liberian Women, whose members had familial ties to the government of President Tubman, focused on women's socioeconomic empowerment (Massaquoi, 2007). President Samuel Doe later banned these organizations for their political ties after he assumed power in a violent coup in 1980. Nonetheless, women's organizations pressured him in an effort to end human rights abuses during his attacks on political opponents in the 1980s (Steady, 2011). However, women's groups did not mount sustained and focused campaigns to pressure the state to address VAW. Instead, activism was reactionary, usually in response to a series of violent attacks against women or to a particularly shocking incident of violence. For example, female residents of the Matadi Estates in Monrovia, in March 1988, criticized the police for poorly handling the investigation of the rape and murder of one of the estate's female residents. They appealed to several government agencies that were involved in the case to make it a priority ("Estate Women," 1988, p. 1). These calls, however, did not gather enough momentum to become subnational or national campaigns against any form of VAW. Furthermore, in the absence of a national women's machinery, the state was not subject to internal pressure to address VAW, particularly to establish specialized mechanisms.

International Pressure

Similarly, international pressure, if it existed, was not significant. Even though VAW had been placed on the UN's agenda through women's activism at the global conferences, the UN's women's rights agenda was still centered on population control and economic empowerment, a reflection of the Women in Development approach that the organization was promoting in developing countries. The international community had only begun to accept that VAW was an issue that required state intervention in the second half of the 1980s (United Nations Economic and Social Council, 1995). Consequently, states, including Liberia, received minimal pressure from IOs to prioritize VAW as a policy problem prior to the early 1990s. In conclusion, VAW was low on governments' agendas prior to the conflict. However, widespread sexual violence by all warring factions placed the problem on the agenda of local women's organizations and IOs. This provoked a dramatic shift in how the state responded to VAW, particularly rape, after the conflict.

The Response to Violence against Women during the Conflict (1989–2003)

As explained in Chapter 3, rebel and government forces perpetrated widespread violence, including sexual violence, against civilians, both male and female, during the 14-year civil war. This placed the problem on the agenda of women's organizations and of IOs, and led them to introduce measures to end this violence and to assist survivors. Women's organizations advocated for the end of the conflict and provided humanitarian assistance and legal services to survivors of sexual violence, with funds from local and international sources. Their advocacy was a source of pressure on all actors during the war, including the UN. UN agencies and international NGOs funded the programs of local women's organizations and built the capacity of members. They also independently launched programs that provided survivors of sexual violence with health care and humanitarian assistance. These initiatives by local and international actors were the first of their kind in Liberia and ushered in an era where VAW, particularly sexual violence, was on the agenda of human rights organizations in the country. They also shaped the post-conflict response to VAW.

Domestic Pressure

Widespread sexual violence during Liberia's conflict served to force the problem into the public discourse. Women, through their activism, also drew domestic and international attention to rape, and in addition to providing health care and legal aid to survivors, encouraged them to patronize these services. Thus, the mobilization of women's organizations resulted in strong domestic pressure on entities that were active during the war, including peace mediators, humanitarian agencies, and even the government of Charles Taylor.

Women advocated for an end to the violence and provided humanitarian assistance, which included medical and psychosocial care to survivors of sexual violence. While some women worked in loosely coordinated groups or well-structured organizations, others contributed as individuals. Together, they constituted a women's movement. Some of their peace initiatives occurred for short periods of time and on a small scale, while others occurred at the national level and lasted for several years. On May 19, 1990, the *Daily Observer*, one of the most widely read newspapers in Liberia, published an appeal by Christian women, led by educator Mary Brownell, for an end to the crisis in Nimba County. In the same month, the Ecumenical Women's Organization appealed to the Organization of Africa Unity (OAU) and the UN to mediate a ceasefire in the rapidly spreading conflict ("Women Call for Ceasefire," 1990, p. 1). They cited the loss of life and the destruction of the country as reasons for their appeal. Hawa Clemens, a woman who had declared her intention to run for president in 1985, also appealed to President Doe and Charles Taylor to lay down their arms ("It Is Time for Peace," 1990).

The women's movement became more organized and members intensified their efforts and diversified their strategies as the violence escalated. The Liberian Women's Initiative (LWI), which was formed in 1994, worked with groups such as the Inter-Faith Mediation Council to organize stay-home days that paralyzed businesses and government institutions in Monrovia in March 1995 and early 1996. This form of protest signaled the women's clout and legitimized their demands to be included in peace mediations (African Women Peace and Support Group [AWPSG], 2004). With personal funds and some raised locally and internationally, women attended local and international peace talks, and though they were sometimes excluded from the official discussions, they persisted in making their case to the warring factions and the international community (AWPSG, 2004). In May 1995, women's organizations sent a three-woman delegation to the Economic Community of West African States (ECOWAS) Heads of State Mediation Committee in Abuja, Nigeria. Initially refused participation in the proceedings, the women intensively lobbied until then ECOWAS chairman, President Jerry John Rawlings of Ghana, allowed them to speak to the attendees. During this meeting, the women demanded a place at all negotiation tables and made recommendations for a government of inclusion and for a disarmament process. They also drew international attention to the VAW that was being perpetrated by combatants. According to a member of the delegation, Theresa Leigh-Sherman:

> I just took that ... paper ... and slowly we talked about the killing and how these men were opening these women's stomachs and betting on the babies. We talked about everything because the women were tired. We were just tired. We were just tired. It was a 30-minute paper. We made recommendations. And I tell you the nine Presidents that were there and ... CNN, BBC, everybody was in tears because these are the facts that these people didn't know about ... but we had gone through it. We had lost everything we worked for. (AWPSG, 2004, p. 26)

Another interfaith organization, the Women in Peacebuilding Network (WIPNET), formed in 2000, protested the war and demanded women's inclusion in the peace process at the final peace talks in Ghana in 2003.

The women's movement also provided humanitarian assistance to survivors of VAW and their families during the war. This assistance came in the form of medical care, food, water, clothing, and shelter. While some of these initiatives were supported with funds from IOs, others were funded by donations from Liberians. For example, in 1993, Ruth Caesar cofounded the Abused Women and Girls project in Monrovia with funds from the United Nations Children's Fund (UNICEF) and support from the National Women's Commission of Liberia.[4] She explained that it took two years to secure funding for the project (interview, Monrovia, June 5, 2011). She had previously approached several international funding agencies without success. Caesar stated that those approached did not support the project because it was not their focus at that time. This, however, changed as the war progressed and reports of rapes became more frequent.

The project was housed in a center called My Sister's Place and consisted of a mobile medical unit that provided gynecological care to rape survivors, a legal arm that educated women on their rights, a trauma team that offered psychological counseling, and an economic empowerment arm to train women in income-generating skills. The project operated in Internally Displaced People's (IDP) camps, and in other communities in Monrovia, and was extended to Grand Bassa County. But women's initiatives were not limited to humanitarian assistance. In 1994, female lawyers formed the Association of Female Lawyers of Liberia (AFELL) to advocate for women's rights, provide legal aid to survivors of domestic violence, rape, and other forms of VAW (United Nations High Commissioner for Refugees, 2001). In November 2000, after intense lobbying, the MoJ granted AFELL a "letter of patent" that allowed the organization's lawyers to prosecute rape cases alongside state prosecutors. Counselor Elizabeth Boryenneh, president of AFELL, explained that "where state prosecutors are not readily available, like in the regions, AFELL can present the letter of patent to a magistrate or judge to initiate prosecution in a case involving rape" (allAfrica, 2000). Their involvement was necessary because the MoJ lacked the prosecutorial capacity, and this was an attempt at creating a specialized mechanism during the presidency of Charles Taylor. This initiative was funded by UNICEF; however, AFELL also raised funds through membership dues, and local efforts such as a football tournament (IRIN Special Report on the Challenges Ahead, 1999).

During this period, women's organizations also began to lobby for the creation of the Ministry of Gender and Development (MoGD). Beginning in 1999, the LWI and other women's groups drew on the Beijing Platform for Action, which called for the creation and strengthening of gender machineries and the mainstreaming of gender in all governmental bodies, and collaborated with the UNDP's gender advisor to petition the government for the establishment of the ministry (Morris, 2005). Although the MoGD was established in 2001 under a government that sanctioned, actively encouraged, and perpetrated atrocities against women and girls, it was still a significant step in institutionalizing women's rights and giving them a voice, however faint, in the state's bureaucracy.

These activities of women's groups placed VAW, particularly rape, on the public agenda in Liberia and contributed to bringing it to the attention of the international community. Though these initiatives were concentrated in Monrovia, this was the first time that physical and sexual violence against women and girls had been publicly and consistently opposed on a national platform and survivors encouraged to seek medical care. This awareness partly influenced IOs in Liberia to fund VAW initiatives developed by local women's groups and to create their own programs to respond to the problem. However, due to the prevalence and the visibility of atrocities committed by the warring factions, the women's movement and the international community were focused almost exclusively on violence, particularly rape, committed by combatants. This affected how the state, NGOs, and IOs structured their initial post-conflict response to VAW.

International Pressure

International pressure was exerted on rebel groups and the Taylor government by actors such as ECOWAS, various UN agencies, and international NGOs. However, these international actors were also the recipients of pressure from women's organizations who sought political as well as financial support from them and their intervention to end the violence. During the early stages of the war, international actors were mostly focused on conflict resolution and providing humanitarian assistance. They sought to protect all civilians from violence without recognizing the unique threats that women and girls were facing. For example, the Economic Community of West African States Monitoring Group (ECOMOG), which arrived in Liberia in August 1990, did not have a plan to address VAW (Olonisakin, 2008). The mission did not provide training and lacked expertise on issues such as child protection and GBV. This weakness limited their ability to prevent VAW and to assist survivors. However, awareness-raising by women's rights activists, NGOs, media reports, and field reports brought international attention to the problem and prompted the UN and other IOs to act. They supported local NGOs in developing and implementing programs. For example, Ruth Caesar said she was influenced to co-develop the Abused Women and Girls project by a 1991 Save the Children workshop that educated participants on the issue of rape and encouraged them to take actions to address the problem (interview, Monrovia, June 5, 2011). The project received funding from UNICEF.

IOs also gave crucial political support to women's organizations. For example, women's organizations lobbied the Taylor government for the establishment of the MoGD with support from the UNDP. IOs also independently implemented anti-VAW programs. They were the primary providers of humanitarian aid, which included medical and psychological care to survivors of VAW. For example, in 2001, the International Rescue Committee (IRC) established "drop-in" centers in Monrovia where female survivors of sexual violence could go to receive medical and psychological care. They also provided these services at IDP camps across the city (Reliefweb, 2006).

Nevertheless, these international actors possessed many shortcomings. International negotiators excluded women's groups from peace negotiations and resisted their efforts to participate in the conflict-resolution process (AWPSG, 2004). Not only was ECOMOG poorly resourced, but its forces were involved in the looting of properties during the war and were implicated in brutality against civilians and the sexual exploitation and abuse of women and girls (Olonisakin, 2008). Their shortcomings left many people vulnerable to violence, including girls and women. Furthermore, IOs working in Liberia were often restricted by the conflict and a lack of resources and were, therefore, unable to access many people who were in need of assistance (United Nations Security Council, 2003). However, despite these shortcomings, the efforts of international actors would contribute to placing VAW on the state's agenda after the conflict.

The Response to Violence against Women after the Conflict

Liberia made some progress in addressing VAW after the conflict ended. Two notable improvements were the adoption of laws and policies and the establishment of specialized criminal justice sector mechanisms. I begin this section with a description of the legal and institutional reforms that were implemented to address rape and domestic violence after the conflict. I then introduce the specialized mechanisms that were created, with a focus on the WACPS of the LNP force.

Legal and Institutional Reforms in Post-Conflict Liberia

Activism by women's organizations, combined with the support of the UN and other international organizations, led to the amendment and strengthening of the rape law in 2005. Two sections of Chapter 14 of the New Penal Code were repealed and replaced in this amendment, resulting in several revisions. One revision was the definition of consent and intercourse. The terms of consent were made more stringent and included in the definition of intercourse was the penetration of orifices other than the vagina.

Another change was the inclusion of gang rape in the definition of rape. The amendment also revised the maximum sentence for rape from 10 years to life imprisonment and made the granting of bail non-applicable in cases of the first degree. With this amendment, all forms of rape were covered under the law. The passage of the amendment was also the first major accomplishment by the women's movement and their allies in the area of VAW after the conflict ended.

The Committee on Gender Equity, Women, and Child Development of the National Transitional Legislative Assembly (NTLA), which was headed by Ruth Caesar, with the support of AFELL, the MoJ, and the UN, introduced the draft amendment to the legislature. While there was support for the passage of the amendment within the male-dominated legislature, with some members describing the offense as a "crime against humanity," it faced some opposition ("Speed Up the Rape Bill," 2005). One major point of contention within the legislature and the public was AFELL's attempt to mandate the death penalty for certain acts. This penalty was also opposed on human rights grounds by organizations such as the Foundation for International Dignity ("Find on New Code for Gang Rape," 2005). A compromise was reached with the removal of the death penalty clause and its replacement with life imprisonment. Nonetheless, the amendment was still criticized. Some lawyers argued that the removal of bail and pre-trial hearing rendered it unconstitutional (Toby, 2010).

Another area of contention was the inclusion of a clause on marital rape. Some lawmakers thought that the criminalization of marital rape was too harsh a measure to introduce and posed a threat to the institution of marriage. According to a news report,

> The male-dominated assembly argued that in fact it is unimaginable that a husband could rape his own wife when both have vowed through marriage that "for better or for worse," adding, "when we both are in bed whatever happens could be her worse and my better." The assembly said, as for the 10-year jail sentence, it is another name for divorce, noting that if a man goes to jail for 10 years on charge of rape by his wife, it is clear that before he is freed, his wife might have already remarried. ("NTLA Passes Bill But...," 2005)

Thus, the clause provoked resistance from lawmakers, resulting in its removal. Nonetheless, female lawyers told me that perpetrators of marital rape could be prosecuted because the law did not explicitly exempt the act from prosecution. Overall, the amendment of the law was a major stride in the campaign to reduce impunity for rape.

However, the women's movement was much slower in lobbying for the passage of a domestic violence law. According to Zeor Bernard, interim president of AFELL, the movement had prioritized rape because of the alarming and frequent reports of the problem in the immediate aftermath of the conflict and because it affected more people (interview, Monrovia, September 7, 2010). The brutality of the crimes reported and the targeting of children also created a sense of urgency. The disparity was evidenced in news stories. Whereas newspapers regularly reported on incidents of rape, especially when the victim was a child, domestic violence was typically reported on when it resulted in grievous injury or death.

In October 2013, the MoGD, with funding from the SGBV Joint Program and the United Nations Population Fund (UNFPA), organized focus group discussions in 11 counties. Several women's organizations, including AFELL, WIPNET, and the Women's NGO Secretariat of Liberia (WONGOSOL), participated in these consultations, along with international partners such as the International Rescue Committee and Kvinna till Kvinna. In July 2014, the MoGD and its partners submitted the draft bill to the office of the president, and to the cabinet in June 2015. The president submitted it to the legislature in July 2015 (Senah, 2016). Members of the legislature began debating the bill in July 2016, and some of them opposed the clause banning FGM contained therein. They argued that instead of an outright ban of the practice, FGM should be practiced on girls at the age of consent (Senah, 2016). Despite criticism from organizations such as WIPNET, the bill was amended in order to be passed. On July 16, 2016, President Johnson Sirleaf threatened to issue an executive order to pass the bill if lawmakers did not move to do so (Senah, 2016). In August 2017, the Senate concurred with the Lower house to pass the bill (Senah, 2016a; Worzi, 2017). However, the removal of FGM understandably led to criticism from the members of the women's movement, some of whom attributed the lawmakers' stance to the influence of secret societies who practice FGM and are key to mobilizing votes during elections (Global News Network, 2016, 2016a). The legislature passed the bill in July 2019 and President George Weah signed it into law in August 2019. These processes underscore the challenges that accompany legal reform, even in a state with a relatively strong women's movement and one that is led by a female president who was outspoken in her support of women's rights.

Women's groups also participated in the drafting of several anti-GBV policy documents, including Liberia's 2006 GBV Plan of Action, the 2009 National Action Plan for the Implementation of Resolution of 1325, and the 2009 National Gender Policy. They also played a direct role in the creation of two specialized mechanisms, the SGBV Crimes Unit in 2009 and Criminal Court E, also in 2009 (Medie, 2012). Both of these mechanisms were within the MoJ, as was the GBV Unit, which was created in 2006 with support from the UNFPA. The staff of the unit was responsible for overseeing all non-sexual violence GBV cases in the judicial system. They were tasked with collecting data on cases and visiting courts across the county to interview staff and judges in order to determine the challenges they faced. The unit's staff was also tasked with representing the interests of GBV victims within the MoJ.

The SGBV Crimes Unit was mandated to assist in the investigation and prosecution of sexual offenses. The chief prosecutor of the unit, counselor Felicia Coleman, explained that her unit also prioritized the welfare of the victim (interview, Monrovia, July 14, 2010). They provided counselors to survivors and their families to prepare them for trial and to support them throughout the trial. The Crimes Unit also provided victims with emergency financial assistance, relocated them to other communities to avoid stigmatization, and referred them to NGOs where they could receive psychosocial support. They also raised awareness of sexual violence within communities, and trained police officers and medical personnel who worked with victims of sexual violence, and ran a 24-hour hotline for victims to report cases and receive advice on how to access medical care and justice. Criminal Court E was also dedicated to the prosecution of sexual violence crimes. It was mandated to exclusively prosecute all cases of sexual violence in Monrovia, the only city in which it was located. Members of AFELL modeled the court after that of South Africa; thus trials were conducted in-camera to protect the victim's confidentiality. The Danish International Development Agency (DANIDA) and the UN funded the establishment of the court in Monrovia. Institutional change also occurred in the police force, which fell under the MoJ. The UN Mission in Liberia (UNMIL) established the Sexual Assault Squad in the LNP in 2004. The first WACPS became operational and replaced this squad in September 2005.

UNMIL created the Sexual Assault Squad within the LNP in Monrovia so that its members could take charge of receiving and investigating rape cases. Police officers whom I interviewed, including one who served on the squad, observed that its personnel lacked the training to handle rape cases. Police officers of the squad often re-traumatized victims and compromised their confidentiality. They also released suspects due to poor investigative procedures and unethical practices. Consequently, the LNP and UN Police (UNPOL) began discussing the establishment of an independent specialized mechanism. UN officials, officials of the MoJ, and senior LNP officers participated in these consultative meetings and arrived at the decision to create the WACPS in concert with the UN. This decision was presented in the LNP's Gender Policy, which was adopted in February 2005. A central directorate was also created in 2005, and the first cohort of WACPS officers, who were exclusively assigned to the new section, graduated from the academy in November 2005. This new section had four divisions: sexual assault squad, domestic violence squad, juvenile violence squad, and information and database unit. Within a year of its creation, a WACPS had been established in six counties, and by December 2008, every county had at least one such unit. The establishment of the WACPS was funded by the UN Peacebuilding Fund and supported by the Norwegian government, which funded the construction and renovation of county police headquarters in which WACPS units were installed. The UN, donors, and international NGOs also supplied equipment such as vehicles and motorbikes to WACPS units. The UN also supported the LNP in providing specialized training to WACPS officers, as did women's organizations and international NGOs. The establishment of the WACPS represents a major shift in Liberia's response to VAW. Indeed, specialized mechanisms, which were nonexistent before the conflict, became a major component of the state's post-conflict response to VAW. With a focus on the police force, I seek to explain why the WACPS was created and institutionalized.

Conclusion

This chapter has described how the state responded to VAW in Liberia. Prior to the conflict, Liberia did not have specialized mechanisms in place to address VAW. This reflects the situation in many African countries, where specialized mechanisms did not exist. Indeed, as was the case in many other African countries, VAW was not recognized as a category of crime within the country's criminal justice system. Rape, domestic violence, and other forms of VAW were mostly adjudicated outside of the formal criminal justice system, reinforcing the importance of informal dispute-resolution mechanisms in this setting during this time. During the conflict, the police and other security sector agencies were implicated in violence, including sexual violence against girls and women. With its role in this violence, it is not surprising that the state agencies did next to nothing to address VAW during the conflict, despite pressure from the women's movement and IOs. However, the end of the conflict gave way to significant developments in this area as the transitional government, as well as the government of President Ellen Johnson Sirleaf, created several specialized mechanisms in the criminal justice system. This mirrored developments in post-conflict states such as Rwanda, Sierra Leone, and Côte d'Ivoire, where specialized mechanisms were also established after the end of conflicts. Liberia established four criminal justice sector agencies, placing it ahead of many post-conflict countries, and African countries more broadly. It is important not only to understand why this change occurred, but also to probe the similarities and differences in how other post-conflict countries established their specialized mechanisms. In the next two chapters, I describe VAW in Côte d'Ivoire and the state's response.

5
Violence against Women in Côte d'Ivoire

This chapter is a presentation of the problem of VAW in Côte d'Ivoire, with a focus on domestic violence and rape. I discuss the occurrence of these forms of violence and attitudes toward them over three time periods in the country's history: pre-conflict, conflict, and post-conflict. I draw on primary and secondary sources that explain that, as in Liberia, domestic violence and rape were prevalent in Côte d'Ivoire prior to the war and were largely dealt with in informal forums such as customary courts. This is partly because of the preference for the reconciliatory approach that prevails in communities in many African countries, but also because of sociocultural norms around both forms of violence, and because of a lack of trust in the formal criminal justice system. I explain that the Ivoirian conflict (2002–2011) exacerbated women's vulnerability to physical and sexual violence and that both formal and informal mechanisms were weakened during this period, further reducing women's access to justice. Women continued to rely heavily on informal mechanisms after the war, and in the case of domestic violence, women who filed complaints usually wanted law enforcement officers to advise their partners instead of arresting and prosecuting them. However, interviews also show that the perceived increase in the level of sexual violence and the services that were provided by the UN, NGOs, and the government encouraged some survivors of rape to report their victimization to the police and gendarmerie and to seek prosecution. The chapter shows that while the majority of survivors sought justice through informal mechanisms, the conflict and post-conflict initiatives introduced by state and non-state actors had begun to gradually increase reliance on the police and gendarmerie.

The chapter begins with an overview of legal systems and shows that like Liberia, Côte d'Ivoire has had a dual legal system since it was colonized by the French and this has shaped access to justice and the type of justice dispensed over several decades. This is followed by comparative sections on VAW in pre-conflict, conflict, and post-conflict Côte d'Ivoire with a focus on the prevalence of domestic violence and rape and society's attitudes toward this

Global Norms and Local Action. Peace A. Medie, Oxford University Press (2020). © Oxford University Press.
DOI: 10.1093/oso/9780190922962.001.0001

violence. This chapter lays the groundwork for the analysis of the state's and civil society's response to domestic violence and rape in Chapter 6.

Legal Systems and Legal Authority in Côte d'Ivoire

Côte d'Ivoire is a former French colony, which gained independence in 1960. The country is situated in West Africa and is bordered on the south by the Atlantic Ocean, on the west by Liberia and Guinea, on the east by Ghana, and on the north by Mali and Burkina Faso. In 2017, the country's population was 24.29 million. Similar to Liberia and many other African countries, Côte d'Ivoire has a dual legal system, consisting of customary laws, which have not been codified, and civil law, which was codified in 1964 and derived from French civil law. Prior to this codification, French citizens—of which there were few—in its African colonies, including Côte d'Ivoire, were governed by French Metropolitan Law, codified in French West Africa in 1896, while the indigenous population was governed by customary laws, which had exclusively prevailed before colonization. The French colonial administration tried to curb the authority of kings, chiefs, family heads, and other traditional leaders, who were the custodians of customary laws administered in palavers and other assemblies, by introducing "indigenous justice" in 1903 (Sekre, 2008, p. 639). This indigenous justice structure included village, canton, and circle tribunals; the first two applied customary laws solely to the indigenous population, while the third applied French civil law and customary laws. Chiefs presided over village and canton tribunals; judges of the latter were appointed by the colonial administration. A French colonial administrator presided over the circle tribunal, which had jurisdiction over French nationals as well as the indigenous peoples. All three tribunals received cases of domestic violence and rape, but village tribunals could only levy a fine of 1–15 francs and impose a prison sentence of not more than five days, while circle tribunals could pronounce harsher penalties.

The French allowed chiefs to adjudicate civil and criminal infractions—such as domestic violence and rape—that did not threaten French interests (Sekre, 2008). Upon independence in 1960, President Houphouët-Boigny did not codify customary laws, as had been done in other African countries, because of the fear that this would "solidify ethnic differences within the country and that national unity would best be served by a single set of principles uniformly applied to all citizens" (Salacuse, 1969, p. 132). Thus, customary laws were not incorporated into the 1964 code of laws. The state's formal court system dealt with civil and criminal cases such as domestic violence and rape, although in practice, the majority of Ivoirians in rural and urban areas continued to rely on customary courts and other informal forms of dispute resolution (Assepo, 2000; Ellovich, 1985; Monni, 2006). This is partly because the population preferred the reconciliatory approach of the customary justice system to the retributive approach of the formal justice system (Monni, 2006; Segui, 1995). Furthermore, the state allowed customary courts and other informal mechanisms to function in a bid to preserve social cohesion and because the formal justice system did not have the capacity to meet the population's needs (Assepo, 2000).

While the warring factions threatened the social order, usurped the authority of chiefs and other traditional leaders, and subjected some of them to physical attacks, customary forms of dispute resolution remained important during the Ivoirian conflict from 2002 to 2011, which consists of the civil wars and the period of "neither war nor peace" that separated them. Indeed, the withdrawal of the state from certain regions placed more pressure on customary justice and other informal dispute-resolution systems. Furthermore, while there were indications that some sections of the population had become more willing to report crimes to the police and gendarmerie after the conflict ended, the majority of Ivoirians referred cases to family heads, chiefs, and religious leaders for adjudication (Medie, 2017).

Violence against Women before the Ivoirian Conflict (Pre-2002)

Violence against women, including domestic violence and rape, was common before the outbreak of the first civil war in 2002. In the absence of prevalence studies, it is impossible to specify the prevalence of these acts and their variation across time and regions. However, anthropological studies reveal the presence of this violence. For example, writing about the Agni, Tauxier (1932) explained that the principal reason for divorce was unjust beatings. Interviews and focus group discussions in Abidjan and Bouaké also revealed that girls and women were subjected to both physical and sexual violence before the conflict that began in 2002.

There was a level of acceptance of these forms of violence within many communities. Tauxier (1932) wrote that a man was forgiven for "correcting" his wife for committing adultery. While family pressure and social expectations led many women to remain in abusive relationships, a woman's relatives sometimes disapproved of this violence and some women left abusive relationships, sometimes with the support of relatives. Indeed, among the Agni, it was common that women left their marriages as a result of this violence during the early twentieth century (Tauxier, 1932). While I am unable to speak about the responses of women from every ethnic and social group, interviews show that even in the 1980s and 1990s, domestic violence was a major source of dispute within the household and was normalized in some settings. For example, a police officer explained that

> before in the village—I mostly grew up in the village—when your wife ran her mouth and her face wasn't bruised, it would mean you do not hit her and people would make fun of you. They'd even say that the husband is encouraging his wife or even that the wife is in control of her husband. But when you bruised her face they'd say "when she does her nonsense, her husband never misses." The people are even happy, they congratulate him. (interview, police officer #31, female, Abidjan, July 3, 2014)

Furthermore, this violence was largely perceived as a private issue to be resolved in the family or in other informal forums. Officer #31 described the situation in the late 1990s:

> in 1998 people preferred to deal with these things within family and it's only recently that I've seen people coming to the police . . . besides when a husband used to beat his wife, she found it difficult to even tell her parents. She was forced to lie, it's only when it went overboard . . . we'd only know when it went overboard. (interview, female, Abidjan, July 3, 2014)

In matters of marriage, most people first used customary law (Assepo, 2000; Ellovich, 1985). They only turned to the formal courts when informal mechanisms failed to resolve their dispute (Ellovich 1985). Thus, many women who were victims of domestic violence prior to the conflict and those who disclosed this violence generally relied on relatives and community leaders to intervene to stop the violence and for support to leave violent relationships. The act of disclosing was even more difficult for rape survivors.

Rape carried a stigma that discouraged most girls and women from revealing its occurrence to relatives. Survivors of this violence were often blamed for the act and faced social consequences such as the loss of their partners. Therefore, they rarely disclosed this violence and when they did, it was to relatives and community and religious leaders. This is partly because Ivoirians generally lacked confidence in the criminal justice system and feared retaliation if they turned to this system for justice (Assepo, 2000). It is also because informal forums emphasized social cohesion and reconciliation, which were preferred to the punitive approach of the formal criminal justice system (Assepo, 2000; Ellovich, 1985). Furthermore, state agents were often happy to allow informal mechanisms to deal with problems such as rape that were not perceived as threats to political power and political stability. In fact, police officers and gendarmes would sometimes transfer cases that had been reported to them to chiefs and other community leaders for resolution, effectively signaling the strength and legitimacy of informal mechanisms (Assepo, 2000). Patriarchal beliefs and practices were strong within Ivoirian society and affected both the occurrence of this violence and survivors' and their community responses to it.

In a reflection of dynamics in Liberia and most other countries, Ivoirian society was founded on deeply patriarchal gender norms. These norms were even salient among the Akan ethnic groups, who practiced matrilineal inheritance. This does not mean that women lacked power within Ivoirian society. Some ethnic groups had female chiefs and leaders, and women participated in political activities. For example, a multiethnic coalition of women marched on Grand Bassam in 1949 to liberate political leaders who had been jailed by the colonial government and were on a hunger strike (Diabeté, 1975). Nonetheless, due to power inequalities between men and women, the latter were heavily underrepresented in leadership positions in informal and formal institutions (Toungara, 1994). Women who migrated to Abidjan and other urban areas during the 1960s and 1970s strived for economic independence but faced resistance from communities that sought to maintain women's subordinate position in relation to men (Vidal, 1977). Indeed, elite women associated with President Houphouët-Boigny's Democratic Party of Côte d'Ivoire (PDCI) who mobilized to change the country's restrictive family laws faced a backlash from men for their "efforts to protect and assert their economic autonomy" (Toungara, 1994, p. 49). These norms remained salient during the nine-year conflict and contributed to women's victimization within and outside of the home.

Violence against Women during the Ivoirian Conflict (2002–2011)

Prior to the outbreak of conflict in 2002, Côte d'Ivoire was one of Africa's most economically developed countries. Migrants, many of them Muslim, from neighboring countries, including Burkina Faso, flocked to the country to work in cocoa-producing sectors and in other sectors of the economy. President Felix Houphouët-Boigny, who had governed the country since independence in 1960, encouraged this migration and employed it for political gain. Political dynamics after his death led to the entrenchment of an indigenous and foreigner divide that corresponded with ethnic and religious division. This contributed to political instability that culminated in an army mutiny in 2002 (Daddieh, 2001). The mutiny evolved into a civil war that lasted from 2002 to 2004 (the first civil war), which led to the division of the country, with the rebels (the New Forces) controlling the north and the government of President Laurent Gbagbo controlling the south (Bah, 2010; Crook, 1990). Both government and rebel forces committed atrocities, including rape, against civilians (Human Rights Watch, 2011). The government and rebels signed the Accra III Peace Agreement in 2004, and the United Nations Operation in Côte d'Ivoire (UNOCI) was deployed in that same year. Backed by French Licorne forces, UNOCI controlled the buffer zone that separated the two factions in the north and south.

From 2005 to 2010, Côte d'Ivoire experienced relative stability. The state functioned in the south while the rebels attempted to build governing apparatuses in their territories. Meanwhile, a low-intensity conflict raged across the country as both factions continued to launch attacks against the opposition, including civilians. Indeed, this has been described as a period of "neither war nor peace." In 2010, President Gbagbo's refusal to step down after losing the presidential race to Alassane Ouattara, a candidate backed by the rebels, led to the second civil war (2010–2011) which pitted pro-government forces against the rebels. An estimated 3,000 people were killed in this war. This second civil war led to more violence against civilians. Government forces targeted pro-rebel communities in Abidjan, and when the rebels entered Abidjan, they also attacked government strongholds and committed atrocities, including rape. Both factions committed atrocities in the volatile western regions of the country. The rebels (the New Forces), with the support of UNOCI and French troops, succeeded in removing Gbagbo from power and in installing the government of his successor, Alassane Ouattara. They handed Gbagbo over to the International Criminal Court in November 2011 for prosecution.

Both domestic violence and non-partner rape were prevalent during the conflict. Eighty-five percent of all respondents in an International Rescue Committee (IRC) survey conducted in the Man, Yamoussoukro, and Abidjan regions reported an increase in VAW during the political crisis, particularly domestic violence and rape (IRC, 2011). Rape was used systematically, and sometimes indiscriminately, by pro-government and rebel forces and by an assortment of criminal gangs, during both civil wars and in the interval between them (UNSC, 2012). The western regions of the country, particularly Moyen Cavally and Dix-Huit Montagnes, which bordered Liberia and were controlled at different periods by pro-government and rebel forces, experienced the highest level of sexual violence (Human Rights Watch, 2010). These regions were the scenes of intense fighting between pro-government and rebel forces at various points in the civil wars. Both parties committed widespread rape during this period (Human Rights Watch, 2011).

Some girls and women who fled this violence faced increased risks. An IRC study found that "[d]isplaced respondents were two times more likely to report an increase in sexual violence against adult women than non-displaced respondents, and three times more likely to report it against girls under the age of 18" (2011, p. 4). However, even after the first civil war ended, the risk of violence remained high. The almost six-year interval between the first and second civil wars was a period of low-intensity violence against non-combatants, including rape. A 2008 survey found that 1.1 percent of women surveyed reported non-partner sexual violence in the preceding year (Hossain, 2014). In the western regions, bandits and militia, who had been aligned with both factions in the first war, and who still had access to arms, relentlessly attacked towns and villages, committing atrocities such as rape (Human Rights Watch, 2010). According to Human Rights Watch,

> Hundreds of women and girls have been sexually assaulted, raped, and gang raped during these criminal acts. Women and girls are systematically pulled off transport vehicles, one by one, and marched into the bush where they are raped while other bandits stand guard. Victims include very young children, including babies, and women over 70 years of age. During home attacks, husbands are tied up and forced to watch as wives, daughters, and other female family members are raped. Women sometimes become

pregnant as a result of these attacks, while underreporting and clandestine, unsafe abortions likely hide many other cases. (2010, p. 5)

Thus, the lull in the conflict did not bring reprieve to many girls, women, and their communities. The second civil war exacerbated this violence.

In the early stages of this war, security forces loyal to President Gbagbo violently cracked down on the pro-Ouattara opposition, leading to many injuries and deaths (Human Rights Watch, 2011). These forces and allied militia also raped women suspected of supporting Ouattara or whose husbands were Ouattara supporters (Human Rights Watch, 2011). In the northern half of the country, the rebel group (New Forces) also committed violence against Gbagbo supporters, including the rape of women, although the scale of violence was less widespread than in the south (Human Rights Watch, 2011). This would change as the rebel movement gained ground and advanced on Abidjan. Indeed, the violence intensified as the conflict progressed. According to Human Rights Watch:

> Until their military offensive began in the country's far west, armed elements loyal to Ouattara were implicated in few serious abuses. However, wherever they met stiff resistance once armed conflict began—primarily in the west and Abidjan—soldiers systematically targeted civilians perceived to support Gbagbo. Men, especially youth, were particularly targeted for their perceived affiliation with militias, but the elderly, women, and children were also killed. In total, hundreds were killed, most along ethnic lines, and dozens of women were raped. These abuses at times implicated high levels of the Republican Forces leadership, either directly or through command responsibility. (2011, p. 75)

Therefore, both sides committed atrocities against the civilian population. Seven women, who were in a group of thousands that was protesting Gbagbo, were gunned down by pro-Gbagbo security forces in the Abobo neighbourhood on March 3, 2011. In the west of the country, retreating pro-Gbagbo forces launched a wave of killings against northern Ivoirians and West African immigrants. The Republican Forces (made up of the New Forces) retaliated with mass killings and rapes in the West (Toulépleu, Doké, Bloléquin, Duékoué) as they gained ground in these regions and "left a trail of killings, rapes, and villages burned to the ground" as they bored down on the capital in the south (Human Rights Watch, 2011, p. 59). Upon reaching

Abidjan, the Republican Forces executed at least 149 people and tortured many more (Human Rights Watch, 2011, p. 64). The pro-Gbagbo stronghold of Yopougon was the scene of much of this violence. Four-hundred and seventy-eight cases of rape were documented between January and September 2011 (UNSC, 2012).

The IRC reported a fourfold increase in the number of women seeking help at its health centers between December 2010 and February 2011. Nonetheless, rape cases were highly underreported. According to participants in an IRC study, the most common reasons for which survivors were unable to access health services were: "'lack of resources,' 'stigma', 'fear of reprisal by the perpetrator,' and 'presence of armed group nearby'" (IRC, 2011, p. 5). It is important to note that health centers were not in close proximity to many survivors, and many others were not aware of the services available to them (IRC, 2011). It is also important to note that the sociocultural norms that contributed to the stigmatization of survivors remained deeply embedded in most communities during this period. Respondents in Man reported that survivors would not disclose rape for fear of not getting a husband in the future (1RC, 2011). Yet, when they did disclose, it would be to relatives (mothers, sisters, aunties) or an NGO or other organization that addresses women's concerns (IRC, 2011).

Survivors of this violence faced emotional distress, isolation, unwanted pregnancies, injury, and stigmatization. The fear of being raped also restricted women's movement and thus caused a loss in income and negatively affected their ability to provide for their family (Human Rights Watch, 2010). However, there was variation in the treatment that survivors received from their families to deal with these problems. The environment in Man was reportedly more supportive and less punitive. According to a study participant, "We say what happened does not put an end to your life. It is because of the war" (quoted in IRC, 2011, p. 29). While in Abidjan and Yamoussoukro, participants reported that survivors were more likely to be blamed for bringing shame to their families. According to a participant in Abidjan, "Rape is disgraceful for women, so they keep their mouths shut in order to protect their lives" (IRC, 2011, p. 31).

Meanwhile, perpetrators mostly acted with impunity (Amnesty International, 2013; Boutellis, 2011; IRC, 2011). The fear of retaliation prevented most survivors and their families from bringing the perpetrators to account through informal or formal mechanisms. The armed groups threatened the social order and the authority of traditional leaders. Indeed, the threat of violence, or actual violence, prevented the functioning of most informal justice mechanisms. Much of the social support traditionally available to women was disrupted by the violence (Blay-Tofey & Lee, 2015). Furthermore, the absence of police officers, gendarmes, and courts in large portions of the country, and their weak capability in some of the areas in which they were present, ensured that the formal system was often not an option (Bovcon, 2014). The environment in the west prior to the second civil war was described thus:

> Police and gendarme officials present another problem, routinely failing to fulfill their duties to protect, investigate, or prevent lawlessness. Victims described how security officials repeatedly refused to pursue and investigate criminal elements, even when attacks were reported at checkpoints only a few kilometers from the scene of brutal physical and sexual violence. Indeed, state authorities often demand bribes from victims to file complaints, most of which languish with authorities who show little interest in investigating or arresting perpetrators. Even when arrests do occur, suspected perpetrators are often freed within 24 or 48 hours, leaving victims disillusioned with authorities and terrified of revenge. (Human Rights Watch, 2010, p. 4)

However, where it was possible, relatives and community leaders attempted to come to an agreement with the perpetrator, which the survivor was often pressured to accept (IRC, 2011).

Domestic violence was another problem that plagued women during this period. The act occurred frequently and is reported to have increased in certain regions, including Man (IRC, 2011). A 2008 survey found that intimate partner violence (IPV) was the most frequently reported form of violence among women after the first civil war; 20.9 percent of women surveyed experienced this violence (Hossain et al., 2014). In this survey, 12.9 percent of ever-partnered women reported having experienced forced sex in the preceding year (Hossain et al., 2014). Indeed, of the 32 percent of women who said they had experienced sexual violence since the age of 15, 24 percent reported that act was perpetrated by an intimate partner (Hossain et al., 2014). Women were more likely to report experiencing severe acts of physical violence by a partner than men (23.9 percent vs. 9.9 percent) (Hossain et al., 2014). The authors operationalized "severe violence" as at least one of the following: kicking, dragging, choking, burning, or threatening with a weapon. This violence was more widespread among some groups and communities. For example, a 2010 study found that the prevalence of IPV was higher among women who identified as Yacouba, Guéré, or Dioula (Falb & Gupta, 2015). This violence had severe impacts on all areas of women's lives. A 2010 study found a significant relationship between IPV and experiences of partner-perpetrated reproductive coercion (Falb & Gupta, 2015). Specifically, women with experiences of IPV were more than "three times more likely to report reproductive coercion than their counterparts who did not report IPV" (Falb & Gupta, 2015, p. 65). Overall, Côte d'Ivoire's conflict was characterized by both domestic violence and rape. Domestic violence (physical and sexual) was more frequently reported and affected women across the country. Non-partner rape, though widespread, was more concentrated in the western regions of the country and was used strategically by some groups, and indiscriminately by others. Pro-government and rebel forces continued to pose a threat to women's security after the end of the conflict in 2011.

Violence against Women after the Conflict (Post-2011)

The official end of the Ivoirian conflict brought a significant decrease in violence against civilians by armed groups in most parts of the country. However, militias and ex-combatants, who had been loyal to both sides in the conflict, continued to wreak havoc in some parts of the country and to prey on the civilian population by perpetrating acts such as rape. However, ex-combatants were not the only perpetrators of non-partner perpetrated rape, and this violence was not limited to areas where they remained mobilized. Furthermore, partner-perpetrated physical and sexual violence remained more prevalent across the country. The sociocultural norms that foster this violence were still deeply embedded in communities. These norms also discouraged survivors from disclosing their victimization and seeking medical attention and justice from the formal criminal justice system. Corruption and the ineffectiveness of this system also discouraged survivors from filing complaints and following their case through to prosecution. Nonetheless, the violence that occurred during and after the conflict, combined with increased awareness-raising, had begun to gradually shift attitudes toward sexual violence and, to a lesser extent, domestic violence. Thus, survivors and their families were reportedly more likely to seek medical attention and report non-partner rape and, to a lesser extent, domestic violence to the police.

Domestic Violence

This was the most prevalent form of VAW in Côte d'Ivoire after the conflict. According to the country's 2011 Demographic and Health Survey (DHS), 22.2 percent of women reported that they experienced physical violence often within their intimate relationships in the year preceding the study (Institut National de la Statistique (INS) & ICF International, 2012). Furthermore, 4.6 percent of women reported sexual violence often and 16.6 percent reported emotional violence often (2012). The types of physical violence to which they were subjected include slapping, shoving, shaking, kicking, dragging, strangulating, burning, and threatening with a weapon. It is important to note that the conduct of the study overlaps with the second civil war. However, studies conducted exclusively after the end of the second civil war confirm the pervasiveness of domestic violence. In a 2012 survey of women in Abobo, a densely populated, ethnically diverse, and low-income community in Abidjan, 53.6 percent of surveyed women reported exposure to physical, sexual, or emotional violence by an intimate partner in the previous year (Shuman, 2016). Emotional violence was most frequently reported (46.4 percent), followed by sexual violence (21.7 percent) and physical violence (17.4 percent) (Shuman, 2016). While these figures were not representative of the entire city or country, they demonstrate the extent of the violence in certain communities. The DHS revealed that this violence was most frequently reported by women in the northwest of the country (48 percent) and in urban areas (34 percent) (2012). Women with primary education (36 percent) and from rich households (34 percent) also reported a higher rate of domestic violence (Institut National de la Statistique (INS) & ICF International, 2012). Furthermore, the survey recorded domestic violence against girls between the ages of 15 and 19, demonstrating the degree to which this violence is normalized.

The consequences of this violence for girls and women are manifold and include physical injuries, trauma, and death. This violence was also disruptive to women's daily activities (Shuman, 2016). Certain cultural practices illustrate the salience of the patriarchal gender norms that undergird this violence.

> In [northern] Côte d'Ivoire, when a father gives his daughter in marriage he gives the husband a cane. In the north, they say, "you're coming to marry my daughter, I'm giving her to you in marriage, I am giving you a cane." It is the tradition.... The current emancipation of women, it goes against that. Generally, when the woman demands a few rights, they beat her. (interview, police officer #1, male, Abidjan, July 8, 2014)

These norms foster this violence. The DHS also shows a correlation between alcohol consumption and the perpetration of this violence. Twenty-seven percent of women whose partner did not consume alcohol were victims of at least one form of domestic violence, in comparison to 36 percent whose partner drank heavily sometimes and 48 percent who drank heavily often (2011, p. 356). Women also believed that the new roles they had assumed as a result of the conflict were also provoking this violence (Cardoso et al., 2016). Indeed, both social and structural characteristics of the post-conflict environment contributed to women's risk of IPV and how they experienced this problem (Cardoso et al., 2016).

> Structurally, urban poverty and with it high male unemployment, food insecurity, financial stress, and cramped housing played a role in women's experiences with partner violence. Socially, fractured social networks, changing gender roles and growing tensions between traditional gender norms and those of the modern city were discussed as important contributors to IPV. (Cardoso et al, 2016, p. 4)

Furthermore, displacement and discrimination rendered internally displaced women particularly vulnerable to this violence. Their status as strangers in their communities prevented them from seeking help, and their neighbors did not come to their aid when they were being beaten (Cardoso et al., 2016).

While more women were reporting domestic violence than before and during the conflict, the majority relied on their family and other informal justice mechanisms to adjudicate the matter. Similar to Liberia, most survivors did not seek to have their partner arrested and prosecuted, but rather for the violence to stop. A police officer explained this practice:

> The victim herself will sometimes come and say that she just brought the case here so that her husband will be given some advice but she does not

want him to be locked up. "I just came for you to give him advice so he does not do it again." It happens a lot. Sometimes they bring a team of religious people to come and plead. (interview, gendarme #27, male, Abidjan, July 8, 2014)

Fear of the family and community's reaction is one reason why women were reluctant to file domestic violence complaints with the police. A police officer summarized this problem: "There are women who desire to lodge their complaints but are filled with fear of having the families on their necks or being rejected. It's very difficult" (interview, police officer #3, male, Abidjan, July 8, 2014). The fear of losing their partner is another reason why most women are reluctant to report domestic violence to the police and gendarmes. Police officer #2 summarized this sentiment:

it's [a domestic violence case] often quite delicate because when a woman lodges a complaint against her husband, the man's family does not take kindly to it because to them doing that implies separation.... For instance when an Ivoirian is summoned, they take it in a bad way and behave as though it is the end of the world. Sometimes they even stop speaking with the woman from that day onwards arguing that the problem they had was between husband and wife so why must the woman report to the police. So it is often taken in a bad way. Nonetheless, when a woman comes to lodge a complaint against her husband, it is usually with the intention to have him corrected so that he doesn't repeat his actions, since her only recourse is the police. She does not come to lodge the complaint against her husband with the intention of engaging in a legal process with him. That's the observation we made. (interview, male, Abidjan, July 8, 2014)

When women officially filed a complaint, these sociocultural factors caused many to try to withdraw the complaint:

That's [domestic violence] a bit more delicate because the women have children. The women want the care because if the man goes to prison the woman is left alone and the children [. . .] psychologically. But there are serious cases, the man poured boiling water and bleach on the woman. When we started the procedure, the man began to take care of the woman. After, the woman refused for her husband to be sent to prison and he escaped us. She refused for us to pursue the man. Domestic violence is extremely difficult, we have not referred them, even severe cases, because the women withdraw. With rape, we convince them because it is a third person. With domestic violence women think of their children; psychologically, the children will know their father has been imprisoned so the women take their children into consideration. They say, "It is to get him to change, you need to encourage him." (interview, police officer #18, female, Abidjan, July 22, 2015)

Women who seek help from the police often face repercussions in the family and in the community. A lack of trust in the police was another barrier to reporting domestic violence. A member of staff of a women's and children's rights NGO explained how the behavior of agents in the criminal justice system affected the decision to report domestic violence:

we've found that the people are afraid of the judicial process. So when there is a problem they do not dare go to the police. This fear is reinforced by the behavior of the police. If a woman who's been beaten goes to report they will say, "what did you do to get beaten, you provoked him." She is revictimized. The behavior makes women afraid. (interview, L.G., Abidjan, July 7, 2014)

They explained that training offered to officers of the police and gendarmerie has reduced, but not eliminated, this problem. Thus, informal mechanisms would appear to be the best option.

However, the conflict had eroded the social support structure available to many women and thus left them more vulnerable to this violence. For example, displaced women in Abidjan were humiliated by their neighbors as a result of the violence they suffered within the home (Shuman, 2016; Cardoso et al., 2016). The women contrasted this reaction to the rural areas from where they originated and where neighbors would intervene to stop this violence. Indeed, in the absence of this support or in its inadequacy, some women were turning to NGOs, social centers, and the police to mediate cases of domestic violence. Officer #31 explained that "[i]n the past a woman will not come and make a report when her husband beats her. But now they come and report because they see the campaigns on TV informing them that it is not normal for them to be abused physically" (interview, gendarme #31, male, July 9, 2014). However, as explained earlier, the majority of complainants sought the intervention of the police to counsel and advise the perpetrator, as opposed to prosecute. While some women did pursue prosecution, they were in the minority. Rape survivors proved more willing to seek justice from the formal criminal justice system.

Sexual Violence

In the country's 2011 Demographic and Health Survey, 5.8 percent of girls and women between the ages of 15 and 19 surveyed reported that they had experienced sexual violence.[1] The figure was 8 percent in the west of the country. A part of the survey was conducted during the second civil war and thus reflects the violence during this period. However, armed groups remained active in Bouaké and in the western regions of the country after the war ended. In Bouaké, ex-combatants committed robbery and raped girls and women (UNOCI, 2016). Many of them remained armed. However, this violence was not limited to these parts of the country, as reports of rape in communities across the country were frequent.

The Human Rights Division of UNOCI documented 1,129 cases of rape across the country between January 2012 and December 2015 (UNOCI, 2016). Of this number, 761 were children between 2 and 17 years old. The majority of these children were raped by individuals within their family and community. Also implicated in this violence against both children and adults were law enforcement officers. In 5 percent of the cases documented between 2012 and 2015, 51 soldiers, three policemen, and one gendarme were identified as the perpetrator. It is important to note that some rebel fighters who participated in rapes during the war were integrated into the army. Girls and women were also vulnerable to violence by those who were closest to them. In 30 percent of the documented cases, the perpetrator was a neighbor or an acquaintance, in 10 percent of the cases the perpetrator was a relative, and in 2 percent it was a teacher. The perpetrator was unknown to the victim in 60 percent of the documented cases.

Similar to Liberia, activists, social workers, police, and gendarmes believed that the incidence of rape was higher than before the conflict. While it is difficult to measure the change in violence due to the lack of pre-conflict statistics, it is clear that many negative attitudes persisted. The blaming and shaming of girls and women remained major problems in Côte d'Ivoire. The Focus group discussions I conducted in Abidjan and Bouaké showed that rape was largely perceived as an act that tarnishes and destroys its victims. Some survivors and focus group participants explained that survivors, particularly those who were Muslim, were viewed as unsuitable for marriage, because rape resulted in the loss of virginity. The fact that a rape can result in injuries that affect a survivor's ability to conceive and bear a child and put her at risk of contracting HIV and other sexually transmitted diseases added to its perceived destructiveness. Their responses demonstrate that the society judged women's social value by their sexual purity and capacity to conceive and bear children. Many people responded to this perceived destructiveness of rape by shaming and stigmatizing victims and their families, thus exacerbating the emotional distress that usually occurs as a result of the act. Victim blaming was also common. Both male and female focus group participants argued that victims' revealing attires and their frequenting of dangerous areas at night were causes of rape. Writing about South Africa, Pumla Gqola (2007) argued that obeying these warnings does not protect from violence and that the discourse communicates to girls and women that public spaces do not belong to them.

Ivoirians relied overwhelmingly on informal mechanisms for the adjudication of rape cases. Survivors and their families settled cases in discussion with the offender's family or turned to community leaders, chiefs, and Christian and Muslim leaders. Although there were many exceptions, the process in these forums usually culminated in the fining of the offender. Chiefs interviewed maintained that fining the offender, instead of handing him over to the state, was necessary to maintain peace and harmony between the affected families as well as within the community. Despite reports of rapists being beaten, chiefs said they did not order violence. Instead, the basic settlement was for the accused to cover the victim's medical expenses. Additional fines might be levied based on factors such as ethnicity and the age of the victim. A community chief in Abidjan argued that the only crime that should go before the state is murder. My interviews with law enforcement officers and the parents of children who had been raped revealed that chiefs and religious leaders often collaborated with offenders' relatives to discourage reporting and to encourage case withdrawal.

The interviews and focus group discussions revealed dissatisfaction with informal forums. This dissatisfaction stemmed from the assessment that settlements failed to punish and deter offenders. Indeed, two community chiefs in Abidjan admitted to settling cases involving serial rapists. With young men taking up arms and the spread of gangs in some communities, chiefs' influence over young men, and thus their ability to deter crime, had diminished (Interpeace, 2015). For survivors, having to continually encounter their rapists within the community (and the pain this caused) was another source of dissatisfaction with extrajudicial settlements. Furthermore, some interviewees accused community leaders in Abidjan of exploiting rape cases for financial gain.

This dissatisfaction occurred in an environment in which people were more conscious of rape, due to sexual violence during the war and post-conflict awareness-raising campaigns, and were of the opinion that the problem had become more prevalent. Both female and male focus group participants revealed that they had been exposed to information about rape from television and radio programs as well as posters. They explained that these materials had conveyed that rape was a criminal offense and that there were mechanisms in place to aid survivors and help them access justice. Indeed, a female participant intimated that Côte d'Ivoire was now serious about rape because it had passed a rape law. However, Côte d'Ivoire's rape law predates the conflict; the change was the education on rape and on accompanying laws being provided by IOs, NGOs, and the state. This awareness-raising campaign seems to have broken some of the silence surrounding rape, such that it was less of a taboo to speak about the act to relatives, friends, and service providers. This change, combined with the perception that informal dispute-resolution forums failed to deter rape, and concern about the prevalence of the act and the harms it caused, led to strong agreement in the focus groups that rape should be reported to the police and gendarmes, although the majority thought that certain cases should be resolved informally. These included marital rape and cases where both the perpetrator and victim were minors. Interestingly, this call for the involvement of the state existed alongside a distrust of the criminal justice system.

There is thus something of a paradox that focus group participants were firm in their dissatisfaction with informal forums and wanted the state to intervene in rape cases, yet they distrusted law enforcement agencies, particularly in Bouaké. For example, female participants complained of police corruption and said that police officers also rape. They stated that the police would insist that the perpetrator in a stranger rape was the victim's boyfriend and would not investigate complaints. They, therefore, argued that the best course of action was for a survivor to bypass the police and report directly to the courts, where they believed there was a better chance of finding honest officials. However, distrust of the police was not the only reason for not reporting. In fact, the majority of women did not report this violence because they were ashamed of what they had experienced. They feared the stigmatization that would occur if they disclosed this violence. Police officer #39 explained (while wrongly implying that women "provoke" rape):

> Yes, that is done [people coming to withdraw rape cases]. They do that because in fact in Africa rape is frowned upon so it happens that when they do not want it repeated, they themselves come because they don't want it to be . . . there are people who have very respectable wives who may not have done anything to provoke but unfortunately for them on their way home they were raped. So in such cases, even when the women come to lodge the complaints, their husbands would not want the case to go far for others to hear and speak about so they themselves would want to pay the officer in charge not to take the case up. (interview, male, Abidjan, July 11, 2014)

However, I found that when women received support from allies (relatives, friends, and social workers), they were highly likely to reverse the decision not to report rape, and to instead lodge a complaint with the police or gendarmerie (Medie, 2017).

Police officers and gendarmes reported that women were less likely to report rape in rural areas because cultural values and social pressures were stronger in that area. Officer #29, in recounting his experience, stated that:

> I was at the [. . .], it is a small village and all cases are handled by the chief of the village. Apart from some few cases that come to us. So in most small towns that does not exist but in Abidjan people come and report. . . . In the rural areas people take their problems to the chiefs, a public figure, etc. It is only when the case is very serious that they bring it to the station. (interview, gendarme, male, Abidjan, July 8, 2014)

In fact, I interviewed a chief in Bouaké (which is partly urban) who revealed that he even adjudicated murder cases in his court and that the police and gendarmes in his area referred cases to him for adjudication. Thus, the majority of survivors continued to rely on informal justice mechanisms, particularly in rural areas. However, I will explain in the next chapter that the UN, in collaboration with the state and NGOs, tried to improve the performance of personnel of the criminal justice system in a bid to increase reliance on the state and reduce impunity, particularly for sexual violence.

Conclusion

Similar to Liberia and many other African countries, domestic violence and rape have affected the lives of women for many years in Côte d'Ivoire. In this chapter I have discussed the causes of these forms of VAW, the prevalence, and societies' as well as survivors' responses. The literature shows that women were subjected to various forms of gendered violence, with domestic violence being the most documented. This is similar to Liberia and other African countries where VAW was not on the policy agenda and was rarely researched. In another similarity to Liberia, the conflict drew both national and international attention to the problem of VAW, particularly non-partner sexual violence committed by combatants and the state's security forces. However, wartime sexual violence was less widespread in Côte d'Ivoire and more concentrated in certain areas of the country. Many survivors lacked recourse to justice during this period, while others relied on informal dispute-resolution mechanisms. Indeed, Côte d'Ivoire bears several similarities to Liberia in terms of the reliance on informal justice mechanisms before, during, and after the conflict. This persisted due to dissatisfaction with the formal criminal justice system, coupled with sociocultural pressures and economic conditions. However, more women began to report domestic violence and non-partner rape to the police, although they exhibited more willingness to support prosecution in rape cases. Furthermore, women were more likely to report rape to the police when they received support from relatives and friends, pointing to societal changes that have accompanied the conflict. In the next chapter I will examine how the state, IOs, and NGOs have dealt with the problem of VAW in Côte d'Ivoire.

6
The Response to Violence against Women in Côte d'Ivoire

This chapter examines how the Ivoirian state responded to VAW before, during, and after the 2002–2011 conflict. I begin with a discussion of the state's response to VAW before the outbreak of the first civil war in 2002. I show that even though women's organizations had placed VAW on the government's agenda, there were no specialized mechanisms in the police force or gendarmerie to address the problem. I continue with a discussion of the conflict-era response to VAW. The deployment of a UN peacekeeping mission to the country and the arrival of several UN agencies during the conflict (2002–2011) led the state to introduce certain measures, including creating the position of a gender focal point in the police force and gendarmerie. The third section traces the post-conflict response to VAW, including the creation of the gender desk. I show that in comparison to Liberia, Côte d'Ivoire has created fewer specialized mechanisms in the criminal justice sector.

The Response to Violence against Women before the Conflict (Pre-2002)

While VAW was not a major policy issue in pre-conflict Côte d'Ivoire, post-independence governments did introduce policies, programs, and institutions to address some aspects of this violence. Some of these initiatives were the result of pressure from women's NGOs and IOs, which sometimes collaborated in pressuring the government and in providing expertise. However, Houphouët-Boigny, the country's first post-independence president, also introduced some measures in a bid to signal his progressivism to the international community (Toungara, 1994).

The country's penal code criminalized but did not define rape. However, the country did not have a domestic violence law; the offense was prosecuted as assault and battery. As in Liberia, the state did not recognize VAW as a

Global Norms and Local Action. Peace A. Medie, Oxford University Press (2020). © Oxford University Press.
DOI: 10.1093/oso/9780190922962.001.0001

category of crime or one that required distinct procedures. The 1998 Law of Reppression of some Forms of Violence against Women, including FGM, Law No. 98-757 of December 23, 1998, was limited to criminalizing FGM and made no mention of domestic violence or rape. It imposed a sentence of 1–5 years and the payment of a fine. If the act results in the death of the victim, it is punishable by 5–20 years in prison, and if the procedure is performed by a physician, he/she may be prohibited from practicing for up to 5 years.

The government also introduced laws that touched on women's social and economic rights, even though not on VAW. Its 1964 Civil Code drew heavily on French law and thus was more a reflection of French, than of dominant Ivoirian values and preferences. The Family Law within the Civil Code covered women's rights within the home. The code "regulated marital obligation, property, divorce, paternity, and inheritance within legally contracted marriages" (Toungara, 1994, p. 46). This code was a product of Houphouët-Boigny vision of a male-led, nuclear family in the Christian mold and elicited opposition from women for the power it gave men, including over household finance (Toungara, 1994). This law was repealed and replaced by the 1983 Law on Equality Between Couples (Act No. 83-800 of August 2, 1983). However, this law contained some discriminatory clauses; for example, it granted men all rights in making important decisions in the household while limiting the role of women to "performing household chores" (Committee on the Elimination of Discrimination against Women, 2010, p. 14). In addition to laws, Côte d'Ivoire also adopted international conventions during this period. The country ratified the Convention on Women's Political Rights in 1995. This pre-conflict period also saw the creation of a women's ministry.

The Houphouët-Boigny government created the Ministry for the Condition of Women in 1976. In 1993 the name would be changed to the Ministry for Family and Promotion of Women; in 2000 it became the Ministry of Solidarity and Women; and in 2011 the name was changed to the Ministry of Solidarity, Family, Women, and Children. As at December 2019, it was the Ministry of Women, Family, and Children.[1] Toungara (1994) argued that the creation of this ministry could not be divorced from Houphouët-Boigny's desire to impress Western observers (Toungara, 1994, p. 51). According to the author, Houphouët-Boigny "has always shown sensitivity to western opinions of the political and economic choices he has made in the formation of the state" (Toungara, 1990). However, while the Western gaze might have influenced the creation of the ministry, it did not lead to the introduction of women-friendly measures in the criminal justice sector.

There were no specialized mechanisms to address VAW in the criminal justice system. Furthermore, neither the police nor the gendarmerie had in place internal policies that instructed on how to handle domestic violence. Neither were officials given training in how to handle domestic violence, rape, and any other forms of VAW. These offenses were subject to the same procedures as all others. Officially, the decision to prosecute domestic violence, rape, or any other offense rested with the prosecutor. Thus, the police officer or gendarme was tasked with receiving and investigating a case, while the prosecutor decided if it merited prosecution or could be withdrawn. Officers interviewed said that even before the war, they were taught to refer all offenses to the prosecutor and not to independently withdraw any. However, they did not always follow these instructions. Officer #32 explained that "[i]t [referring rape cases to court] was done but at the time tradition was followed and the family had the upper hand. Not many cases were sent to the court" (interview, male, Abidjan, July 12, 2014). Domestic violence was often not perceived as a serious offense and was, therefore, trivialized.

> Before the officers began the training, there were things that we the officers thought were normal, I hope you get it. A woman does not cook, or she insults her husband, he gets hold of her and beats her. It is true that there is violence and simple assault, but even though we are gendarme we also believe in our customs and traditions but with time, as I was saying, nowadays things are not as they used to be. . . . Right now when they come we explain to them to desist from such acts. We explain to them that beating women and children is no longer allowed. (interview, male, gendarme #31, July 9, 2014)

Furthermore, the re-victimization of survivors of both offenses was normalized in the police and gendarmerie. According to police officer #2,

> One of my colleagues recalled a case where formerly when a girl or a lady lodges a complaint at the police station that she has been raped, it's almost as if she's harassed by the police. They hurl questions like "what did you do? where were you? you went after him yourself and so on." Everyone wants to know what happened; "did he penetrate you?" . . . They do this in front of everyone and that is very frustrating. (interview, male, Abidjan, July 8, 2014)

Women's organizations began to call on the government to address this problem in the 1990s.

Domestic Pressure

Domestic pressure, mainly from women's organizations, was present in Côte d'Ivoire, even if it was not always strong, or the focus on VAW. For example, the Association of Ivoirian Women's (AFI) opposition to the 1964 Family Act did not touch upon the issue of VAW. The organization was founded in October 1963 by the first lady, Marie-Thérèse Houphouët-Boigny, and was mostly made up of politically active and conscious Akan women who had ties (sisters, daughters, wives) to the Democratic Party of Côte d'Ivoire (PDCI), which was the ruling party (Toungara, 1994). This is an organization that fits the model of state feminism, which existed in Ghana, Nigeria, and other African countries (Mama, 1995; Prah, 2003). Mama (1995, p. 41) defines state feminism, or femocracy, as "an anti-democratic female power structure which claims to exist for the advancement of ordinary, but is unable to do so because it is dominated by a small clique of women whose authority derives from their being married to powerful men, rather than any actions or ideas of their own". Their activism led to backlash from some who criticized their attempts to empower women, but resulted in an amendment of the family code. They were succeeded by women's organizations such as the Ivoirian Association for the Defence of Women's Rights (AIDF), which worked with external actors such as Amnesty International and with the Ministry of Women Affairs and Family to successfully lobby for the criminalization of FGM. In 1999, the AIDF began a campaign to advocate for the passage of a domestic violence law.

International Pressure

The AIDF and other women's NGOs worked closely with external actors, including UNICEF, Amnesty International, and the US Embassy to advocate for the criminalization of FGM. These actors supported women's NGOs by sharing information, training, and funding their programs. International actors also supported the campaign to draft and pass a domestic violence law.

However, international actors would become more visible with the outbreak of the first civil war.

The Response to Violence against Women during the Conflict (2010–2011)

Côte d'Ivoire experienced civil war from 2002 to 2004 and from 2010 to 2011. The period between these wars has been described as "neither war nor peace," with the government controlling the south of the country and rebel forces controlling the north. Control of the volatile western regions would change hands several times during this period. Unlike Liberia, the presence of the state in certain sections of the country meant that the police, gendarmerie, and courts functioned (to a degree) in these areas. In fact, the police recruited during this period (Boutellis, 2011). Thus, during the wars and in the intermediate period separating them, certain measures were introduced to address VAW in the police and gendarmerie. They were often introduced under pressure from and with the support of the UN and other international actors working in the country. Women's organizations also protested the violence, with many of them protesting one faction or the other in the conflict. Indeed, unlike Liberia, where women mobilized across political and ethnoreligious lines, the most visible protests by women's groups occurred along partisan lines. However, there were women's groups that condemned the violence by both factions in the conflict.

Some of the policies, programs, and institutions introduced during the conflict were specific to VAW, while others concerned women's rights or human rights more broadly. In 2007, the government, in collaboration with partners such as the United Nations Population Fund (UNFPA), the United Nations Development Program (UNDP), and the United Nations Development Fund for Women (UNIFEM), formulated and adopted Côte d'Ivoire's National Action Plan for the Implementation of UNSC Resolution 1325 on Women, Peace, and Security, making Côte d'Ivoire the first African country to do so. On August 20, 2008, about 60 women's organizations, with the support of the UN, met to discuss an action plan to combat violence against women and girls. The government did not adopt this plan until after the conflict. The Association of Female Lawyers of Côte d'Ivoire (AFJCI) and other organizations also began to lobby the government for the removal of discriminatory texts within the law.

On another front, the UN trained police officers and gendarmes in both rebel and government-controlled areas throughout this period. One such training from UN Women led a police prefect in Korhogo to create a gender section in the prefecture. The government agreed to assign gender focal persons (called gender focal points) to police stations and gendarmeries in 2009, under pressure from UNFPA, the Ministry of Solidarity, Family, Women, and Children (MSFFE), and the National GBV Platform.[2] The GBV platform was established by the MSFFE, the UN and other IOs, and NGOs in 2004, and police officers and gendarmes were members of this platform. Similar to Liberia's GBV taskforce, this platform was a forum to discuss various forms of GBV and how to address them.

Measures were also introduced outside of the criminal justice sector. The National Committee to Fight Violence against Women and Children was created in 2005. On July 15, 2005, the government established the National Human Rights Commission of Côte d'Ivoire, which is an independent body "tasked with promoting and protecting human rights and thus deals with issues of violence against women. Its powers are limited as it has an advisory role, and it is not well known to the public. It cannot take binding decisions, but can only make recommendations" (Committee on the Elimination of Discrimination against Women, 2010). The MSFFE established the Centre for Prevention and Assistance for Victims of Sexual Violence in the community of Attécoubé in 2008, with funding from the UN. The government began to establish listening offices to provide psychosocial care and legal support to women and child victims of violence in 2003. Thus, in contrast to Liberia, the state functioned and collaborated with the UN and other international organizations to introduce one specialized mechanism (gender focal points) and programs to address VAW. Civil society organizations, including women's organizations, also sought to influence the government's response to VAW.

Domestic Pressure

Women's and children's rights organizations pressured the government to address VAW. Women's organizations worked independently, and sometimes collaboratively, to protest the violence, and to call on the state to respond to VAW, particularly rape, during this period. For example, in 2004, the AFI released a statement calling on the government to cease hostilities.

On May 14, 2007, the AFJCI issued a statement that condemned sexual violence against women, among other violations, and called on the police and gendarmerie to take adequate measures to combat this violence. The Women in Peacebuilding Network also called on the government to bring an end to the violence; its members met with the director general of the gendarmerie to convey this message. Some of this protest targeted the police and gendarmerie. The Federation of Women's Organizations in Côte d'Ivoire protested police brutality and condemned police rape of women (Badmus, 2009). Women's groups also used demonstrations to protest the violence. One of the largest was in Abobo in 2009 where seven women were killed by state security forces (Human Rights Watch, 2011). However, unlike Liberia, where women's organizations mobilized across political, ethnic, and religious, women's activism in Côte d'Ivoire was politicized such that women's protests were often against one side in the conflict. Thus, while there were many women's organizations that did not support any faction in the conflict, others clearly had political allegiances. For example, the march in Abobo was against the government by women who supported the opposition.

As in Liberia, civil society organizations faced barriers to participating in the peace process. While a few of them participated in peace negotiations, they were not prominent voices at the peace table (Hudson, 2009). Women's organizations were also mostly absent from the mediation processes surrounding the various peace agreements that were signed during the conflict (Hudson, 2009). The exclusion of women's organizations cannot be disassociated from the strength of the women's movement. The Ivoirian women's movement has been categorized as weak due to its relative inability to command public support and attention (Htun and Weldon, 2012). It is likely that the divisions in the movement contributed to its weakness, as members could not speak with one voice and thus struggled to be heard.

However, women's organizations did not limit their work to peace activism. They also provided services to women. The AFJCI continued to operate the legal aid clinics with UN support as the US embassy's funding had dried up. Women's organizations also collaborated with the UN to train law enforcement officers and to educate women on their rights. They also ran programs that provided psychosocial support in both government- and rebel-controlled areas. The MSFFE often worked with women's NGOs and IOs in demanding that the government implement measures to address VAW and in developing specific programs. In 2005, it called on the government to establish specialized units in the police and gendarmerie to address VAW.

According to the National Action Plan, officers were not trained to deal with rape, and corruption undermined the entire public sector (Republic of Côte d'Ivoire et al., 2007). However, senior officials of the ministry could only go so far in their criticism of the Gbagbo government. Furthermore, as is the case with women's ministries across Africa, it was severely underfunded and was not a major player in the government (MSFFE, 2005). It, therefore, had to work closely with international actors to have an impact.

International Pressure

There was some international pressure on the government to address VAW. International focus on VAW was fairly limited for most of the conflict in Côte d'Ivoire. Beginning in 2003, the UN and other IOs condemned sexual violence by both pro-government and rebel forces. Numerous UN reports released during the conflict raised awareness of sexual violence, and condemned the government's and rebels' role. Working with the MSFFE and other members of the GBV platform, UNFPA lobbied for the creation of the position of gender focal point within the police and gendarmerie. The government agreed and assigned gender focal points to some stations in Abidjan. This assignment was not done systematically; not all stations had them, and they were often transferred and not replaced. In 2010, Human Rights Watch urged the government to assign gender focal points to stations in the west of the country (2010). The IRC began lobbying the government for the creation of a specialized section (an independent mechanism) in 2009 and met with the leadership of the police force and gendarmerie; however, the government took no visible action on this front. Overall, there was international pressure on the police and gendarmerie to address VAW, particularly sexual violence. However, the UN's gender programming was, at best, moderate for most of this period. UNFPA, which was the lead agency on gender, barely had a program on VAW until the latter part of the first decade of the 2000s, and a 2007 UNICEF report showed that gender was missing from most of the agency's work during this period. UNDP personnel reported that the agency had a gender program, but their emphasis seemed to be on training law enforcement officers. Thus, although there was pressure on the Gbagbo government, it was moderate. Furthermore, there is no indication that UN agencies pressured the government to create a specialized independent mechanism in the police force or gendarmerie.

Response to Violence against Women after the Conflict (Post-2011)

While the post-conflict Ivoirian government did put measures in place to address VAW, it introduced fewer specialized mechanisms in the criminal justice sector in comparison to Liberia. I use this section to discuss the legal, programmatic, and institutional changes that occurred in country after the end of the conflict. I then describe the gender desk, the specialized independent mechanism created in the police force and gendarmerie in 2014.

Legal and Institutional Reforms in Post-Conflict Côte d'Ivoire

The legal and institutional changes in Côte d'Ivoire are less extensive than those that occurred in Liberia after the conflict. Unlike Liberia, Côte d'Ivoire had not amended its rape law as of December 2019 and had not passed a domestic violence law. However, women's organizations lobbied the government to amend discriminatory texts in the code of laws, to define rape in the penal code, and to pass a domestic violence law. While this activism had not produced the intended outcomes, the government adopted related policy documents. In 2014, it adopted the National Strategy to Combat Gender-Based Violence. Within the criminal justice sector, the police introduced a charter that reserved a special welcome for victims of gendered crimes. This demonstrates their recognition of GBV as a category of offenses.

In 2015, pressure from the UN led to the integration of the National Gendarmerie so that for the first time in the country's history, women were accepted into the Gendarmerie School. The UN continued to train the police and gendarmerie, increasing the number of officers who had received GBV training. By September 2017, officials of the police and gendarmerie had taken over this training. The police and gendarmerie also continued to select and assign gender focal points to stations in Abidjan and across the country. However, not all stations had a focal point, and many had only one. Furthermore, focal points were often reassigned without being replaced, such that their posts were left vacant. UN and NGO personnel claimed that this was a result of poor organization on the part of the security sector; the police and gendarmerie hierarchy did not know which of their officials had received GBV training and thus could not take this into consideration when reassigning them. This illustrates the state of GBV activities within the police force and gendarmerie and it extends to the gender desk, the first of which was created in 2013.

UN Women supported the police to set up the first gender desk in Yopougon in 2013. This gender desk consisted of one office, partly equipped and furnished by UN Women and the Organization for Children, Women, and Family (ONEF) and was staffed with two female police officers who worked exclusively on VAW. In June 2014, the gender desks were formalized and in December 2014, the UN announced that more gender desks would be created. In 2016, UNOCI announced that 12 gender desks would soon be opened (Oumar, 2014; United Nations Operation in Cote d'Ivoire, 2016). As of September 2017, gender desks had not been installed in each of the country's 14 districts. This relatively slow pace of institutionalization was also observable at the administrative level. Neither the police nor the gendarmerie had a gender directorate tasked with overseeing the operations of the gender desks. Instead, officials who worked in other areas were tasked with providing support for gender desk programming. For example, the police's Office of Training, Projects, and Evaluation served as liaison between the UN team working on establishing gender desks and the police force, and also coordinated gender-related training in partnership with UN officials. The situation was similar in the gendarmerie, where there was no central office or an official with oversight of the gender desks. Consequently, gender focal points on the ground did not have a central authority to whom they reported. Instead, their reports on VAW were included in general reports as opposed to being separated and analyzed. Côte d'Ivoire, therefore, is a case that is different from Liberia in many aspects. While both countries created a specialized section after their respective conflicts, the rate of institutionalization was much slower in Côte d'Ivoire.

Conclusion

I have discussed the state's response to VAW over three time periods in Côte d'Ivoire and have compared it with Liberia. Before and during the Ivoirian conflict, the government made some strides in addressing VAW, often in response to activism by IOs and women's organizations. Thus, the position of gender focal point was created in the police force during the conflict. The MSFFE, the women's machinery within the government, also advocated for state action, including reforms in the security sector. Indeed, Cote d'Ivoire had a women's ministry before the outbreak of the conflict. The situation was different in Liberia, where state action to address VAW was minimal before the war and practically nonexistent during. However, the Liberian state outpaced Côte d'Ivoire in the post-conflict period by amending its rape law and creating several specialized criminal justice mechanisms, including a specialized unit within the police force. Furthermore, Liberia institutionalized its specialized unit, WACPS, more rapidly than the gender desk in the police and gendarmerie in Côte d'Ivoire. These two countries are illustrative of the differences in the implementation of the international women's justice norms in post-conflict states in Africa, and of the implementation of norms more broadly. In the next section of the book, I analyze how varying domestic pressures and domestic conditions explain this disparity, and in Chapter 8, I theorize the impact on street-level performance and women's access to justice.

PART III

NATIONAL AND STREET-LEVEL IMPLEMENTATION OF THE INTERNATIONAL WOMEN'S JUSTICE NORM

7
Establishment of the Specialized Units in Liberia and Côte d'Ivoire

In 2005, two years after the end of the country's 14-year conflict, the National Transitional Government of Liberia (NTGL) signed a Memorandum of Understanding with UNICEF to create the Women's and Children Protection Section (WACPS), a specialized police unit mandated to deal with all forms of GBV. In 2014, three years after the Ivoirian conflict ended, the Ivoirian government signed an agreement with the UN mission to construct 12 gender desks in the country with funding from the UN Peacebuilding Fund and the European Union. The creation of these specialized units in both countries marked an important step in the efforts to reduce the re-victimization of survivors and impunity for GBV crimes.

However, a closer examination of these mechanisms reveals disparities in how they were institutionalized; Liberia institutionalized its specialized mechanism at a significantly more rapid pace than Côte d'Ivoire. Thus, while Liberia created a central directorate and assigned officers to work exclusively in the WACPS in the same year that the section was created, four years after the first gender desk was created in Côte d'Ivoire, neither the Ivoirian National Police nor the National Gendarmerie had a central directorate for this specialized unit, and officers assigned to the gender desk also received and processed non-GBV cases. Furthermore, while Liberia had installed WACPS units in all 15 counties within three years of the creation of the first section (2008), Côte d'Ivoire had yet to do the same after four years (2017). This chapter, therefore, investigates the creation and the variation in the institutionalization of these specialized units in Liberia and Côte d'Ivoire. I operationalize creation as a written statement by the government or the UN, announcing that the government has decided or agreed to create a specialized unit. Institutionalization describes the formalization of the unit as a section of the force. It includes the setting up of a central directorate, the installation of units in all administrative regions of the country, and the assignment of officers dedicated exclusively to GBV to work in these units.

Global Norms and Local Action. Peace A. Medie, Oxford University Press (2020). © Oxford University Press.
DOI: 10.1093/oso/9780190922962.001.0001

In this chapter I answer two related questions that probe the process of implementing this international practice and the international women's justice norm: (1) Why did Liberia and Côte d'Ivoire create specialized GBV units in the police force, and why did Côte d'Ivoire create one in the gendarmerie? (2) Why did Liberia institutionalize its specialized unit at a significantly more rapid pace than Côte d'Ivoire? I explain that both countries faced high levels of international pressure from UN agencies and from other international organizations (IOs). However, Côte d'Ivoire faced low domestic pressure from its women's movement and political and institutional conditions of moderate favorability. Conversely, the Liberian government was subjected to a high level of domestic pressure from the women's movement and had political and institutional conditions of high favorability. While these factors combined to facilitate the creation of Liberia's WACPS, the creation of Côte d'Ivoire's gender desk was primarily driven by a high international pressure. Thus, despite low domestic pressure and moderately favorable political and institutional conditions, Côte d'Ivoire created its gender desk. However, high international pressure was not enough for its institutionalization. Thus, while high international pressure combined with high domestic pressure and favorable political and institutional conditions to propel the institutionalization of the WACPS in Liberia, high international pressure in Côte d'Ivoire was not sufficient for the rapid institutionalization of the gender desk.

This comparison shows that while high or strong international pressure was the most important factor in the creation of the specialized mechanism, it was not sufficient for its rapid institutionalization. The comparison also underscores the analytical leverage that is gained from disaggregating the stages of implementation at the domestic level; international and domestic factors are not uniform in their effect on the creation and institutionalization processes. Domestic actors and conditions were more critical at the institutionalization stage. Indeed, the findings demonstrate the influence as well as limits of a powerful international actor on the domestic implementation of a best practice and a norm. They also show that the influence of women's movements extends beyond policy adoption to the implementation stage of the policy process.

I draw on data gathered during fieldwork between 2010 and 2017 in both countries to provide support for these arguments. I first describe and analyze the process of creation in both countries and continue with a description and analysis of the process of institutionalization. I conclude the chapter with a comparative analysis of the influence of international and domestic factors on the establishment of the specialized mechanisms, and on the implementation of the international women's justice norm at the national level.

Creation of the Specialized Units in Liberia and Côte d'Ivoire

Both Liberia and Côte d'Ivoire faced high international pressure at the creation stage. However, domestic pressure was stronger in Liberia and political and institutional conditions more favorable. In this section I describe the dynamics in each country and show that while a combination of high international and domestic pressures and relatively favorable political and institutional conditions led to the creation of Liberia's WACPS, high international pressure had the most influence on the creation of the gender desk in Côte d'Ivoire, even though creation occurred at a slightly slower pace (approximately 2 years after the conflict in Liberia vs. 3 years after the conflict in Côte d'Ivoire) (see Table 7.1).

Table 7.1 Creation of Specialized Units

Factors	Liberia	Côte d'Ivoire
International Pressure	High	High
Domestic Pressure	High	Low
Favorability of Political Context	High	Moderate
Favorability of Institutional Context	High	Moderate

Liberia: Creation of the Women and Children Protection Section

After the Liberian conflict ended in 2003, women's organizations, children's rights organizations, and the media reported that sexual violence, including sexual violence against children, was prevalent in the country. However, the criminal justice sector lacked the capacity to adequately deal with sexual and other forms of VAW. The police force under Charles Taylor had been an instrument of terror that committed atrocities, including rapes, within the population. The 14-year conflict had destroyed police infrastructure, and the existing force lacked basic training. The August 2003 Comprehensive Peace Agreement called for the restructuring of the Liberian National Police (LNP), and UN Security Council (UNSC) Resolution 1509 (2003), which created the United Nations Mission in Liberia (UNMIL), tasked the peacekeeping mission with assisting the transitional government in monitoring and restructuring the force. The resolution also reaffirmed the importance of a gender perspective in post-conflict peace-building and called on Liberian parties and UNMIL, which was deployed in October 2003, to address violence against women and girls as a tool of warfare. However, the NTGL, under the chairmanship of Charles Gyude Bryant, lacked the capacity to independently reform the LNP; the reform was led by UNMIL. It is within this climate of frequent reports of sexual violence, weak state capacity, and UN-led police reform, that the WACPS was created in 2005 through a memorandum of understanding between the transitional government and UNICEF. In September 2005, UNICEF, in collaboration with UNMIL and the LNP, officially launched the newly created section. In this section I demonstrate that the creation of the specialized unit in Liberia can be explained by high international and domestic pressures and relatively favorable political and institutional conditions.

International Pressure

The transitional government faced strong ideational and material pressures from international actors to address impunity, particularly for sexual violence, but also for other forms of VAW. State action on this issue was deemed necessary for the protection of women and children in the aftermath of the war and for strengthening the rule of law. This international pressure came primarily from the UN (including the Secretary General, UNMIL, and UNICEF). The UN employed ideational tools (awareness-raising, advising, lobbying) to exert pressure on the Liberian government. In addition to highlighting the problem and making a case for why perpetrators should be brought to justice, the UN proposed the creation of a specialized unit in the LNP that would enable the force to meet this objective. The UN also employed capacity building (training), which combines ideational and material power, to facilitate the establishment of the WACPS. I discuss these ideational and material tools in detail in the following paragraphs.

The UN **raised awareness** of sexual violence and conveyed that it was a major problem. This was done through documents as well as in meetings with senior government officials. The UN Secretary General submitted four reports on Liberia to the Security Council between September 2003 and June 2005. Three of these reports highlighted the problem of sexual violence. The September 2003 report pointed to "widespread sexual violence against women and children" that required special attention (UNSC, 2003, p. 27). The Secretary General's Sixth Progress Report, published in March 2005, criticized the inadequacy of the criminal justice response to sexual violence against children: "Secondly, reports of rape and sexual assault against young children are not always being investigated or prosecuted in accordance with the law" (UNSC, 2005). A September 2004 report by the World Health Organization (WHO) revealed the prevalence of sexual violence in Montserrado and Bong counties and characteristics of the victimization (Omanyondo, 2004). In a joint press conference with the Minister of Gender and Development in July 2005, Joana Foster, UNMIL's Senior Gender Advisor, discussed how daily reports of rape had overshadowed post-conflict reconstruction (Reliefweb, 2005).

In addition to raising awareness, international actors, led by the UN, also **advised** the government on how to address VAW. Officials of UNMIL recommended the creation of a specialized unit during meetings with receptive senior LNP officers who agreed with the idea. These discussions with senior officers informed, and were informed by, the country's security plans. The UN Country Team and the World Bank led the development of the country's 2004 Joint Needs Assessment and assisted the chairman and senior members of the NTGL in the assessment process. One action-point specified in the Needs Assessment was the establishment of a family support and/or women and children protection unit by December 2004 (NTGL, 2004). UNMIL officials also contributed to the drafting of the 2005 Gender Policy of the LNP, which listed the creation of a specialized unit as one of the force's objectives. The advice to create a specialized unit was in line with the UN's promotion of specialized mechanisms in various forums and documents, including the General Assembly's 1998 resolution on Crime Prevention and Criminal Justice Measures to Eliminate Violence against Women.

UN officials also **lobbied** the Liberian government to act. UNSC Resolution 1509 (2003), which created UNMIL, called on the peacekeeping mission and the government to address VAW. The resolution

[r]eaffirms the importance of a gender perspective in peacekeeping operations and post-conflict peace-building in accordance with resolution 1325 (2000), recalls the need to address violence against women and girls as a tool of warfare, and encourages UNMIL as well as the Liberian parties to actively address these issues.

UN agencies were not the only international actors lobbying the government to act. International NGOs, multilateral organizations, and donors also highlighted the problem and urged the government to end impunity. For example, Amnesty International asked the NTGL to "... state publicly and unequivocally that rape and other forms of sexual violence against women and girls are criminal offences and that the perpetrators will be brought to justice" (2004, p. 36). However, international actors were not limited to written statements when lobbying the government. UN officials met with senior government officials, including the chairman of the NTGL, and urged them to address sexual violence and other forms of VAW in the country. At a two-day consultative meeting on legislative reform co-organized by UNMIL in April 2005 and attended by senior government officials, including Chairman Gyude Bryant, Special Representative of the Secretary General Jacques Paul Klein urged reform of the legal framework, including the rape law (Bryant Proposes Stiff Penalty 2005). At this meeting, Bryant supported the proposal for the reform. These engagements, and the accompanying reports and discourse, were sources of pressure on the government. Furthermore, due to the UN's leading role in the country's reconstruction, their statements to the government carried weight. Indeed, the influence of UN officials in Liberia has been criticized (Fayemi, 2004). However, it meant that senior NTGL officials were likely to listen, and take action, when they were addressed by UN officials.

The UN did not rely solely on ideational factors. It also combined ideas with material power to **build capacity**. Police officers began receiving **training** on human rights in 2004 when the reform began. Senior officers who participated in this training were exposed to the UN's message of a stronger criminal justice sector response to sexual violence and best practices for dealing with the problem. This training served to introduce them to initiatives that had been adopted in other African countries and ensured that UN officials were in talks with senior police officers who had already been sensitized to the issue of VAW and specialized mechanisms.

Overall, the UN employed awareness-raising, lobbying, advising, and training to pressure the NTGL to create the WACPS. Through these strategies, they drew the attention of senior government officials, including the chairman of the NTGL, to VAW, and urged them to bring perpetrators of sexual violence to justice. In policy documents and meetings, they also identified a specialized unit as an important measure that had to be introduced in the LNP and trained police officers in this issue area. Senior government officials and police officers responded to this international pressure from the UN. However, the creation of the WACPS cannot be attributed solely to international pressure. Domestic pressure and the political and institutional conditions also influenced the section's creation.

Domestic Pressure

High domestic pressure also influenced the government's decision to create the WACPS. This pressure also fed into the UN's gender programming. It came primarily from women's organizations, which called for the state and UNMIL to prevent sexual violence and punish perpetrators. Research has shown that a strong, autonomous women's movement determines government responsiveness to VAW (Weldon, 2002). In Liberia, women were able to place credible pressure on the NTGL and the police force to arrest and punish perpetrators of sexual violence because of the strength of the movement and its autonomy. I draw on Htun and Weldon (2012) to assess the strength of the women's movement. They describe a strong women's movement as one that can command public support and attention, while a weaker movement struggles to convince the media and others that its opinions are important for discussion. The authors define an autonomous movement as one that is "devoted to promoting women's status and wellbeing independently of political parties and other associations that do not have the status of women as their main concern" (2012, pp. 553–554). I draw on their operationalization of independent variables to measure the strength and autonomy of the women's movements in Liberia and Côte d'Ivoire. A strong movement (1) has a strong media presence; (2) is able to mount massive protests; (3) is described in "narrative accounts as being strong, influential, powerful, mobilizing widespread public support, and the like" (Htun & Wledon, 2012, appendix). An autonomous movement (1) has its base outside political parties and other political institutions; (2) has activists located outside the government; (3) does not take its ideas and initiatives from the women's wing of a political party or faction.

The women's movement in Liberia employed protests, awareness-raising campaigns, and lobbying to exert pressure on the NTGL. Its relatively **strong media presence** ensured that the public as well as senior government officials were made aware (more so than in Côte d'Ivoire) of movement activities and demands. Both the national and international media began covering the women's movement during the civil war, and this coverage continued after the war ended. A Lexis Nexis search showed that women's organizations in Liberia were significantly more visible than women's organizations in Côte d'Ivoire in the three years preceding the creation of the WACPS. Women's organizations were mentioned in 28 local and international new stories on rape in the country. This is in contrast to five news stories on women's organizations in Cote d'Ivoire. This coverage demonstrates the visibility of women's organizations and of the movement during this period. The newspapers covered efforts by the movement and by member organizations to place sexual violence on the public agenda and demand action. For example, on May 21, 2004, allAfrica carried a story on the five-day National Women's Conference in which Liberian women condemned rape and urged the government to take appropriate action to address rape, trafficking, and other forms of VAW (Liberian Women Recommend Severe Punishment, 2004). The media also reported on protests by the women's movement.

The women's movement organized two large **protest** marches between September 2003 (when the peace agreement was signed) and September 2005 (when the WACPS was launched) to condemn sexual violence, to criticize the inadequacy of the NTGL's response, and to demand action from the government and the UN. Smaller marches were also held during this time. It is notable, and an indication of the strength of the movement, that these large protests were acknowledged and addressed by senior government officials, including the chairman of the NTGL. In November 2003, hundreds of women marched on City Hall to demand an end to post-conflict criminality, including rape. Led by Leymah Gbowee, the women demanded the swift disarmament of combatants. In presenting their demands to Charles Gyude Bryant, chairman of the NTGL, Gbowee stated, "We the women of Liberia will no more allow ourselves to be raped, abused, misused, maimed and killed. . . . Our children and grandchildren will not be used as killing machines and sex slaves" (Paye-Layleh, 2003). Bryant received the women and acknowledged the strength of the movement: "When these women put their hands behind something, they will not stop 'til it is finished" (Paye-Layleh, 2003). The movement organized another march in January 2004, this time on the Ministry of Justice, where their spokesperson, Ruth Caesar, presented their concerns to the Minister of Justice, Kabineh Ja'neh.

> Madam Ruth Caesar said their protest is meant to draw the state's attention to the prevailing state of insecurity, especially what they as women are faced with at the hands of the suspected criminals. She recounted how every second in a day and night, a woman is robbed or raped by suspected criminal and nothing but apparently, nothing is being done to stop it. "We are raising this concern to government and demand that immediate measures be taken because the situation is gradually getting out of hand. Why should we live in fear in our own country with the huge presence of the United Nations Mission that is responsible for security, together with our own security forces?" she asked. Madam Caesar reiterated that in the districts of Paynesville, Duala, Gardnersville, Sinkor, Central Monrovia and other environs, women are either mobbed or raped, and the situation has generally become too dangerous for residents. (Women Decry Criminal Activities, 2004)

The Minister of Justice told the women that action would be taken within 72 hours to deal with the criminality in the country. However, protest marches were only one of the mediums through which women's organizations voiced their discontent. They also held meetings with government officials and organized briefings. In a press conference at the Ministry of Gender and Development, Counselor Lois Lewis Brutus, president of the Association of Female Lawyers of Liberia (AFELL), urged the government to "attach serious importance" to rape, which was a crime against humanity and undermined "the future of its victims" (Punish Rape, 2005). The ability to mount large protests that garnered the attention of senior government officials and to have one-on-one discussions with these officials demonstrates the strength of the movement.

Narrative accounts have also described the strength and influence of the movement. Indeed, Chairman Bryant's 2003 statement about the tenacity of the movement illustrates how it was represented in narrative accounts. The contributions of the Women of Liberia Mass Action for Peace, which sought an end to the war through a variety of strategies, including a sit-in outside the presidential mansion, has been documented and discussed, nationally and internationally. The Mano River Women's Peace Network (MARWOPNET) is another group that gained domestic and international recognition for its efforts. Scholars have argued that the movement was strong in its advocacy for peace during the conflict (Badmus, 2009; Fuest, 2008). This vibrancy continued into the immediate aftermath of the conflict. According to Fuest (2008b),

> The war appears to have generated a perhaps unusual level of collective female peace activism compared to women's peace movements in other African countries. Observers' reports and anecdotal evidence suggest an extraordinary level of persistent determination and militancy among Liberian female peace-building NGOs, whose members share a uniform of white T-shirts and head-ties.... Unlike women in other war and post-war situations, Liberian women appear to have achieved some voice in national peace-building endeavours in spite of resistance from male politicians. (pp. 213–214)

One of the leaders of the movement, Leymah Gbowee, would later share the 2011 Nobel Peace Prize with President Ellen Johnson Sirleaf and Tawakkol Karman of Yemen. She was awarded the prize for the movement's "nonviolent struggle for the safety of women and for women's rights to full participation in peace-building work" (Nobel Prize, 2011).

The structure of the movement was key to its strength. The women's movement, which began to mobilize during the war, was **autonomous** from political factions. Women's groups crossed political, ethnic, and religious lines in order to become a part of the movement (AWPSG, 2004); thus, even though political and social divisions existed in the movement, they were less salient during this period. The movement's base was **outside of** political parties and other political institutions prior to the creation of the WACPS. Most (but not all) of the well-known activists who urged the government to bring perpetrators of sexual violence to justice, including Leymah Gbowee, were **not located within** the government. The movement's **ideas and initiatives** did not originate from within the government. Instead, the protests organized and statements released by the movement were fueled by reports from within communities about rapes. Not only were they targeted at the government, but they were also critical of its weaknesses in enforcing the law. Similarly, women's protests during the war had condemned the violence by the government of Charles Taylor as well as by the rebel factions (AWPSG,

2004). Thus, the women's movement in Liberia was autonomous and, therefore, a source of strong domestic pressure on the NTGL, and even the UN, to hold perpetrators of sexual violence accountable. The political context in Liberia in the period leading to the creation of the WACPS allowed the movement to have access to senior government officials.

Political Context

Scholars have argued that the domestic political context conditions the impact of international actors who promote an international norm (Betts, 2014; Cardenas, 2007; Cortell & Davis, 2000; Deere, 2009; Simmons, 2009). The political context affects how international pressure is received and also affects the ability of social movements to mobilize and be heard. In Liberia, the inauguration of a transitional government with an agenda to strengthen the rule of law positively mediated international and domestic pressures.

Government's Adoption of Rule of Law Agenda
The creation of the WACPS aligned with and was thus aided by the transitional government's rule of law agenda. In his inaugural address, Gyude Bryant, chairman of the NTGL, promised that his government would implement the peace agreement and that governance would be based on the rule of law. Violence against women and the creation of the WACPS fit squarely into this rule of law agenda. The country's 2004 Joint Needs Assessment undertaken by the NTGL, the UN, and the World Bank linked human rights, including VAW, to the rule of law and described the restoration of the rule of law and human rights as a key priority. It recognized the need to protect women from human rights abuses:

> xxx. Human rights, protection and gender. After years of widespread and severe human rights abuses, the priority of enhancing protection for civilians, especially women, requires that programmes are focused on realising the human rights of the most vulnerable groups. Human rights and gender considerations must be kept to the fore as interventions within different sectors—at the institutional and community levels—are coordinated.

Deputy Inspector General of Police Assatu Bah-Kenneh explained that "[i]t was important to establish WACPS especially in this post-conflict situation where so many women and children walk around with wounds of abuse" (UNMIL Focus, March 2007). In his presentation of the draft rape bill to Gyude Bryant in July 2005, Kabineh Ja'neh, the minister of justice, summarized the government's assessment of the problem of post-conflict sexual violence:

> the issue of human rights has been one of the critical factors the Liberian nation has been faced with. "By this [the issue of human rights], we are referring to rape and sexual violence being perpetrated against women and children, especially children as young as one year old," he said. The Liberian Justice Minister gave instances of rape and sexual violence that apparently have given rise to the preparation of the Bill on Rape and Sexual Violence. According to Minister Ja'neh, in June 2005, two children, 8 years each, were raped; one by a 58-yrs old man, while two other children 11 and 12 were also allegedly raped by a 30-yrs old man. Minister Ja'neh said as ghastly and horrifying as these stories have been for victims and their loved ones and the larger society, perpetrators of the heinous crime against women and children, have dully exercised their rights to bail as guaranteed under current legislation. (Rape, Sexual Violence in Check, 2005)

It is, however, important to note that the UN and other international actors played a key role in crafting this rule of law agenda, beginning with the 2003 Comprehensive Peace Agreement that ended the war. Thus, the main advocate for the creation of a specialized mechanism participated in crafting the rule of law agenda that favored the creation of the WACPS. It is also important to note that rebel groups that displaced, raped, tortured, and murdered Liberians were included in the NTGL, due to the terms of the peace agreement. Therefore, this was not a government made entirely of human rights champions. Relatedly, the government's adoption of a rule of law agenda does not mean that the actions of leaders of the NTLG always reflected the principles of democracy and good governance. Indeed, ECOWAS found that the NTGL was riddled with corruption (Dube, 2008). In 2009, Gyude Bryant was tried for the alleged embezzlement of one million US dollars from the state oil refinery that occurred during his tenure as chairman and was acquitted due to the state's failure to provide evidence in support of this charge. Nonetheless, the transitional government recognized the importance of strengthening the rule of law, and this contributed to shaping a political environment in which there was support for the creation of the WACPS and in which advocates for a stronger criminal justice response were given an audience.

Institutional Context

A relatively favorable institutional context mediated the creation of the WACPS. The institutional context describes properties of the implementing agency that condition international and domestic pressures. While key policy decisions are often made at the presidential and ministerial levels, conditions within the implementing agency can either boost or constrain the effects of pressure from international and domestic actors. In Liberia, the LNP was undergoing extensive reform that began in 2004. Article VIII of the Comprehensive Peace Agreement had tasked the National Transitional Legislative Assembly (NTLA), UN, ECOWAS, and the International Contact Group on Liberia with restructuring the force. However, due to the capacity gap in the Liberian government, UNPOL led the reform of the police force. Indeed, a senior rule of law official said that the state existed in name only in the immediate aftermath of the conflict (interview, Z.M., Skype, February 15, 2016). The Secretary-General assessed the criminal justice security sector in the immediate aftermath of the war thus:

> Judicial institutions throughout Liberia have suffered an almost complete breakdown as a result of years of violent conflict and the disregard of the Taylor Government for the rule of law. The Liberian national police is said to have functioned more as an instrument of repression than as an enforcer of law and order. Its 3,500 officers lack training and have not been paid since early 2002. Corruption has been endemic. Similarly, the judiciary sometimes does not enjoy public confidence and has suffered from corrupt practices and political interference. Most courts are not functioning and much of the infrastructure has been destroyed or looted. It also appears that various prisons throughout the country are empty and dilapidated, and that former prisoners are on the loose. (United Nations Security Council, 2003b, p. 6)

UNMIL, which led the reform process, had its own internal gender guidelines. VAW was recognized in the mission's mandate, which

[r]eaffirms the importance of a gender perspective in peacekeeping operations and post-conflict peace-building in accordance with resolution 1325 (2000), recalls the need to address violence against women and girls as a tool of warfare, and encourages UNMIL as well as the Liberian parties to actively address these issues. (UNSC 2003c)

UNMIL's Office of the Gender Advisor sought to "facilitate gender sensitive approaches to the implementation of the Mission's mandate, drawing on the provisions of the UN Security Council Resolutions on women, peace and security" (UNMIL, n.d.). Thus, the creation of the WACPS occurred in an institution that was undergoing reform—a reform in which UNMIL was playing a leading role.

Police Reform Led by the United Nations
The destruction of state institutions meant that the NTGL largely lacked the capacity to govern and to reconstruct institutions without assistance from the UN and donors. This assistance came in the form of funds, the training and equipping of police and other personnel, advice, and the assigning of UN personnel to work within Liberian institutions and to support Liberian officials. This level of involvement enabled the UN not only to shape the agenda in collaboration with Liberian officials, but also to place VAW, and more specifically, a specialized unit on the reform agenda. The UN's leading role also meant that UNPOL officers had access to senior LNP officials and met regularly with them to promote the idea and to offer advice, based on the UN's experiences in other countries.

However, it is important to note that the UN did face resistance from some quarters. For example, the UN Secretary General reported that the NTLG was slow in implementing salary reform that had been approved by the Rule of Law Committee (UNSC, 2005). Also, Chief Justice Johnnie Lewis resisted pressure from AFELL and the UN to establish Criminal Court E, which he argued was not necessary, as existing courts could handle rape cases (IRIN, 2008). This resistance delayed the establishment of the court and also shows that despite the government's reliance on the UN and donors, international actors could not effect change without the consent of veto players. Describing the nature of the relationship between the government and the UN, a senior official in UNMIL's Rule of Law Department explained that theirs was an advisory mission that could only make recommendations to the government (interview, L.I., Accra, August 11, 2014). Indeed, a senior Liberian police officer who participated in the discussions to create the WACPS explained that although the idea to create the section originated with UNPOL personnel, LNP officers liked, supported, and agreed to it in the course of several meetings. Thus, it was not an imposition on the LNP or the Liberian government (interview, L.Q., Skype, July 1, 2016).

Nonetheless, UNMIL's leading role in the reform process removed many bureaucratic barriers to institutional change. Joseph Kekula, acting director of the LNP in 2004, discussed LNP officers' attitudes toward the reform:

> The CPA mandated the reform and restructuring of the police so that was not anything they had choice [the transitional government] over, whether they liked it or not. In the CPA, it was an agreement from Accra. So it was a priority, the reformation of the police was a priority. The document mandated the United Nations to do that, to do the reform and restructuring of the police.... The relationship with the UN, especially the UN police was very cordial I can say from the top even though from the beginning a lot of people were against the change. It took us a long period of time to make some of these officers understand that these changes have to go on whether they like it or not. At first we had a lot of opposition from within the police itself regarding the change process. Then when everybody became convinced it is going to go on, everybody was in line. (interview, May 14, 2008a, p. 12)

The reduction in institutional resistance enabled UNMIL advisors to shape the institutional agenda and promote the creation of the WACPS.

Liberia is a case where strong international and domestic pressures conditioned by relatively favorable political and institutional dynamics led to the creation of the WACPS. The evidence shows that activism by the women's movement generated a sense of urgency within the Liberian government. Although this domestic pressure did not explicitly call for the creation of a specialized mechanism, it demanded an improved police performance that could bring perpetrators to account and reduce impunity. This call was very much in line with the UN's agenda to address VAW in post-conflict countries and to establish specialized mechanisms. Thus, when the UN raised awareness, lobbied, advised, and built capacity, it was sowing seeds in fertile soil. The political and institutional conditions further facilitated the creation of the section. I compare this to the creation of the gender desk in Côte d'Ivoire in the next section. In Côte d'Ivoire, domestic pressure was low and levels of political and institutional favorability for the creation of the gender desk were moderate. I, therefore, investigate how the gender desk was created in these conditions.

Côte d'Ivoire: Creation of the Gender Desk

Reports by NGOs and IOs such as the UN drew attention to sexual and other forms of VAW before, during, and after the Ivoirian conflict, which ended in April 2011. As in Liberia, the criminal justice sector lacked the capacity to effectively deal with the problem, but unlike Liberia, the destruction of the sector had been less extensive. In areas controlled by the Gbagbo government, the National Police, National Gendarmerie, and courts had functioned for most of the conflict, albeit inadequately. In fact, there was an attempt at gender-responsive policing during this period; Côte d'Ivoire began the process of establishing an embedded specialized mechanism. Lobbying by the Ministry of Family, Women, and Social Affairs (MFFAS)[1] and the Organization for Children, Women, and Family (ONEF) led to the introduction of gender focal points in some police stations and gendarmeries beginning in 2009, although this role was not formalized. The country's Security Sector Reform strategy was adopted by the National Security Council in September 2012, after the second civil war. However, in contrast to Liberia, where the UN played a leading role in reforming the police force, SSR in Côte d'Ivoire was led by the Ivoirian government.

Furthermore, Côte d'Ivoire had three overlapping specialized mechanisms after the end of its nine-year political and military conflict. First, the police and gendarmerie continued to assign gender focal points. However, this was not done consistently, and focal points were frequently transferred without being replaced by similarly trained officers. Second, UN Women created one gender desk in the 17th arrondissement police station in Abidjan in 2013. This gender desk consisted of one office with a female police officer, who was later joined by a second. However, it was a stand-alone initiative that was not replicated by UN Women. Third, in 2013, the police and gendarmerie informally agreed to create the gender desk (renamed Bureau d'Accueil Genre [BAG] in 2017) after a November visit to Rwanda's specialized police unit. The creation was formalized with the June 2014 signing of an agreement for the construction of 12 gender desks with financing from the UN's Peacebuilding Fund and the European Union. This 2014 creation occurred about three years after the end of the second civil war, which is a year longer than it took to create Liberia's WACPS.

I explain that Côte d'Ivoire faced high international pressure to create the gender desk after the second civil war. However, in contrast to Liberia, this was paired with low domestic pressure and political and institutional conditions of moderate favorability. The domestic pressure and conditions did not prevent, but rather, slightly delayed the creation of the specialized unit. Thus, creation was primarily due to high international pressure.

International Pressure

Strong pressure from the UN, working through several of its agencies after the second civil war, was key to the creation of the gender desk. Similar to Liberia, the UN employed ideational tools (awareness-raising, advising, and lobbying). However, in contrast to Liberia, the UN also used naming and shaming to pressure the Ivoirian government. These strategies were combined with capacity building (training and learning visits), which is a combination of ideational and material factors. This subsection details these dynamics.

First, the UN **raised awareness** of VAW in Côte d'Ivoire, particularly sexual violence, through reports, press releases, and statements delivered by UN officials. This served to draw the government's attention to the problem of VAW. The message from the UN focused not only on post-conflict VAW, but also on widespread sexual violence committed during the conflict by ex-rebels, who had been absorbed into the army, the Republican Forces of Côte d'Ivoire (FRCI). Seven out of nine reports of the Secretary General to the Security Council in the three years preceding the creation of the gender desk stressed that VAW was a problem in post-conflict Côte d'Ivoire; four reports underscored sexual violence by the Republican Forces of Côte d'Ivoire (FRCI). For example, the Secretary General's June 2012 report stated that "[e]lements of FRCI and dozos (traditional hunters) were also involved in cases of arbitrary arrest and illegal detention, sexual violence and rape" during the reporting period (UNSC, 2012, p. 8). UN agencies also issued press releases and gave speeches in which they drew attention to and condemned post-conflict sexual violence. For example, on December 29, 2011, the United Nations Operations in Côte d'Ivoire (UNOCI), through its spokesperson, voiced "deep concern" about human rights violations, including rapes, by the armed forces (UN Voices Concern, 2011). These statements drawing attention to the problem were sometimes accompanied by advice on how the state could address sexual and other forms of VAW.

UN officials **advised** senior officers of the police and gendarmerie in meetings. After the government approached UNOCI for advice, UNPOL officers in the section on Gender, Human Rights and the Protection of Vulnerable Groups met with senior Ivoirian officials in the police and gendarmerie and recommended the creation of a specialized unit in 2013. They developed a document that specified the reforms needed in the police and gendarmerie to create the specialized unit.

The UN and other international actors also **lobbied** the government to address sexual and other forms of VAW. In January 2011, Margot Wallström, the Special Representative of the Secretary-General on Sexual Violence in Conflict, released a statement condemning sexual violence in the conflict and called on the authorities to prevent the problem and to protect civilians (UN 2012). In November 2011, she met with senior government officials to urge action on conflict-related sexual violence. Hers was only one of several voices that urged the government to act.

The special rapporteur's visit was linked to the blacklisting, and thus, the **naming and shaming** of Côte d'Ivoire. In 2012, the UN placed Côte d'Ivoire on the list of countries whose security forces perpetrated sexual violence during conflict. A United Nations Development Program (UNDP) official revealed that this blacklisting accelerated government action (interview, A.A., Skype, April 19, 2017). A senior police officer at the Ministry of Interior and Security confirmed that placement on the list was a major push factor for the creation of the gender desk within the national police (interview, A.L., Abidjan, September 22, 2017). She explained that the blacklisting was particularly impactful because it came from outside the country. Indeed, in direct response to this blacklisting, Minister of Interior Hamed Bakayoko participated in the Global Summit to End Sexual Violence in Conflict held in London in June 2014 and committed Côte d'Ivoire to certain steps to address the problem in the security sector. This is notable because elements of the former rebel force that backed President Ouattara during the conflict and perpetrated sexual violence during this period had been integrated into the army. Thus, naming and shaming of the Ivoirian army contributed to compelling the state to begin to introduce measures to address sexual violence, even though members of the security sector were implicated. Risse, Ropp, and Sikkink (2013) have argued that the effectiveness of naming and shaming is dependent on the audience's belief in the social validity of the norm. The Ivoirian government recognized the international significance of the norm and of the norm promoter. This was particularly relevant because President Ouattara sought to move past the country's violent history and to boost its international standing (Piccolino, 2018).

The UN also invested in building the capacity of the police and gendarmerie through training and learning visits. UNOCI began **training** officers of the police and gendarmerie on how to handle GBV before the outbreak of the second civil war and continued to train them after the war ended. UNDP and UNOCI spent about 180 million CFA francs to provide training on gender, human rights, and the rights of children. A senior UNPOL officer estimated that 800 officers had been given such training and had been deployed to gendarmeries and police stations by July 2014 (interview, M.K., Abidjan, July 14, 2014). This training, which was given to both senior and junior officers, contained information on specialized services for victims of GBV. UNOCI also organized **learning visits** in which senior police and gendarmerie officials visited specialized units in other African countries. Officials from the gendarmerie and army visited Senegal in 2012. A senior delegation from the police and gendarmerie visited Rwanda's specialized unit in November 2013. These visits were opportunities for UN officials to promote specialized units and to convince Ivoirian officials of the benefits of creating one.

Thus, similar to Liberia, the Ivoirian government was subjected to strong international pressure. This ideational and material pressure served to convey information on VAW and on specialized units to senior officials in the gendarmerie and police and to urge the government to act. It was, however, paired with low domestic pressure and political and institutional conditions of moderate favorability.

Domestic Pressure

Women's organizations did draw attention to VAW in the three years preceding the creation of the gender desk. However, the women's movement in Côte d'Ivoire was not as strong as the movement in Liberia. Once again, I draw on Htun and Weldon (2012) to measure the strength of the movement. While women's organizations employed awareness-raising campaigns and some lobbying to pressure the government, they were less visible in the media. Indeed, after the second conflict, the movement in Côte d'Ivoire was not as visible in the media as the movement in Liberia. While national and international media covered the war and there were some mentions of women's organizations, their efforts in the area of VAW from April 2011 to June 2014 received significantly less coverage than women's organizations in Liberia (28 new stories in Liberia versus 5 in Cote d'Ivoire). Furthermore, more than half of the articles that mentioned women's organizations were stories of seven women killed in a March 2011 anti-Gbagbo protest in Abobo.

While women's groups organized large **protests** during the conflict, protests became smaller after the April 2011 end of the second civil war. During the war in March 2011, women marched in support of Ouattara, calling for President Gbagbo to step down. Pro-Gbagbo forces opened fire on the protesters, resulting in seven deaths and injuries to many more. Women also marched in support of Gbagbo during this period. For example, in February 2011, the pro-Gbagbo Coordination of Patriotic Women of Côte d'Ivoire, led by Genevieve Bro-Grebe, organized a sit-in in front of the UN mission. The women expressed their support of Gbagbo's victory in the presidential elections and condemned the actions of the UN and French forces, whom they accused of destabilizing the country. They also protested the rebels, stating that "atrocities are committed by a certain invisible commando unit that wants to impose, at all costs, Alassane Ouattara as president" (BBC, 2011). However, in contrast to Liberia, such large demonstrations mostly ceased with the end of the conflict. Instead, protests became smaller and localized. For example, the Coalition of Female Leaders of Duekoué marched in 2011, 2012, and 2014 to protest rape in the town and to pressure the police and gendarmerie to effectively address the problem (Moussa, 2016). Thus, while women's organizations were drawing attention to VAW in the immediate aftermath of the conflict, it was not being done through large protests.

Narrative accounts of the Ivoirian women's movement have been mixed. While some accounts have concluded that the women's movement is strong and impactful, others have argued otherwise. Based on a 2003 protest mounted mostly by pro-Gbagbo women and others by the Women's Organization in Côte d'Ivoire, as well as social initiatives by women's organizations, Isiaka Badmus concluded that "women's organizations have been highly instrumental in ensuring that peace returns to their country right from the beginning of the war" (2009, p. 828). In discussing women's contribution to peace-building in Côte d'Ivoire, Heidi Hudson also stated that women's groups made "small but significant steps in the right direction" (2009, p. 290). However, she also noted that "civil society has always been rather divided and weak and women's movement are struggling to be the exception" (p. 313). Meanwhile, Htun and Weldon (2012) coded the movement in 2005 as "weak" in their study of states' responses to VAW. Narrative accounts after the conflict (between May 2011 and June 2014) were mixed (see Moussa, 2016). Furthermore, the movement did not receive the same level of international recognition as the movement in Liberia, where one of the leaders was awarded the Nobel Peace Prize.

One factor that possibly undermined the strength of the Ivoirian movement was its lack of **autonomy**. Autonomous movements are more influential, partly because autonomy provides them leverage to make policy demands of government and allows them to serve as a watchdog (Tripp, 2001). However, major protests by women's groups during the conflict were mostly organized along political lines. Thus, as explained earlier, pro-Ouattara groups protested Gbagbo and vice versa. The pro-Gbagbo Coordination of Patriotic Women of Côte d'Ivoire, which organized sit-ins, was allied to the Young Patriots, a pro-Gbagbo movement that had been implicated in violence, including sexual violence, against his perceived opponents. This does not mean that all women's organizations were aligned to one faction or the other; there were some autonomous organizations that were critical of all factions in the conflict. However, women's groups' alignment with factions in the conflict fractured the movement and undermined its autonomy. Furthermore, this division did not end with the conflict. Evidence of this is the October 2012 protest of Dominique Ouattara, the first lady, by the Femmes Patriotes in Paris. This alignment with political factions meant that after the conflict, the movement's base was not entirely **outside of** government or the opposition, and leaders of this splintered movement were **located within** these opposing political factions. Consequently, while there were many women's organizations that were not aligned with any political faction, the organizational **ideas and initiatives** of some women's groups could not be divorced from the political factions they supported. This politicization of women's groups and of civil society more broadly weakened the movement and stifled activism. Leaders of some women's organizations explained to me that they preferred to provide services to survivors of VAW, instead of criticizing the inadequacy of the government's response, for fear of being labeled anti-government. Overall, a picture emerges of a splintered and politicized women's movement in Côte d'Ivoire that received relatively less coverage in the media and less recognition, in comparison to the movement in Liberia. Thus, the movement in Côte d'Ivoire was weaker than the movement in Liberia before the creation of the specialized unit and exerted relatively less pressure on the post-conflict government.

Political Context

The post-conflict political context offered a mixed environment for the creation of the gender desk and was therefore moderately favorable. While the post-conflict government's rule of law agenda prioritized reform of the police force and gendarmerie, the politicization of the security sector proved a hindrance to this reform.

Government's Adoption of Rule of Law Agenda

The post-conflict government of President Alassane Ouattara sought to strengthen the rule of law, particularly as a buffer against a relapse into violent conflict. Ouattara, who wanted to elevate Côte d'Ivoire's standing in the ECOWAS region, also wanted to demonstrate to the international community the progress that his country was making; a strong rule of law was central to this story. While this led the government to prioritize issues that were viewed as threats to national security, it also meant that the government was open to other programs that sought to strengthen the rule of law. Therefore, in 2012, the Ouattara government initiated the reform of the country's security sector with partners such as the UN, German Corporation for International Cooperation (GIZ), and the French government. "Gender" was one of the issues included in the reform strategy. The government's concern with its international image also meant that blacklisting from the UN was an unwanted mark that it sought to erase. However, while this rule of law agenda, which was partly crafted by the international community, meant that senior officials of the police and gendarmerie were now more likely to pay attention to issues of gender and VAW, there were political barriers that limited the extent to which this attention could lead to concrete changes such as the creation of the gender desk.

Politicization of the Security Sector

A major challenge was the politicization of the relationship between the government and the police and gendarmerie. The Ouattara government viewed the police and gendarmerie as pro-Gbagbo and thus, anti-Ouattara (Lebeouf, 2016). There was, therefore, significant distrust between the government and the two agencies. There was also distrust within and between the security and defense forces (UNSC, Dec 2013). This state of affairs undermined SSR. Indeed, some members of the gendarmerie interpreted efforts to integrate women into the force as an attack on their identity, a consequence of their support of Gbagbo during the conflict (Lebeouf 2016). They, therefore, resisted this measure. Even where reform was not perceived as retaliation, politics was salient. Comparing Liberia to Côte d'Ivoire, a senior UNPOL officer reported that while the former was pragmatic (when deciding on the establishment of a specialized unit), the latter was political (interview, A.B., Abidjan, July 14, 2014). Political calculations disproportionately framed all aspects of the reform process.

Institutional Context

Although Côte d'Ivoire's institutions were stronger than Liberia's, they were not necessarily more conducive for the creation of a specialized unit. The government began reform of the security sector in 2013, after several false starts under Gbagbo. Peace agreements signed during the conflict had mandated this reform. However, while the UN led the reform in Liberia, SSR in Côte d'Ivoire was led by the government, with UN support. This affected the extent to which the UN could shape and drive the agenda. Thus, although the UN was active in the reform process, it was not leading the process, contributing to the creation of a moderately favorable political environment.

Security Sector Reform Not Led by the United Nations

The relative strength of Ivoirian institutions offered the UN fewer opportunities to impact what happened within the government and its institutions. As previously explained, the capacity gap in the NTGL necessitated a leading role for the UN in the reform of Liberia's security sector. The situation differed in Côte d'Ivoire, where UNOCI met a police force and gendarmerie that had functioned throughout the war in government-controlled areas. Indeed, the police held recruitment drives during the conflict. Furthermore, the Ivoirian police was rated as one of the best in Africa prior to the conflict and had trained forces in other African countries (Boutellis, 2011). Thus, although the Ivoirian police and gendarmerie had been weakened by the conflict, a large section of the institution remained operational after the end of the conflict in 2011. In 2012, the government announced an SSR strategy developed in consultation with UNOCI but also with the National Security Council and with President Ouattara at the helm. The UNOCI was responsible for three aspects, including gender. Thus, although the UN was playing a key role in the reform of the Ivoirian security sector, it was mainly a supporting role. Consequently, the organization's ability to push its agenda was more circumscribed in Côte d'Ivoire. UNOCI officials had to lobby senior police and gendarmerie officers more intensively and over a longer time period. Being less embedded in the police and gendarmerie meant that it was harder to accelerate the decision to create a specialized unit. Furthermore, the UN was perceived as anti-Gbagbo by pro-Gbagbo elements within the security sector. This is due to various actions it took during the conflict, including in the post-electoral struggles that brought Ouattara to power. Consequently, UNOCI was viewed with suspicion in some quarters, further curbing the organization's ability to introduce major changes in the police and gendarmerie and to prompt Ivoirian officials to act quickly.

Despite the moderate favorability of the political and institutional conditions and the low domestic pressure, the police force and gendarmerie formally created the gender desk in June 2014, demonstrating the role of international pressure at the creation stage. However, the next section shows that while strong international pressure can be sufficient to drive the creation of this mechanism, domestic pressure and conditions become more critical at the institutionalization stage.

The Institutionalization of the Specialized Units

Liberia institutionalized its unit at a much faster pace than Côte d'Ivoire. Thus, within three years of the creation of the WACPS, a central directorate had been created, a WACPS had been installed in each county, and WACPS officers worked exclusively on GBV cases. This is in contrast to Côte d'Ivoire, where three years after the creation of the gender desk in the National Police and National Gendarmerie, officers were not exclusively signed to the unit, a central directorate had not been created, and sections of the country did not have gender desks. I attribute this variation in institutionalization to the levels of domestic pressure and the favorability of political and institutional conditions. International pressure on Liberia and Côte d'Ivoire remained high after the creation of the specialized units. However, within three years of the creation of the specialized units in both countries, domestic pressure

Table 7.2 Institutionalization of Specialized Units

Factors	Liberia	Côte d'Ivoire
International Pressure	High	High
Domestic Pressure	High	Low
Favorability of Political Context	High	Moderate
Favorability of Institutional Context	High	Moderate

was higher in Liberia than in Côte d'Ivoire, and political and institutional conditions were more favorable in the former. I argue that these domestic factors explain the variation in the rate of institutionalization of the specialized units (see Table 7.2).

Liberia: Institutionalization of the Women and Children Protection Section

After the creation of the WACPS, the media, women's and children's rights organizations, and international organizations reported that incidents of VAW were still rampant. Studies conducted in 2006, 2007, and 2008 pointed to an epidemic of sexual violence. Meanwhile, domestic violence was the most reported crime to the police after the creation of the WACPS. Reasons given for the continued reports of sexual violence included deficiencies in the newly created WACPS and the absence of the section in some parts of the country.

The WACPS became operational in September 2005. A central directorate was created at the police headquarters in 2005 and the section's officers worked exclusively on GBV cases and on cases that involved children. Six months after the launch, units had been established in eight counties, and three years after, all 15 counties had at least one WACPS unit. By December 2010, there were 56 units across the country, with Monrovia having the most units (23) and six counties (Bomi, Grand Cape Mount, Grand Kru, River Gee, River Cess, Sinoe) having only one WACPS. New LNP buildings constructed by UNDP with funding from the Norwegian government had a WACPS attached (de Carvalho and Schia, 2009). While the buildings had a separate structure for the specialized section, in most police stations, the WACPS did not have a separate structure. Consequently, most of the 11 WACPS units I visited in Liberia in 2010 and 2011 consisted of one WACPS office housed in the police station, alongside other sections of the LNP. This demonstrates the government's willingness to install WACPS units, even in the absence of the required office space and resources. Indeed, a senior UN Rule of Law official pointed to the government's willingness to use every "little space" available to set up a WACPS unit as an indication of its willingness to implement this best practice (interview, L.I., Accra, August 11, 2014).

In this section, I explain the institutionalization of the WACPS. Specifically, I analyze why the WACPS was institutionalized across the country at a relatively accelerated pace, in comparison to Côte d'Ivoire. In explaining this phenomenon, I do not seek to assess the street-level performance of the officers within these units, which I examine in Chapter 8.

International Pressure

International pressure on the government was important for the institutionalization of the section. This pressure came primarily from UN agencies and was in two main forms: (1) ideational (awareness-raising, lobbying, advising) and (2) capacity building (learning visits; training; constructing, renovating, and equipping units). The UN and other international actors continued to draw the government's attention to the problem of VAW, particularly sexual violence. Through reports, statements, and meetings with senior government officials, the UN shone a spotlight on VAW and identified areas in which police performance was inadequate and had to be improved. UN officials lobbied for the institutionalization of the section in meetings and coordinated with other international actors to provide funds to construct, renovate, and equip the section, to train its officers, and to organize learning visits.

First, the UN **raised awareness** of the problem by stressing that VAW, particularly sexual violence, was a major security, rights, and developmental challenge that needed to be addressed. All 11 of the Secretary General Reports released between September 2005 (when the unit became operational) and August 2008 (three years after it became operational) underlined the issue of sexual violence. Mirroring the reports that preceded the creation of the section, these reports identified areas in which the police's response to VAW was inadequate and called on the Liberian government to take action. For example, the Secretary General stated in the December 2006 report that

> I am deeply concerned by the high incidence of sexual violence, including rape committed against women and girl children in Liberia, as well as by the spate of violent crime in Monrovia and elsewhere in the country. . . . Every effort must be made to ensure that criminal justice is rapidly and fairly addressed and that widespread violence against women and children is brought to an end. (UNSC 2006, p. 16)

Thus, the UN continued to underline VAW through these and other documents and to urge the government to act.

Indeed, UN officials **lobbied** the government in discussions with senior government officials. They sometimes applauded the progress that had been made by the LNP and pointed to areas in which the force could be further strengthened. In October 2006, the head of UNMIL's human rights section, Dorota Gierycz, criticized weaknesses in the judicial system and urged the government to "ensure that the anti-rape legislation is fully implemented by taking steps to ensure that all allegations of rape are fully and independently investigated and that suspected perpetrators are brought to justice in trials that meet international fair trial standards" (UNMIL Raises Concern, 2006). In a November 2006 press release after an 11-day visit in which she met with government officials, Charlotte Abaka, the UN Independent Expert on the Promotion and Protection of Human Rights in Liberia, stated:

> I commend the Government for its adoption in January of the Act amending the Penal Law in relation to the definition and penalties for rape. However, I am saddened to learn that there has been as yet little noticeable impact on the prevalence of rape in Liberia, including rape of very young children. . . . Rape is one of the greatest challenges to human rights enjoyment of Liberia's women and girl children and I call on the Government, civil society and the international community to make all efforts to ensure the law is enforced. (Liberia's Judiciary Must Be Strengthened, 2006)

Speaking at an August 2007 event that was attended by the vice president and the minister of gender, the special representative of the Secretary General, Alan Doss, emphasized the need to address rape and presented a six-point proposal that included increasing the number of women in the LNP. These and other events were forums in which UN officials urged senior officials of the government and the LNP to improve the criminal justice response to VAW.

In addition to lobbying, they **advised** the government and the LNP directly. UNMIL officers, who were embedded in the LNP and assigned to the WACPS, continued to emphasize the importance of this specialized unit. AFELL, UNMIL, and other international actors drafted the LNP's Sexual Assault and Abuse Police handbook, released in 2009, which underlined the need to provide specialized services to victims of GBV and served as a training manual in the police academy. This pressure from powerful international actors cannot be discounted, given the extent to which the government relied on them for resources to reconstruct the country's institutions.

International actors also built the capacity of officers of the new section. This was partly done though **learning visits**. The UN brought Kaki Fakondo of Sierra Leone's Family Support Unit to train and share best practices with WACPS officers in 2005. The UN, in collaboration with the Liberian government, completed the **training** of the first cohort of WACPS officers in November 2005, two months after the section was created. After this, successive cohorts of WACPS officers underwent specialized training at the police academy. International organizations and women's and children's rights organizations also mounted training sessions for officers of the unit.

The international community also **constructed, renovated, and equipped** WACPS units. UNICEF had renovated and furnished six WACPS units, provided one jeep, eight motorbikes, stationery, and statement-taking forms as of January 2011. UNMIL constructed several police stations through its Quick Impact projects, while the Norwegian government constructed LNP county headquarters with attached WACPS in 11 of Liberia's 15 counties. With this international support, the government used less of its scare resources to set up WACPS units across the country. Overall, this strong international pressure was influential in the institutionalization of the WACPS across the country.

Domestic Pressure

Strong domestic pressure, mainly from women's organizations, also contributed to the institutionalization of the WACPS. The women's movement in Liberia, though less mobilized and cohesive than during and immediately after the war, remained a major voice in Liberian politics and society. It mobilized to support the election of Ellen Johnson Sirleaf in 2005. Women's rights activists and organizations maintained a relatively strong media presence between 2005 and 2008. Women's organizations were mentioned in 63 news stories on rape between September 2005 and August 2008. In news stories, leaders of women's organizations underlined the problem of VAW, particularly sexual violence, and criticized the government for not doing enough to prevent sexual violence and bring perpetrators to justice. For example, in January 2007, Counselor Lois Lewis Brutus lamented the problem of rape in Liberian society (Government, Women's Groups Decry, 2007).

There were also **protests** by women's groups, although they did not match the size of the protests that preceded the creation of the WACPS. For example, women under the auspices of the Liberia Shelter for Abused Women and Children mounted a candlelight vigil in 2006 in front of Monrovia's City Hall to protest alarming levels of rape and to memorialize victims (Shelter for Abused Women, 2006). Women also protested violence at the community level across the country. One possible explanation for the absence of large protests in which women's organizations came together under one umbrella is that the movement's strategy was shifting as a result of the election of a woman president who championed women's rights. Thus, confrontational strategies were no longer needed as the women had an ally in the executive mansion who welcomed their activism. Another possible explanation is that the movement was becoming more fragmented over time and therefore was no longer cohesive enough to organize large protests (see Debusscher and de Almagro, 2016).

Indeed, while some **narrative accounts** underlined the influence and strength of the movement (Tripp, Casimiro, & Kwesiga, 2008), others pointed to its decline (Debusscher and de Almagro, 2016; Fuest, 2009). Tripp, Casimiro, Kwesiga, and Mungwa (2009) have theorized the role of the movement in the adoption of gender policies. Nonetheless, it has also been argued that the movement became fragmented over time. Fuest (2008a) describes a crumbling movement that was characterized by differences in the interests of its members and had been "turned into a branch of the peacebuilding and development business" (p. 136). Therefore, there were competing narratives of the strength of the movement after the creation of the WACPS.

While leaders of some member organizations worked closely with government agencies, the movement remained **autonomous** from political factions, with its base being outside of political parties. Furthermore, while some activists transitioned into working for the government, most activists were **located outside of** the government, and while some organizations collaborated on various VAW initiatives with state agencies such as the Ministry of

Gender and Development, **ideas and initiatives were not driven** by any political faction. Indeed, activists and leaders of women's organizations were openly critical of the government even when they were collaborators. For example, AFELL was critical of the government for the failure to implement the rape law (Government, Women Decry Sexual Violence, 2007). The evidence suggests that the movement was not as strong as it was during the period preceding the creation of the WACPS. It, however, remained a major voice in the anti-VAW campaign in Liberia. I will also explain that it was stronger than the women's movement in Côte d'Ivoire.

Political Context

The political context in Liberia steadily improved after the creation of the WACPS. Armed groups posed less of a threat, even though the security situation was described as fragile into 2008. The government's rule of law agenda remained intact and conducive to reform in the police force. Furthermore, Liberia elected a leader who was an advocate for women.

Election of a President Who Was a Women's Rights Advocate

An element of the political environment that favored the institutionalization of the WACPS was the election of President Ellen Johnson Sirleaf in November 2005, three months after the launch of the first WACPS in Monrovia. President Sirleaf Johnson, through her words and actions, contributed to shaping a criminal justice sector in which VAW was a priority and in which there was more willingness to engage with external actors (IOs and civil society organizations). Before her tenure, she coauthored the UNDP's 2002 "Independent Experts' Assessment on the Impact of Armed Conflict on Women and Women's Role in Peace-Building" and was an outspoken advocate of women's rights. The women's movement backed her presidential campaign, during which she flagged the problem of VAW in the country. In her January 2006 inaugural address, she further recognized the problem and pledged to enforce the rape law:

> And now I would like to talk to the women, the women of Liberia, the women of Africa—and the women of the world. Until a few decades ago, Liberian women endured the injustice of being treated as second class

citizens. During the years of our civil war, they bore the brunt of inhumanity and terror. They were conscripted into war, gang raped at will, force[d] into domestic slavery. Yet, it is the women, notably those who established. . . . We will support and increase the writ of laws that restore their dignities and deal drastically with crimes that dehumanize them. We will enforce without fear or favor the law against rape recently passed by the National Transitional Legislature.(allAfrica, 2006)

After her election, she urged the women's movement to do more in support of rape victims and to make more demands of the government. Speaking at a workshop on the enhancement of women's leadership skills organized by the Hunt Alternatives Fund, the president urged AFELL to

take a stronger role in making its presence felt in rape cases in the country. Women lawyers President Johnson-Sirleaf noted, must reach out to victims of rape and identify with them. The President assured the women that government would support any campaign aimed at curtailing rape in the society. (Rape Cases Must Claim the Attention of All, 2006)

According to a senior UN rule of law official who oversaw the installation of several WACPS units across the country, the government did "as much as it could" including seeking funds from donors (interview, L.I., Accra, 2014). President Johnson Sirleaf also demonstrated her commitment to women's rights and gender equality by appointing women to senior positions in the police force. She appointed Beatrice Munah Sieh to the post of inspector general of police (IGP) in 2006. This marked the first time that a woman was the highest-ranking police officer. In 2007, the president named Assatu Bah-Kenneh deputy IGP. Although these measures were not matched by government financing of the WACPS and other anti-VAW initiatives, President Johnson Sirleaf communicated to the police and the public that VAW (and gender equality more broadly) was a priority, welcomed external involvement in the policy process, and served as an ally of the women's movement in the government.

Institutional Context

The UN's leading role in the reform of the security sector also favored the institutionalization of the WACPS by lowering political and institutional barriers. The reform of the LNP continued after the creation of the WACPS. Consequently, the institution was undergoing change as mandated by the CPA. Indeed, reform was high on the agenda of the LNP, and the MoJ more broadly. Justice Philip Banks, minister of justice and attorney general from 2007 to 2008, discussed the priorities during his tenure:

> The second thing that I really had looked forward to was improving the security of the country. Now you know, the Ministry of Justice currently has responsibilities for most of the security agencies in the country. The Liberian National Police is under the Ministry of Justice.... And ours was to see if we could improve the security elements of all of these agencies so that the performance would be better, particularly given the fact that we had just emerged out of a civil crisis.... Prosecution was key on my agenda. It was also important because we thought that if we didn't have—well, I thought that if there was not an adequate machinery in place to prosecute criminals, the temptation for people taking the laws into their own hands would be great. (interview, July 24, 2009, ISS–Princeton University)

Prosecution was therefore prioritized on the ministry's agenda, including in dealing with rape cases. The prioritization of reform reduced the institutional barriers to change. Nonetheless, reformers continued to face some resistance and criticized the role of politics in the LNP. Mohamed Idris, UNPOL's operations coordinator in 2008, described one aspect of the problem:

> I'm just giving you an example of how politics plays in the appointment of some of the leadership of these agencies. Someone who was somewhere, he messed up. You move him, you find him another agency. He messed up, he moved out, you find another. They are just moving them around, just like all the previous, because they are political appointees. The only thing we can do is to recommend to government, say these guys are unsuitable. But in most cases I think the President has the prerogative to appoint who [sic] she wants to work with. But that is one of the greatest challenges we are facing in the LNP now. I think this transcends most of the security agencies in this country. (interview, Monrovia, March 14, 2008, ISS–Princeton University)

Such practices on the part of the government created obstacles to change as they forced reformers to work with personnel who, for a variety of reasons, were not suited for the job. The decisions and actions of UN personnel also stymied reform. For example, the UNPOL training team was criticized for being composed of too many countries with diverse policing traditions such that classes of recruits graduated with distinct drilling and saluting techniques (Malan, 2008). Nonetheless, the government's commitment to police reform remained strong, and the process continued despite these challenges. The UN played a key role in driving the process; this favored the institutionalization of the WACPS.

Reform Led by the United Nations

Similar to when the WACPS was created, UNMIL continued to lead the reform of the LNP. The mission continued to be guided by its mandate which called for the restructuring of the police force. UNPOL officers were embedded in the LNP and worked closely with the leadership in making decisions and in building the capacity of officers to implement these decisions. Paavani Reddy, a civil society officer for UNDP, seconded to the Ministry of Gender and Development (MoGD), aptly described the relationship between UN personnel and government institutions: "Sometimes it becomes difficult to differentiate where my role as a UN staff and my role as a Ministry staff ends and begins" (interview, May 17, 2008, ISS–Princeton University). While this does not describe all UN-government partnerships, it illustrates the degree to which some UN personnel were embedded in institutions such as the MoGD and the LNP.

> Several high-level U.N. Police officials sat with LNP counterparts in LNP headquarters from 2005 to 2011 to provide on-the-job training and guidance, including six U.N. Police officers assigned to the Women and Children Protection Section. One of these officers who made particular strides was Vildana Sedo of Bosnia-Herzegovina, who served as acting U.N. Police gender adviser and worked closely with Liberia's police to improve responsiveness to sexual assault, domestic violence and crimes against children. (Bacon 2012, p. 5)

Thus, their presence in the LNP facilitated their participation in decision-making and implementation, including in the decision to install WACPS units across the country.

Overall, the institutionalization phase in Liberia was characterized by strong international pressure and strong (but declining) domestic pressure. Political and institutional conditions were also favorable. In the next section I show that while international pressure was strong in Côte d'Ivoire, domestic pressure was weak and political and institutional conditions were moderately favorable. I argue that this explains the difference in the rate of institutionalization.

Côte d'Ivoire: Institutionalization of the Gender Desk

While low domestic pressure and less enabling political and institutional conditions did not prevent the creation of the gender desk, they significantly slowed its institutionalization; in other words, high international pressure was not sufficient for the rapid institutionalization of the specialized unit. Thus, almost four years after the gender desk was created, the unit had not been formalized through a decree or any such measure. As of September 2017, there was no central directorate in the police or gendarmerie that oversaw the operations of the unit. Similarly, with one exception, gender focal points assigned to the gender desk were not devoted exclusively to VAW or GBV and therefore were tasked with investigating and processing other types of offenses. Finally, four years after the creation of the first gender desk, units had not been installed across the country. This is in contrast to Liberia, where the creation of a central directorate and the assigning of officers devoted exclusively to VAW happened at the time of the creation of the WACPS and there was at least one WACPS in each county within three years of the creation of the first unit. The point of this comparison is not to argue that Liberia's WACPS was successfully institutionalized. Indeed, in Chapter 8, I discuss many of the problems in the section, including the crippling lack of resources. Rather, the purpose of this comparison is to analyze how international pressures and domestic pressures and conditions can lead to varied implementation outcomes, depending on the stage of implementation.

International Pressure

International pressure on the Ivoirian government remained high. The UN continued to work with the police and gendarmerie to develop more gender desks. The UN still used ideational tools (awareness-raising, lobbying, advising) and capacity building (training and constructing and equipping units) to pressure the government to institutionalize the gender desk.

The UN **raised awareness** through several reports and publications, including the UN Secretary General's quarterly report. These reports emphasized that sexual violence, including sexual violence by the FRCI, was rampant and that the government's response was inadequate.

All four of the Secretary General's reports released between June 2014 and May 2017 mentioned the issue of sexual violence. In the March 2016 report, the Secretary General described the problem and what the country had done thus far:

> Côte d'Ivoire remains on the list of countries examined by my Special Representative on Sexual Violence in Conflict, and continues to face serious challenges with respect to sexual and gender-based violence, including against children. A national strategy to combat sexual violence was adopted by the Government in 2014, but implementation has been limited to the initial steps, such as community mobilization. (p. 21)

A July 2016 report by UNOCI documented the problem of sexual violence and implicated state forces in perpetrating 7 percent of this violence (UNOCI, 2016).

UNOCI also **lobbied** the government to act. Based on this July 2016 report, UNOCI recommended that the Ivoirian government "[c]ontinue to appoint and train focal points on women and children's rights in police stations and gendarmerie brigades, as well as law enforcement officers, including court officials, on sexual violence" (UNOCI, 2016, p. 3). In May 2016 the Special Rapporteur on Sexual Violence in Conflict visited the country to assess the progress made in addressing sexual violence crimes and announced that Côte d'Ivoire was the first country to be removed from the Report of the Secretary General on Conflict-Related Sexual Violence, due to progress made by the armed forces in addressing sexual violence (United Nations News, 2016). She met with senior officials, including the prime minister and minister of state of interior and security, and reported that her office would continue to monitor the country's performance.

UN officials also **advised** the government. For example, in August 2017, the UN organized a workshop and invited officials of the police and gendarmerie and other government ministries to brainstorm how to improve the gender desk. Among other things, they discussed the need to formalize the specialized unit within the police and gendarmerie. This was one of many forums in which UN officials interacted with and advised Ivoirian officials.

The UN also **built the capacity** of the police and gendarmerie, mainly through **training**. Selected officers participated in specialized training offered with the support of the UN at the police and gendarmerie training schools. Furthermore, the UN, through the Peacebuilding Fund, **constructed** nine gender desks in 2016. The European Union also funded the construction of gender desks, which were in various stages of completion in 2017. Therefore, similar to Liberia, the UN was using a variety of strategies to convince the government to institutionalize the gender desk. However, in contrast to Liberia, this pressure was not as effective in accelerating institutionalization. The explanation for this disparity can be found in the level of domestic pressure and the moderate favorability of the political and institutional conditions.

Domestic Pressure

The level of domestic pressure on the government did not change significantly from pre-2014. Though women's organizations urged the government to address VAW and collaborated with government ministries in some issue areas, they had not become more visible and, therefore, were not much stronger than in the period preceding the creation of the gender desk.

Pressure from the Women's Movement

Several women's organizations called on the government to address VAW. However, they mostly focused on providing legal aid and psychosocial services. For example, the Association of Female Lawyers of Côte d'Ivoire (AFJCI) ran a legal aid clinic with UN funding. However, their visibility, and thus the strength of member organizations, had not increased significantly since June 2014, when the gender desk was formally created. Women's organizations remained relatively less visible in the national and international media (63 news stories in Liberia versus 8 in Cote d'Ivoire). The poor visibility of women's organizations reflects the extent to which they were less of an influential voice in the reform of the security sector in comparison to the women's organizations in Liberia.

Women's organizations continued to mount small, localized **protests** such that the country did not witness the mass protests that occurred during the conflict. While **narrative** accounts noted the efforts made by women's organizations in peace-building, they also underlined the weakness of the women's movement and of civil society in general and also noted the divisions within the movement. Indeed, the movement remained divided along political lines, even though many activists and member organizations had no political leaning. Nonetheless, the politicization of the movements undermined its **autonomy** and led to political factions driving some ideas and initiatives.

Political Context

The favorability of the political context within Côte d'Ivoire remained moderate. President Alassane Ouattara, who was re-elected for a second term in 2015, sought to strengthen the rule of law, but former rebels posed credible threats to political stability. President Ouattara emphasized the importance of the rule of law and remained committed to rehabilitating Côte d'Ivoire's image internationally (Abidjan.net, 2016). He elaborated a vision of "emergence" that rests on three assumptions: emergence is a stake in the future; emergence is planned; and emergence is constructed in peace, security, dialogue, and social cohesion (RoCI, 2015). This vision underlined efforts to promote economic growth; indeed, Côte d'Ivoire was Africa's fastest growing economy in 2016. The government recognized that the rule of law is necessary for economic growth, making this vision conducive for institutionalizing the gender desk. However, certain political dynamics stifled this reform.

Major Threats to Political Stability

While the opposition was fragmented and thus weakened, Côte d'Ivoire faced major threats to its political stability from former rebels, some of whom were integrated into the army (United Nations News, 2014). These threats stymied reform. There were several mutinies after the end of the conflict, and four of them occurred between January and October 2017. The first, which spread across nine cities, occurred on January 6. To avoid an escalation, the government agreed to pay the equivalent of US $19,000 each to 8,500 soldiers (Bavier, 2017). This agreement did not bring an end to the mutinies; there was another mutiny in October 2017 by soldiers who were excluded from the January agreement (Jeune Afrique, 2017). In some quarters the mutinies were linked to the former rebel leader, speaker of the National Assembly, and presidential aspirant Guillaume Soro, who allegedly continued to wield control over former rebels. Soro sought to succeed Ouattara but had been gradually edged out of the line of succession, and it was believed that these munities were his way of signaling that he still commanded power. In October 2017, one of his aides was arrested on suspicion of arming mutineers against the government, a charge that Soro denied (Aboa, 2017). Nonetheless, these dynamics created a tense political climate that detracted from reforming the security sector. Thus, these threats to political stability diverted attention and resources away from issues such as the gender desk, which were not seen as a priority by the government. UNDP officials revealed that senior officers of the Ivoirian police and gendarmerie showed preference for vehicles, communication equipment, and equipment to maintain law and order, as these were perceived as more immediate and necessary, given the political situation in the country. Thus, when approached with funding to set up gender desks, Ivoirian officials expressed that it could be better spent on priority issue areas. While gender bias contributed to constructing the hierarchy of needs, these security threats were also important in this regard and thus constituted a barrier to the creation of the gender desk.

Institutional Context

The post-creation institutional context did not change significantly; the UN continued to play a secondary role in the SSR process. In 2012, the government released its SSR strategy in which addressing VAW was categorized as a long-term goal. In comparison to Liberia, the UN was more constrained in directing the reform process.

Reform Not Led by the United Nations

The government continued to lead the SSR process, with the support of the UN and other international actors. UNSC Resolution 226 of June 25, 2015, tasked the peacekeeping mission with helping the government to implement the SSR, assure coordination among implementing partners, and build the operational capacity of security institutions (UNOCI, n.d.). While the UN played an advisory role and built the capacity of personnel of the security sector, it faced resistance in advancing the gender agenda. UNDP officials described the process of convincing the police and gendarmerie to institutionalize the gender desk as long and challenging, because senior officials did not view the unit as a priority. In fact, even senior officers within the police and gendarmerie interviewed for this study recognized this problem and lamented the slow pace of reform. The UN's position in Côte d'Ivoire can be contrasted to its leading role in Liberia's SSR process, which ensured that UN officials often worked with senior officials they had recruited and trained, ensuring that they had a cohort of allies who were mostly sympathetic to the gender reform agenda. These differences across countries affected what could be accomplished within the implementing institutions and how it was accomplished.

Conclusion

Liberia and Côte d'Ivoire are two examples of countries that have established specialized units to address VAW. However, this study shows differences in how these units have been established: Liberia created and institutionalized its unit more rapidly than Côte d'Ivoire, although the gap in timing of creation between the countries was not as wide as the gap in timing of institutionalization. I argue that the differences between the countries can be explained by the domestic context.

At the stage of creation in both countries, international pressure was high. However, there were major differences in the domestic context. The level of domestic pressure was higher in Liberia due to the strength of the country's women's movement. There were major challenges in the political and institutional contexts in both countries. However, political and institutional conditions were relatively more favorable in Liberia: the government had a rule-of-law agenda and the UN was playing a leading role in the police reform process. While there was also a rule-of-law agenda in Côte d'Ivoire, the security sector was significantly more politicized than in Liberia and the UN was not leading the reform process. This constrained the extent to which the UN could accelerate the creation of the gender desk. These domestic conditions slightly slowed down (by one year, in comparison to Liberia) the creation of the WACPS. This comparison shows that international pressure played an oversized role at the creation stage. Even though the domestic conditions in Côte d'Ivoire were not as favorable, they did not significantly stymie creation. This finding suggests that unfavorable or moderately favorable domestic factors and conditions pose less of a barrier to the creation of specialized mechanisms and, more broadly, to government's agreement to implement an international norm. However, domestic factors and conditions become more important at the institutionalization stage.

Indeed, the comparison shows that less favorable domestic factors and conditions were more influential at the institutionalization stage and slowed the implementation process. There are several important lessons here. First, it demonstrates the limits of international pressure. The peace-building literature has drawn attention to the influence of international actors in the peace-building process, who have promoted a liberal peace-building agenda. This study shows that domestic actors and conditions are key to the institutionalization of the peace-building agenda. Thus, while international pressure might be significant for the initial stage of implementation where governments agree on paper to take action, it does not unilaterally determine all stages of the implementation process. This finding corresponds with the literature that has underlined the importance of domestic factors. However, it advances this literature by showing that domestic factors become more important at the institutionalization stage. It also demonstrates the importance of disaggregating the implementation process. The comparison of Liberia and Côte d'Ivoire also shows that social movements can be influential in the implementation process. The gender and politics literature has shown that women's movements are key to the adoption of women-friendly policies. This study shows that they also have an impact on the implementation process; at the creation and institutionalization stages in Liberia, pressure from the women's movement pushed the government to prioritize the establishment of the WACPS. In the next chapter, I show that women's organizations also had an impact on street-level behavior. I also examine how the variation in institutionalization affected street-level performance.

8
Street-Level Implementation in Liberia and Côte d'Ivoire

Police officers and gendarmes are street-level actors who deliver policy in their daily interactions with the populace. They reshape policies according to a variety of factors, including their beliefs and the institutional structure within which they work. Consequently, one cannot take for granted that street-level actors will follow the rules and norms of their institution. Therefore, it is essential to ask how the establishment of the specialized units in Liberia and Côte d'Ivoire has impacted street-level policing. Specifically, how has the degree of institutionalization of the specialized units affected officers' withdrawal of rape and domestic violence cases and their re-victimization of survivors? In other words, how has the variation in the institutionalization of the units in both countries affected the implementation of the international women's justice norm at the street-level?

I draw on interviews with police officers in both countries and gendarmes in Côte d'Ivoire as well as with UN and government officials, women's rights activists, and survivors of violence in both countries to answer these questions. I argue that there has been an improvement in street-level policing in Liberia and Côte d'Ivoire as a result of the establishment of the specialized mechanisms. There was a greater understanding and acceptance of the importance of bringing perpetrators to justice and of treating victims with sensitivity. These changes can be directly linked to trainings provided by the UN and, to a lesser extent, by women's organizations in Liberia, as well as new policies and structures that they have supported. Nonetheless, the difference in the extent of institutionalization affected street-level behavior. It meant that survivors in Côte d'Ivoire did not always meet officers who had received specialized training, increasing the chances of re-victimization and of being subjected to unethical practices. The international women's justice norm, especially concerning the prosecution of sexual violence cases, was more salient in Liberia due to the degree to which the specialized unit and the accompanying practices such as specialized training had been

Global Norms and Local Action. Peace A. Medie, Oxford University Press (2020). © Oxford University Press.
DOI: 10.1093/oso/9780190922962.001.0001

institutionalized. However, because institutions in Côte d'Ivoire had been stronger before the war and had escaped much of the destruction witnessed in Liberia, there was a level of professionalism that also emphasized formal accountability (investigation, arrest, and prosecution), even if the international women's justice norm was not as entrenched as in Liberia. I also argue that, despite the manifold improvements, significant weaknesses in the specialized units and in street-level implementation exist in both countries, and these raise questions about these specialized mechanisms, including about their sustainability after the UN and donors withdraw from post-conflict countries.

Liberia: The Women and Children Protection Section

The establishment of the WACPS (a specialized independent mechanism) marked a major step for the LNP. As of January 2011, the section had 215 officers who had undergone four weeks of women and children's training and were assigned across the country. They were trained in how to respond to sexual violence to ensure that perpetrators would be brought to trial. The training on aggravated assault (domestic violence) also emphasized the prosecution of offenders. Thus, officers worked in a specialized institution that was created to increase the arrest and prosecution of suspects in rape cases, and in some other VAW cases, and were trained accordingly. Therefore, it is important to ask if officers were indeed referring cases to court for prosecution, as opposed to using their discretion to withdraw cases because they did not think a case was serious, they blamed the victim, the victim did not want to corporate, they were in collusion with the suspect, and so on. I argue that even though case withdrawal persisted for all of these reasons, officers of the WACPS were less likely (in comparison to the pre-conflict and immediate post-conflict periods) to use their discretion when handling rape and domestic violence (aggravated assault) cases. This is due to how they perceived these offenses and the policies of the WACPS. Police perception was shaped by their cultural beliefs, the framing of the law, the training they received, and the WACPS's policies. The WACPS's policies were shaped not only by the LNP and the UN, which oversaw the establishment of the section, but also by women's organizations that pushed for a tougher response to rape and participated in crafting the 2009 Sexual Assault and Abuse Police Handbook. This case demonstrates how the international women's justice norm that aims to end impunity for sexual violence was translated into action at the domestic level by the UN and by domestic actors. However, before discussing the performance of officers, it is important to understand the environment in which they worked, particularly the challenges they faced. Perhaps the most pronounced of these challenges was the lack of the infrastructure and equipment needed for law enforcement.

Infrastructural and Resource Constraints

WACPS officers mostly lacked the basic infrastructure and equipment needed to enforce the law. This was most glaring at the central headquarters in Monrovia. When I visited in May 2010, the headquarters shared a building with other sections. They would be relocated to a new building in 2011. However, during my first visit, the WACPS was relegated to one large room, separated by plywood to create small offices and a cramped waiting area. This is where all major WACPS work was done. Crimes were reported and suspects were brought to this office for interrogation. On my first visit, all chairs were occupied and some people were standing. The small space made it difficult to maintain confidentiality, as everyone could see who went in and out of the offices, and conversations within the offices were sometimes audible in the waiting area. Most troubling was a teenager handcuffed to a desk in the waiting area. I was told that she was unwell and was trying to leave the police station before staff of a safe home could come to pick her up. However, the manner and location in which she had been restrained amounted to further victimization. When I arrived, she had urinated on herself and was seated in a puddle of urine on the floor of the waiting area. A host of people—officers, complainants, offenders—came through the office, saw her, and commented on her state. All of this was happening in full view of officials who on that same day would speak to me about how the section prioritizes the welfare of women and girls. The WACPS headquarters was relocated to a new, multistory building, funded by the Norwegian government, within a year, but not all units in the country were as fortunate.

My visit to the WACPS unit in West Point further revealed how the lack of infrastructure led to the re-victimization of girls and women who sought help. West Point is one of Monrovia's poorest and most crime-affected communities, and girls and women who live there are particularly vulnerable to sexual and physical violence. A narrow and dim corridor connected the

West Point police station's front desk to the WACPS's one-room office. On one side of this corridor was a wall, and on the left were cells that held men who had been accused of crimes such as armed robbery, rape, and murder. Not only were these men visible, but they could also reach outside the cell to touch a person in the corridor. Yet, children and women who had been victimized were required to walk in front of these cells each time they sought to visit the WACPS office. I was only able to walk down this dim corridor after officers at the front desk assured me that I would not be harassed or harmed by the prisoners. Putting women and children, many of whom were already traumatized, through this undermines the objectives of a specialized unit. The WACPS officers at West Point explained to me that they had only been allocated one room in which they conducted all WACPS's affairs and housed (sometimes overnight) women and children who were waiting to be conveyed to safe homes. A few days before I came, prisoners had broken out of the cell and knocked a hole into the wall of the unit in order to escape. Fortunately, no women or children were sleeping in the office when this happened. Officer #2 described the challenge of inadequate infrastructure:

> And when you get missing children, lost and found children, when you call OSIWA [NGO] they do not come immediately. Then the boys that come in conflict with the law, we call Don Bosco [NGO], they don't come immediately.... And even when they are sleeping here there is no sleeping place, we don't have office space, interrogation room. When we want to interview somebody, we have to go ask for the next person's office when this office is packed. (interview, female, Monrovia, October 4, 2010)

In some places, it was not inadequate infrastructure that was the problem—it was nonexistent infrastructure. Many small towns and villages did not have WACPS units. For example, Bong County had a WACPS in only three of its eight districts. Six counties, including Grand Cape Mount, had only one WACPS. Thus, victims had to travel long distances, often on motorbikes, in order to access police stations. Most of these roads were impassable, especially during the long rainy season in the country. Poor infrastructure, coupled with the lack of basic equipment, caused officers to take actions that violated victims' confidentiality and re-victimized them.

The most common complaint from officers was that they did not have vehicles to visit crime scenes. Officer #14 summarized this logistical constraint:

The challenges presently that we are facing, I will not say my depot but the entire Women and Child Protection unit in Liberia presently, mainly is logistics. Because, some cases like rape case, statutory rape, when that case is reported, we the police officer in this kind of case, you are not supposed to ask the victim party or complainant party to transport you the officer and other people to go out. We the police officer try our possible best to transport them and it is against us to because there is no fund provided for us to be doing it. So most of the time when our cases come to us, we try our possible best and pay their way to make a follow up on the case. (interview, male, Monrovia, September 15, 2010)

Although the UN and donors had supplied the section with vehicles, they were not enough; most of the WACPS units visited in Monrovia did not have an assigned car or motorbike. UNPOL officers and personnel of the SGBV Crimes Unit sometimes drove WACPS officers to crime scenes, but these individuals were not always present and the SGBV Crimes Unit had only one vehicle at its disposal for this purpose. In the absence of transportation from UNPOL or the SGBV Crimes Unit, their options were to rely on the complainant, pay the transportation fare out-of-pocket for which they would not be reimbursed by the LNP, or not visit the crime scene. Officer #11 explained that this lack of vehicles also delayed their response to reports:

We don't have a mobile [vehicle] to respond on the crime scene immediately, that makes the work so difficult most of the time. For example, maybe a complainant will come to the Zone and say "Oh officer, a fellow raped my daughter just now and he [is] at the house, so officer I need you to go there now." Before we leave from here to go, the perpetrator has already gone. Most of the time, they escape. But if we had logistics, like motorbikes and vehicles, we could respond on the scene immediately and have that perpetrator arrested. Sometimes when we reach the scene we can't meet the perpetrator, the perpetrator always absconds from the scene, so sometimes we fail. It makes the job so difficult for us. (interview, male, Monrovia, October 4, 2010)

Officers also paid for phone calls out-of-pocket and, in most police stations, operated in offices without electricity. The absence of computers led them to sometimes give confidential case files to commercial typists, an act that is against the formal rules of the WACPS. The absence of filing cabinets in most offices meant that record-keeping was poor, as was the confidentiality of records. A unit I visited in Monrovia stored files in a modified suitcase. Officers complained that they were dependent on the UN for office supplies, and in Gbarnga, relied on the Norwegian Refugee Council (NRC) to cover transportation costs. This lack of equipment, combined with the low pay, was a source of frustration for officers of the unit and undermined their ability to gather evidence and meet the needs of complainants.

Another weakness in the force was inadequate training, particularly in how to handle cases of non-sexual VAW. For example, during the interviews, while officers were knowledgeable about the crime of rape, some struggled to distinguish between the crimes of human trafficking, kidnapping, and child abuse. Thus, while the WACPS held the promise of improving women's access to justice and how they were treated by the police, it had yet to meet most international standards of policing. The Liberian government largely lacked the ability to allocate adequate funds to the WACPS, and to the LNP in general, and relied heavily on the international community, which in turn provided some, but not all, of what the WACPS needed. This illustrates how the local political and economic conditions affect street-level implementation. Indeed, with inadequate resources, WACPS officers struggled to perform their duties and sometimes took actions (e.g., asking victims to cover a taxi fare, sharing confidential case files with commercial typists) that contravened the principles of good policing and of gender-sensitive policing. Senior officers were aware of these limitations and of how domestic political, economic, and social conditions affected law enforcement. They, therefore, structured the unit's policies to circumvent some of these constraints.

Rules Guiding the Response to Rape and Domestic Violence

The effect of international and domestic pressures, as well as socioeconomic conditions, was evident in the formal and informal rules of the WACPS. The section had a firm no-withdrawal/mandatory referral policy for rape. In other words, a police officer could not unilaterally decide to withdraw a rape case. Instead, this decision rested with the prosecutor. On the other hand, while the WACPS mandated that the decision to prosecute a case rested with the prosecutor and not the police or the victim, it allowed officers, in conjunction with complainants, to (under certain circumstances) decide on whether or not domestic violence cases (aggravated assault) should be prosecuted. The latter response was a deviation from the training that officers received in the academy. Officers were taught that domestic violence should be prosecuted. However, senior officers argued that a blanket mandatory referral policy could prove injurious to some victims, thus the need for discretionary decision-making in aggravated assault cases. They argued that poverty in Liberia, which compels some women to stay in relationships with men on whom they are financially dependent, combined with sociocultural norms that discourage women from reporting and punish them for reporting violence and supporting the prosecution of their partners, justified the decision not to refer all aggravated assault cases for prosecution. Conversely, the section did not give precedence to sociocultural norms that discourage the reporting and prosecution of rape.

Police officers in the WACPS learned in the academy that rape was a crime that was "above" the police. They were taught that the decision on how a case should progress rested with the state's prosecutor and not with the officer(s) in charge or the complainant. This message was reinforced by the section's leadership, which did not formally or informally give officers competing instructions for how they should handle rape cases. Officers were, therefore, required to consult with their superiors and the prosecutor; the latter decided whether or not sufficient evidence had been collected to proceed with prosecution. While this did not rule out the official withdrawal of the case by a complainant who no longer wished to cooperate with the state, it took this decision out of the hands of the police. A senior officer explained that a rape case could be withdrawn, but only at the prosecutorial level:

> Legally all rape cases need to be prosecuted but under the law we have private prosecutors and cases reach the court the private prosecutor needs to go and explain what actually happened but most of the time when the victim is not willing to cooperate with the investigation they give the prosecution a difficult time. So even with the SGBV [Crimes] Unit they have the issue called waiver, most times people waive cases but it is at the court level. We try our possible best to send issues to the court. (interview, officer #10, Monrovia, July 12, 2010)

Senior officers gave three interconnected reasons for this no-withdrawal and pro-prosecution policy: (1) the section's mandate, (2) the gravity of the offense, and (3) the agenda of IOs and local NGOs. First, they explained that because the section was created specifically to end impunity for rape, any policy that empowered officers to decide against prosecution would contravene this mission. Second, they argued that rape was a grievous offense, due to its classification under the law and its health and social effects on victims, and thus should be prosecuted. A senior officer offered the first two explanations while differentiating between the WACPS's rape and domestic violence policies:

> it [rape] is the issue of focus. Rape damages the image of a human being, of a woman. It is a grave offense, it is a very grave offense, so we take it very seriously, we put in all our time and effort in the issue of rape ... we all know it [rape] is one of the focus points of this section. Because this section came into being because of the high level of sexual violation, if you look at the establishment of this section, the focus point of the establishment of this section is to combat rape in this country. (interview, A.A., Monrovia, 2014)

These first two reasons explain the section's non-withdrawal policy for rape, but they do not tell the full story. Rape was perceived as a grievous offense in Liberia before the war and was even a first-degree felony then, but these things were not sufficient for the police force to institute a strong non-withdrawal policy. Widespread rape during the civil war was also not enough to adequately change the way the police force dealt with the problem, as evidenced by the deficiencies in the Sexual Assault Squad that was established immediately after the war and by the need to create the WACPS. Instead, strong emphasis on prosecution (through international and domestic pressures) was necessary for instituting this no-withdrawal/mandatory referral policy. A senior officer succinctly made this point:

> there are so many reasons for this [why rape is a priority] but you know donors, our NGOs, UN partners, this is where they feel we should actually address, because they bring the money and they decide what to emphasize and then the national government also joins them and emphasizes [rape] as well. (interview, officer #29, Monrovia, July 12, 2010)

Thus, the influence of IOs, particularly UN agencies and, to a lesser extent, NGOs, did not end with the establishment of the WACPS. Instead, these actors strived to shape procedures and behavior within the new section, to varying degrees and effect. They reinforced this mandatory referral message in the training given to officers and lobbied and advised senior officials to make it the norm within the section. They also emphasized the prosecution of rape in the 2009 Sexual Assault and Abuse Police Handbook. Furthermore, UN Police (UNPOL) officers paid daily visits to police stations, including the central headquarters where decisions were made, where they reviewed case files, urged officers to refer cases for prosecution, and helped them in achieving this goal by providing them with expertise and logistics. The UN also emphasized the prosecution of domestic violence (aggravated assault) in their discussions with the police, and the offense was one of the crimes that UNPOL personnel monitored and supported police officers in investigating during their visits to police stations. Nonetheless, the section allowed officers to use their discretion in the handling of domestic violence cases, when it was deemed in the best interest of the victim.

Officers were taught at the academy that aggravated assault should be prosecuted by the state and not mediated in police stations or communities. There were, however, some differences in what was taught at the academy and the rule within police stations. The section informally allowed and even encouraged officers to mediate simple assault cases. At the central headquarters, a special squad, headed by a female officer, counseled such couples, and the police typically tried to refer the case for prosecution only when the offender was a repeat offender or refused to cooperate with their attempts at counseling and mediation. A senior officer summarized the section's approach to simple assault:

> Most especially the suspect that will beat on a woman, we provide more sensitization than prosecution, in the interest of the victim . . . sometimes she [the complainant] comes with begging, she doesn't want to go to court, that is her husband, than we take the overture by advising the man, talking to him that beating on your wife is wrong, it is a crime and most of them do it unknowingly, they don't know that they are committing a crime. Because they feel that when they were small, when they were coming up as a child, they saw their parents [father] beating on their mother, they saw other men beating on their women and nothing came out of it so they feel that now that they are men and they have their women, they need to beat on their wives. . . . Most times we don't charge, we advise, we tell the man it is wrong, it is a crime under the law, it leads to jail. If you are a repeat offender, we don't compromise the issue even if the woman doesn't want to go to court, we insist on the case going to court. (interview, officer #10, Monrovia, July 12, 2010)

The aggravated assault policy, on the other hand, was to refer cases for prosecution with the understanding that it was sometimes necessary to honor complainants' preference for the withdrawal of their cases. Officer #10 explained the unofficial policy:

> Really you see, we have academic and we have practical. Usually at the academy we tell you the strict thing, we don't compromise rape cases, we don't compromise assault, we don't compromise XYZ. But we come on the field, the physical reality, you take into consideration the setting you find yourself in, then definitely you have to use your discretion. . . . The police is [sic] given discretionary power, in certain instances you use your discretion. So most times, letting domestic violence assault cases going home, not going to court, we use our discretionary power . . . the constitution of Liberia also cautions the police officer that whatsoever discretion you choose to use, ensure that you are using it wisely and it should not create problems so if that discretion creates problems then definitely, you will be held liable. But some people use discretion for personal gain, for personal interest, so if you use your discretion for personal gain, then definitely, it will catch up with you. But use discretion to the best interest of the people, the surrounding of the situation, then anybody can look into it and say yes, you acted at least in line. (interview, male, Monrovia, July 12, 2010)

Thus, officers were told that the crime should be referred to the magisterial court for prosecution, but the section's leadership accepted discretionary decision-making—the withdrawal of cases by the police—when it was judged to be in the best interests of the victim.

Although senior officers recognized that the act was a crime, they reasoned that the high rate of poverty in Liberia that compelled some women to stay with abusive partners who financially supported them, coupled with the social pressures that women faced when they reported domestic violence to the police and when they supported prosecution, justified not referring some of these cases for prosecution. Furthermore, despite the official training, neither the UN nor women's organizations were strongly promoting a mandatory referral policy for domestic violence, except in the most extreme cases. This allowed senior officials more latitude to craft an informal rule that deviated from the academy's training. This aligns with the literature which has emphasized how external factors such as target-group behavior impacts street-level performance. Despite the difference in the approaches to domestic violence and rape, the WACPS's rules represent a major transformation in how the Liberian police dealt with VAW. For the first time, there was a firm mandatory prosecution policy for rape and aggravated assault was viewed as a crime, though not always a crime that should be prosecuted. These formal and informal rules signaled to street-level implementers how the WACPS prioritized the prosecution of perpetrators of these offenses.

Street-Level Implementation: Performance of Officers

The behavior of street-level bureaucrats does not always align with the laws they are tasked with enforcing or with the rules of their organizations. It is for this reason that they are described as "bureaucrats who not only deliver but actively shape policy outcomes by interpreting rules and allocating scarce resources" (Meyers and Vorsanger, 2007, p. 154). The implementation literature has recognized that conditions at the implementation stage, in addition to the policy agenda and external factors, affect how implementers behave. The informal rules of the WACPS and the behavior of street-level officers confirm this. In line with the formal rules, police officers accepted that rape was a crime that should always be prosecuted. Therefore, in comparison to the pre-conflict and the immediate post-conflict periods, they were less likely to withdraw cases in the police station as opposed to referring them to the prosecutor. While this does not mean that every police officer was referring every rape case to the prosecutor, it demonstrates that the international women's justice norm in regard to the crime of rape was being internalized within the WACPS. The referral of aggravated assault cases had also increased in comparison to the pre-conflict and early post-conflict periods, although close to half of the officers interviewed reported that they used their discretion to withdraw these cases. I argue that this is because the WACPS had placed less emphasis on the prosecution of domestic violence cases. In the following, I explain the dynamics of street-level behavior in police stations in Monrovia and one in Gbarnga.

Police Performance in Rape Cases

Officers, both male and female, agreed that rape should be prosecuted, and they reported that they always referred rape cases to the prosecutor. They claimed that they did not use their discretion to make decisions in rape cases. Contrary to what had been done prior to the establishment of the unit, officers said they did not weigh rape cases to see if they were serious enough to be referred for prosecution. Thus, while the rape of minors generated the most anger and urgency, officers reported that they did not treat the rape of an adult as a minor offense that should not be referred to the prosecutor. Data provided by the WACPS supports the claim that police officers were referring more cases of rape to court. Between January and June 2010, 44.3 percent of rape cases were sent to court. 3.4 percent were withdrawn, 1 percent were transferred to another agency other than the court, and 51.1 percent were pending.

There were two main reasons for this: (1) officers' perception of the offense as one that was above the jurisdiction of the police, and (2) the WACPS's non-withdrawal policy in rape cases. This perception and policy existed before the conflict but were shaped, reinforced, and promoted in its aftermath by the UN and other international actors and by women's and children's rights organizations in the country. Officers' perception was a product of their sociocultural beliefs, the training they received within and outside of the police academy, the WACPS's policies, the signal sent by the creation of the WACPS and other specialized mechanisms, and the framing of the rape law.

In explaining why the offense was above the police, officers argued that the act was a felony, a crime against the state, a major crime, and a "non-bailable" offense, and thus had to be prosecuted. For example, officer #36 stated:

> We have been receiving cases where the [victim's] parents just do not want to prosecute the person but then for the police, we look at the crime committed, it's a state crime. So we tell them that since you do not want to prosecute this person, but for us you will be serving as a state witness, even though you serve as a complainant in our document. Once we have evidence linking this man to the crime, whether you do not want to prosecute, we will still send this man to court and the state will prosecute him. (interview, male, Monrovia, September 15, 2010)

This assessment of the crime was a product of the training and instructions that they received in the section. The training given to WACPS officers underlined the magnitude of the offense and placed emphasis on the prosecution of offenders. Also important was the reform of the law, which made rape an unbailable offense. This amendment signified the importance of prosecution. While rape had always been a first-degree felony, this was not sufficient in the past to normalize case referral.

The effect of the act on its victims also bolstered the perception that it was above the police and should be referred to the prosecutor instead of being settled in the police station or community. Officers explained that rape was a crime that destroyed the lives of its victims, particularly children, unlike any other form of VAW. They pointed to physical and psychological injuries, sexually transmitted diseases, stigmatization, and infertility that could result from this violence. This underscored the need to prosecute the crime. Similar to features of the law, concerns about the effect of the crime had also been taught in training sessions and been communicated in documents given to officers. Furthermore, some of these ideas about the effect of rape—such as the injuries it causes—were found among the larger population, and would have been held by officers to some extent and with some degree of accuracy before they entered the section.

The WACPS's non-withdrawal policy, which was conveyed in training sessions and passed down through senior officers during meetings and other interactions, also cemented the message that rape was an offense that could not be withdrawn and was like no other form of VAW. For example, officer #1 stated that "[r]ape cases are first degree felonies and aggravated assault is a second-degree felony. For rape aspect we can't make our own decisions, we have to consult our superiors or the courts" (interview, male, Monrovia, July 10, 2010). This policy was emphasized during weekly meetings at the central headquarters and was passed down to street-level officers. It thus shaped officers' perception of the crime, in addition to providing guidelines on how they should respond to it.

Overall, officers in the unit appeared to mostly eschew discretionary decision-making in rape cases and instead followed the rules of the WACPS. Consequently, preferred behavior (the referral of rape cases) was more routinized in the section. I argue that this attitude shows that the international women's justice norm was strong within the section. The collaboration among the state, the UN, and women's NGOs to amend the rape law, establish specialized mechanisms, and develop the WACPS's policies, therefore, impacted how officers perceived the act. The institutionalization of the WACPS was also important as it strengthened the institutional structure and reinforced the message that rape was a major offense. The section's policies guided officers' behavior. An alternative explanation for officers' attitudes toward rape cases is the widespread sexual violence during the conflict. That is, officers were more willing to refer cases because they were sensitive to the victimization of women during the civil conflict. However, this alternative argument is not sufficient to explain this attitude. First, the creation of the WACPS was necessary because the police had been unable to address sexual violence immediately after the conflict. In other words, widespread sexual violence during the conflict did not automatically lead to a change in police performance. Second, a comparison of officers' attitudes to that of the public (described in Chapter 4) shows a sharp difference. That is, widespread sexual violence during and after the conflict had not removed all objections to the prosecution of rapists within communities. Thus, widespread sexual violence did not automatically lead to a change in the attitude of all Liberians in regard to the prosecution of rape cases. Therefore, police attitude cannot be isolated from the post-conflict transformations that have occurred in the LNP.

However, I am careful not to argue that all police officers have experienced a change in attitude and did not sometimes go against the formal rules to withdraw cases for personal gain or bias. Indeed, as recently as 2015, the inspector general of police warned officers against "compromising" rape cases (Johnson, 2015). During my interviews, staff members of NGOs accused the police of accepting bribes to release rape suspects. A women's rights advocate explained that the police accepted money to withdraw cases when they knew that these cases were too weak to end in prosecution. It is beyond the scope of this study to explain when individual officers were more or less likely to accept bribes or to adopt unethical behavior that put prosecution in jeopardy and went against the international women's justice norm. However, it is clear that officers continued to withdraw cases, and sometimes for personal gain. But it is also clear that the international women's justice norm in the WACPS was entrenched and had increased case referral.

It is also important to recognize the challenges that economic conditions, particularly a high poverty rate, and sociocultural norms posed to the referral of rape cases. Because of the sociocultural norms against reporting rape and the stigmatization of survivors, many complainants and their relatives often had second thoughts after reporting rape. Poverty heightened the effects of these norms on poor survivors as it caused them to fear the financial costs of seeing a case through the criminal justice system. Furthermore, this rendered them unable to escape the stigmatization and possible revenge that would follow the decision to cooperate with the police. They, therefore, chose not to continue to support prosecution. Some preferred to accept payment from the rapist in exchange for refusing to cooperate with the investigations. Police told of complainants providing false telephone numbers and relocating in order to prevent the continuance of a case. This unwillingness to cooperate delayed and in some cases derailed investigations. It also contributed to case withdrawal because the SGBV Crimes Unit was usually unable to prosecute a case in the absence of a complainant. Combined with resource constraints, they presented barriers to prosecution. They also demonstrate the effect of economic conditions and sociocultural norms on the implementation of progressive international norms. While the efforts of international and domestic actors succeeded in improving attitudes within the police force, the informal norms remained strong and undermined the implementation of the international women's justice norm. The effects of sociocultural factors were more salient in domestic violence.

Police Performance in Domestic Violence Cases

Officers interviewed felt that simple assault (which is a misdemeanor, not a felony) was a minor offense that could be withdrawn if the complainant wanted. They saw themselves as peacemakers and educators in simple assault cases. They, therefore, preferred to counsel offenders and teach them that battering was a criminal offense. Officer #10 explained:

> So the issue of domestic violence where a woman was beaten by her husband or boyfriend, we handle it very carefully. Because number one, we look at the protection and interest of the victim, the woman. So most times for our Liberian setting, the females take it to be a normal thing to be assaulted by their husbands and when we look back in Liberian history, women were subject to their husbands. Their husbands beat on them anytime and they take it to be a normal life. So coming to modern day reality, issues of women's rights have taken precedence now in Liberia ... most women still bear in mind that their husbands beating on them is not anything major so most of the time most of them cry to the police that "I don't want to go to court, in fact, don't put the man in jail" and other things. So most domestic violence cases, we embark on the advice and educative measure. (interview, male, Monrovia, October 14, 2010)

However, officers were divided on whether or not aggravated assault (a second-degree felony) should be referred to court. Out of 24 street-level officers who discussed how they dealt with domestic violence, 11 reported that they always referred aggravated assault cases, while 13 reported that they sometimes withdrew such cases. The second group explained that they did not always refer aggravated assault because of complainants' reluctance to support prosecution. They argued that compelling poor women to go to court would only cause hardship for them and lead to discord in the community. Furthermore, such complainants would not show up in court and the case would have to be dropped. A male officer captured the conflict between the formal rules and the street level:

> Because we have to be discretional. You know at the [police] academy, it is the theory, but when you come out the practical is difficult because if you want to go according to the theory it won't be easy to do your work.... Yes that's what it says [agreeing that the formal rules state that aggravated assault should always be prosecuted], but when you want to send the man to court, you will have more enemies, because the person will say "I did not want to go to court but the police officer forced me and this and that," and anytime you [are] walking [by] they will be insulting and attacking you personally. (interview, Monrovia, September 20, 2010)

They explained that compelling a reluctant complainant to go to court was a fruitless endeavor as they would not show up in court and the case would have to be dropped. Indeed, officer #10 explained that

> [w]ith this domestic issue the complainant will come and say, "I don't want to go anywhere with this case because this person is the breadwinner for the house and I don't want to carry this case [to court], if he and myself go to court, when he comes from there, he and myself will no more be together." So they say right there they don't want to go to court and so long [as] the person [is not] willing to go to court, even if you carry the accused to court they will ask for the complainant and if the complainant [is] not available they will not see the person [accused], that is the reason why when the complainant is saying that they don't want to go to court we make them solve the problem. (interview, male, Monrovia, September 15, 2010)

For those who reported that they always referred aggravated assault cases, the seriousness of the offense and the implications of withdrawal for the police and the victim were the two main reasons for this course of action. They asserted that aggravated assault was a serious case that should be referred to court because of the physical harm it causes but also because of the seriousness of the offense under the law. For example, officer #2 stated:

> Aggravated, you know is a felony crime. Aggravated assault cases we don't take sides with it, we send it to court. Whereby you hurt the person, the person takes ten stitches, five stiches, then those kinds of cases we don't compromise, we send it to court. (interview, Monrovia, October 4, 2010)

They were also concerned about the consequences of not referring cases. They worried that the victim in an aggravated assault case that was withdrawn by the police could be re-assaulted by the same offender or could suffer complications from the initial assault that could result in death. They explained that if this happened, the WACPS and the victim's family would hold them responsible. They, therefore, were not referring cases solely because they thought it was the right thing to do, but also because they feared the consequences of case withdrawal. Their attitudes show that the efforts by the UN and NGOs to emphasize the gravity of the act through training and their emphasis on prosecution (more so for rape than domestic violence) have affected street-level behavior. Nonetheless, the withdrawal of aggravated assault cases shows that socioeconomic factors still affect street-level implementation.

The response to rape and domestic violence shows that police officers were increasingly viewing these acts as crimes to be prosecuted by the state. While rape had been a first-degree felony before the conflict, officers had typically assessed cases for their seriousness, a basis upon which they pursued their duties. This appeared to be changing with the creation of the WACPS. This meant that cases that were not perceived as serious (e.g., rape of sex workers, rape of adult females, rape that did not leave visible injuries) were still investigated and referred for prosecution. Furthermore, police were less likely to blame such women or compel them to settle cases. This change is evident in the proportion of rape cases referred for prosecution. Interviews with women's rights advocates also confirmed that despite the many weaknesses that I have highlighted, the performance of the WACPS had improved in this regard.

Côte d'Ivoire: The Gender Desk

The gender desk was the second of two specialized mechanisms created in the police and gendarmerie to address VAW. The first was the position of gender focal point (an embedded specialized mechanism) created in 2009. Gender desks (designed to be specialized independent mechanisms) were staffed by gender focal points, who were tasked with opening and investigating cases of VAW, in addition to other non-VAW offenses. Some police stations and gendarmeries without a gender desk also had focal points. The gender desk is a major shift from the pre-conflict period, when neither the police force nor gendarmerie recognized VAW as offenses that required specialized responses. The gender focal points assigned to the gender desks had all received some form of specialized training in how to handle gendered violence. For the majority of officers, this training was offered in workshops and other continuous professional development forums organized in collaboration with the UN and other international agencies. More than half of the officers interviewed had participated in some form of training and were selected by their superiors. A police commissioner in Abidjan discussed the training offered to them:

> We received training by way of a seminar. With these seminars, people came in, they did a seminar for us, sometimes two or three seminars. They laid out the stakes for us, training with regards to this subject. Because we, we are policemen, and there are policemen who are violent and who hit their wives, I don't know... so they taught us about this subject. And it's not good, there are policemen who beat their wives, they exist. So we learned about this during the seminars. This was done by way of seminars. The training doesn't come from here actually. People come from the UNOCI, they come to give us lectures and then they leave. (interview, police officer #37, male, Abidjan, July 8, 2014)

Police officer #21 provided more detail on the training:

> I myself did the training. I did 21 days of training organized by the UNOCI human rights cell and the Japanese cooperation. For 21 days, they put documents at my disposal, documents that allowed us to know how to receive victims of gender-based sexual violence, victims... well people who are victims of different cases of violence, especially children and women. So

it allowed us, on a practical level, in practice it allowed us to know how to receive people who may even have been raped. With regards to women because it is not in the same manner, their reception. That is, when someone comes to say that I was a victim of fraud it's different . . . we receive them differently than how we would receive a woman who may have been sexually abused or who was subjected to physical violence at the hand of her husband or someone she loved. (interview, male, Abidjan, July 31, 2015)

Some of those trained were then designated gender focal points in their respective stations.

Meanwhile, some officers who had not received training reported that they learned about GBV from their colleagues who attended these training sessions. For example, police officer #24 stated:

Yes, there was a training session but not everyone was invited there. We were given the information on a pen drive which we saved on our computers. Truly not everyone was invited to the police academy but those who were at the training sent the information to those of us who were not there so we saved it on our computers. (interview, male, Abidjan, July 3, 2014)

Thus, some of those not selected for training were still benefiting from the sessions organized by the UNOCI and other international actors.

It is important to ask how the creation of the gender affected street-level behavior in Côte d'Ivoire, specifically the decision to refer cases to the prosecutor and the re-victimizing of girls and women who sought help from the police and gendarmerie. The officers interviewed generally perceived rape and aggravated assault as serious offenses. They described rape as a crime, a serious act, and a difficult case that could not be resolved at the station. According to police officer #10, "When you rape someone it is like murder!" (interview, male, Abidjan, July 22, 2014). Officer #35 echoed these sentiments:

For us, it is an act which is very serious because there is an effect on the physical integrity of the person as well as on her moral integrity. Rape can be likened to armed robbery, to a murder, in fact to a homicide. So rape cases are quite serious ones which we do not joke with at all. (interview, male, Abidjan, July 4, 2014)

They also viewed aggravated assault as a serious offense, although not on par with rape. Sixteen of the 48 officers interviewed in 2014 and 2015 reported that they sometimes withdrew cases of aggravated assault. Five of them (none of them focal points) reported that they sometimes withdrew rape cases. The majority explained that they always referred rape cases to the prosecutor and only withdrew on his/her authorization. Officer #32 explained the rules:

> You can withdraw the charges, but that doesn't erase the infraction since all our legal proceedings have to go through the prosecutor and the judges. We are not judges, so we provide the information or pass on the fact that the plaintiff wants to withdraw charges but that's all there is. (interview, male, Abidjan, July 3, 2017)

My interviews with victims of violence showed that some officers did collude with the accused to withdraw cases (Medie, 2017). Thus, as in Liberia, officers' responses cannot be taken at face value. However, interviews with UN officials and activists revealed that police performance had improved.

Infrastructural and Resource Constraints

While officers in Côte d'Ivoire also faced infrastructural and resource constraints, they were better resourced than officers of Liberia's WACPS. Most police stations and gendarmeries visited were well maintained, had electricity, and had space for interviewing suspects. Officers had computers and air conditioners, although many reported that they had purchased these themselves. The gender desks were new buildings furnished with desks, chairs, and filing cabinets, all provided by the UN and the European Union. The new buildings had three offices with adjoining toilets and a large waiting area. None of the waiting areas was furnished. In Abobo, other officers were using the gender desk because there was only one gender focal point in the station. In Bouaké, there was no room dedicated to the gender desk. None of the gender desks visited had an assigned vehicle. Officers explained that they used vehicles from other sections to conduct investigations. One officer reported using her personal vehicle to conduct this police work. Others relied on victims to transport them to and from the crime scene.

Rules Guiding the Response to Rape and Domestic Violence

Officers were directed by the criminal procedure penal code to refer all assault cases to the prosecutor. They explained that the rules had not changed since before the conflict. According to police officer #24:

> This is not because of the training [the referral of cases]. This is business as usual. That is, this is the police's job. We're not there to resolve matters amicably. We're not here to resolve, especially since nowadays, gender issues are getting complicated. Whatever the case we don't settle it amicably. Be it fraud, breach of trust, assault and battery, whatever it is we don't settle it amicably. (interview, male, Abidjan, July 3, 2014)

Thus, the new focus on GBV had not changed the rules. Although some officers said that their superiors had begun emphasizing prosecution in meetings, there had not been an official policy change in the referral of domestic violence cases. In comparison to Liberia, there were no formal and informal rules. The rule was that officers should consult with the prosecutor in all cases and officially, there was no room for discretionary decision-making. However, I will explain in the following that some officers did use their discretion when handling these cases.

However, the major change that seems to have occurred is in the area of re-victimization. Officers said that in training, they had learned not to re-victimize complainants and to treat them with sensitivity. Officers of the police and gendarmerie explained how they had learned not to question victims in public, not to place them in the same room as the accused, not to accuse them of causing the violence, and to avoid all other actions that would exacerbate their suffering. Gendarme #26 explained how the training was changing behavior:

> There was no distinction between the victims that is a woman, a child and a man, everything was put together in the criminal code. But now we are trying to make a distinction especially between the most vulnerable people. All the training we go through, all the capacity building we have at the brigade are now sensitive to the vulnerable people, that is, women and children. Evidently, there is a way or procedure for handling these cases. (interview, male, Abidjan, July 8, 2014)

Police officer #10 underscored the importance of training:

> Yes, there's indeed a change because the policeman of the past and the policeman of today do not do the same things. Formerly, when you go to the police station, let's say a woman who has been assaulted by her husband goes to the police station, even the policemen would chase her away but that is not the case in our day. Today, if a woman who has been assaulted by her husband goes to the police station to lodge a complaint the police themselves go look for the man. . . . The police are trained for that and also they know that it's not normal to assault a woman. . . . Everything has changed. Our mentality begun to change; i.e. when we leave our homes for work we come as policemen and not heads of families. If you are a policeman and you assault your wife you have a problem but when at service you must desist from it so when you see a woman that is assaulted you must go to her aid. There are a lot of things but it's a lot better now; even the police have come to understand. (interview, male, Abidjan, July 22, 2014)

In some cases, commanding officers instructed officers on how to treat victims of VAW, ensuring that those who had not been trained would also get this information. An officer who had not received training described the instructions he received from his commanding officer:

> So it's like a discussion to help us understand . . . how to correct our attitude so that when someone comes here, the person would not be frustrated. That is first of all the reception; how to receive people. When you receive people well, then they feel safe but when you receive them badly, they are afraid to even confide in you because they think that even if they tell their problem it would be taken wrongly, otherwise, before they come in they wait a while at the entrance to observe. When we see them we invite them to come in. When you see that she doesn't want to, you go closer to her because there are things that cannot be said unless you bring the person close. When you realize that their demeanor is a sad one, then you know right away that there is a problem, so you invite them to sit and talk. (interview, A.C., Abidjan, July 11, 2014)

Where these practices were discussed by commanding officers, they also served to reinforce the importance of treating victims with sensitivity.

The policy on rape was similar to domestic violence, all rape cases were to be referred to the prosecutor, who would decide whether there was enough evidence to proceed with prosecution. However, officers stated that there was more emphasis on the prosecution of rape cases because rape was a "crime." Similar to domestic violence, they explained that this had always been the rule within their respective agencies, even before and during the conflict. They were at pains to point out that the emphasis on prosecution that came with specialized training and the gender desk was not new. What was new was the message that complainants had to be treated with sensitivity. Officers, including some who had not undergone specialized training, said that they had been told not to revictimize women who reported rape and other forms of sexual violence. Officer #26 described the new instructions on how to treat rape victims:

> Rape for example is a crime in the criminal code, we look for the prosecutor and then the case is sent to court. Now what happens to the woman who is the victim? Nothing. In the station, we do not have the structures and now we are being asked to keep them in special structures to protect them. If a woman comes to complain that she has been raped what do we do? Most often they are embarrassed and suffering within so they cannot speak in public. The new directive states that we should take them aside to an office and listen to them. In there, they can speak to you to get the burden off their shoulders. If you question them in front of everyone, they will not respond to certain specific questions. This is what has changed a bit in the manner in which proceedings are done. That is, isolate the victim for questioning, if need be give her social aid. (interview, gendarme, male, Abidjan, July 8, 2014)

Police officer #24 officer articulated the new rules of the force:

> it's [training] changed things. Police officers now treat cases with more care—not that they didn't handle them with care before—but now they attend to their cases with more care. For example, if a girl in distress walks into the station right now, they taught us that if a girl comes in in distress and has been raped, and there are many other people who've also come in to file a complaint, it's not in front of these people that you'll start to ask your questions. You bring her in, take her into an office where the officer can ask his questions because if you do this in front of people, there are things she

won't be able to say. You see? There are things she won't be able to say in front of people, they could cause her shame and pain so you call her into the office and then you try to find the right words to calm her down, to reassure her. Because by coming here she expects not only for her rapist to be arrested, so you have to reassure that the man who hurt her will be brought in. That's one. That regardless of where he goes you will arrest him. You also need to reassure her that thanks to the advances in medicine these day[s], nothing will happen to her, she will be cured, we will do the medical exams, she won't catch any disease. We have to reassure her or else [unclear]. So in addition to these seminars, we've also learned new things, new measures. (interview, male, Abidjan, July 3, 2014)

Counselors reported an improvement in police behavior after they received this training. However, they noted that some officers still re-victimized girls and women who came to report rape. Indeed, in my interviews with female survivors of rape in Abidjan and Bouaké, at least half reported some form of re-victimizing behavior from the police and gendarmes, sometimes in a bid to prevent them from filing a complaint or to get them to withdraw a complaint. Thus, even though there was an improvement in comparison to the conflict and pre-conflict period, some negative attitudes and behaviors persisted, and they were more common among officers who had not undergone specialized training and were not assigned to the gender desks.

Police and Gendarmes' Performance in Rape Cases

Forty-three of the officers interviewed reported that they always referred rape cases to the prosecutor. Officers attributed their decision to the gravity of the crime, the age of the victims, the desire to avoid blame, and monitoring by the UN and their superiors. Similar to Liberia, officers explained that rape was a major offense and therefore had to be referred to the prosecutor. Officer #28 illustrated how the gravity of the crime affected decision-making:

Rape is a crime, we do not even want to hear about that. If the issue is verified and a medical certificate is provided by the doctor stating that the rape did occur, you the man will be arrested, you just leave like that. . . . That means that she is no more a plaintiff [a victim who does not want to prosecute]. She can say that she is withdrawing the case but that does not mean that the problem has been solved because the complaints are already with the prosecutor and the officers cannot joke with that. We do not joke with rape cases at all. (interview, gendarme, male, Abidjan, July 8, 2014)

The fear of being blamed in the future also contributed to the decision to refer cases to the prosecutor. Officer #26 gave an example of when an officer could be blamed in a rape case:

> Once we make up our mind we follow through with it [referring a case] even when they plead. Most often they are not happy with it but we also remain firm because at our level there are cases we cannot resolve. When you do not resolve a case properly and later there is a setback, the court will hold the station or the police responsible so there are decisions that we cannot make. For example, if a girl is raped and you set the perpetrator free because people are pleading, and later we find out that the perpetrator raped her without a condom and the girl has been infected with HIV, it will affect her in the future. When the court finds out about that later, it means the officer or the station did not do their work, for that reason when we have very delicate cases we send them to court so that the perpetrator will be punished. (interview, gendarme, male, Abidjan, July 7, 2014)

Similar to Liberia, the emphasis on prosecution was stronger when the victim was a minor. Officer #2 demonstrated the emphasis placed on prosecution when the victim was a minor:

> In all cases we refer them; we send them to court, yes . . . especially if the victim is a minor then that's even more serious. With that also there is no pardon. Order from our boss is that if it's a rape case we should arrest the culprit and keep him in police custody. (interview, Abidjan, July 8, 2014)

The instructions of superior officers and of UN officials who regularly visited police stations and gendarmerie brigades to monitor performance also contributed to the decision to report rape. However, a small number of officers (5) reported that they sometimes withdrew rape cases. Four of them were gendarmes and none was a focal point. While officers in Liberia did not admit to withdrawing rape cases, it is possible that their denial of this action was driven by the institutional norms; the WACPS was created to end impunity for sexual violence. Thus, officers working in such an environment would be highly aware of the norm and would not openly admit to going against it. Officers in Côte d'Ivoire who were not gender focal points and did not work in a gender desk were not subject to the same norms and thus would be more likely to admit to this behavior. While officers argued that they had always referred cases, the evidence did not support this assertion. However, it shows that the end of the conflict and the UN's efforts to address VAW by providing training, assigning focal points, and creating the gender desk had affected attitudes.

Police Performance in Domestic Violence Cases

As in Liberia, officers were more willing to withdraw domestic violence cases than rape cases. Those who did not withdraw cases attributed their decision to complainants' unwillingness to support prosecution, while those who claimed to always refer cases pointed to the law, the gravity of the offense, and the fear of blame as justification. Police officer #21 explained that the decision to withdraw a domestic violence case rested with the prosecutor:

> You know, domestic violence is common blows and the woman comes here to file a complaint but the mere fact that she came to the police to file a complaint means that a decision was taken. She informs the appropriate authorities that she was a victim of violence done by her partner or by her husband. Anyway, it is illegal. We arrest the individual and then we refer the case. Now if she says she doesn't want that, she doesn't want that well, we're under the obligation to report this to Mr. Prosecutor who can tell us over the phone that "well listen, since she says doesn't want this, try to reconcile them." Just as he can say, "despite her refusal to have her partner or her husband referred, just defer the individual so he can be reprimanded." The fact remains that this is all as to discourage, to dissuade all those who might be tempted to violence wherever they may be. (interview, male, July 31, 2015)

At the same time, the victim's preference, which is often driven by social pressures, was a major reason for not referring a case. Officer #11 gave an example of when this would happen:

> The parents of a lady may come here and sometimes in our office wanting to beat up their daughter for having sent the case to the police station. They

do not joke with the police station. So when there is summons, then it's an extreme case. So when it happens like that and we realize that by referring the man, we are destroying an entire family, we don't do it. We demand that the woman be treated so we send her to the hospital and we follow up but we have never had a case where the man assaulted the woman with a machete, it's always with a cane. So, most of the time she has some marks on her back, and for that, we will not destroy a family . . . if we send the man to prison who will take care of his children? And considering the fact that it is the wife herself who sent her husband to prison, are you sure that the parents of this man will take care of the children? We can also send him to court instead of the prison. The judge can decide in this case to set the man free. The time he has spent in cell during all this process is already a shame. So are you sure that if he keeps that in mind, his children can succeed in life? (interview, police, male, Abidjan, July 22, 2015)

Thus, as in Liberia, police officers and gendarmes sometimes withdrew domestic violence cases when the victims demanded it. Their assessment of the impact of arrest and prosecution of the offender played a major role in this decision. This assessment could be influenced by personal biases and sociocultural beliefs surrounding domestic violence, particularly when officers had not received specialized training. Withdrawal was sometimes done in consultation with the prosecutor. As explained in Chapter 1, international policy documents emphasized arrest and prosecution for sexual violence more than they did for domestic violence. This is reflected in the response to both forms of violence in Liberia and Côte d'Ivoire.

Conclusion

There have been significant changes in street-level policing in both Liberia and Côte d'Ivoire. In Liberia, officers were more likely to refer rape and, to a lesser extent, aggravated assault to court. Similarly, Ivoirian officers reported sending more cases to court and to treating victims with sensitivity. These changes can be clearly traced to the reforms that have followed the conflicts in both countries. Pressure from the UN led the police force in Liberia and Côte d'Ivoire and the gendarmerie in Côte d'Ivoire to introduce new structures and policies for addressing VAW. In Liberia, the women's movement also played a role in pressuring the state to address gaps in policing.

These findings show the centrality of the UN and the women's movement in changing street-level implementation in post-conflict societies. By pressuring the government to create and institutionalize the specialized units, the UN had a major effect on how VAW laws were enforced. In Liberia, but less so in Côte d'Ivoire, women's organizations also impacted how police officers and gendarmes performed their duties in regard to VAW. However, the greater degree of institutionalization of the specialized unit in Liberia contributed to a deeper salience of the international women's justice norm in that country. Thus, police officers and gendarmes in Côte d'Ivoire were more likely to admit to withdrawing rape cases.

These findings advance the IR and gender and politics literature by demonstrating how an international actor like the UN can affect street-level behavior. It also demonstrates the role that social movements can play in street-level implementation. The gender and politics literature has shown that women's movements influence policy adoption in Africa. This comparison of Côte d'Ivoire and Liberia shows that they can also have an impact on street-level implementation. It illustrates that IOs and social movements shape how global norms are implemented domestically.

However, the discussion also clearly shows multiple weaknesses in these specialized units. In both countries, officers still withdrew cases for personal gain and also re-victimized survivors. In Liberia, acute resource constraints affected all aspects of policing and contributed to re-victimizing practices. The Liberian government relied overwhelmingly on the UN and international actors to build and equip the WACPS. Thus, while there appeared to be local ownership, this ownership did not extend to investing scarce resources into the section. These issues present serious problems, as the UN mission completed its mandate in March 2018. As international actors move to other conflict-affected areas, international assistance and pressure will be less, leading to questions about the sustainability of the specialized section. In Côte d'Ivoire, the UNDP took over the construction of the gender desks after the withdrawal of UNOCI. Nonetheless, it is still important to ask what happens after these international actors are no longer actively promoting, supporting, and monitoring specialized mechanisms in Liberia and Côte d'Ivoire and in other countries in Africa where they have been established.

In conclusion, this study has shown that the international women's justice norm was more salient in Liberia than in Côte d'Ivoire. I argue that this is mostly because of how the specialized units were institutionalized in both countries. Rapid institutionalization in Liberia served to entrench the notion that rape should be prosecuted. Due to the fact that Côte d'Ivoire had a more professionalized force, prosecution had also been emphasized, but because gender issues had received less attention than in Liberia, there was still some tolerance of the withdrawal of rape cases. This demonstrates that the variation in implementation observed at the national level has implications for street-level implementation.

Conclusion

Specialized Mechanisms and the Campaigns to End Violence against Women in Africa

The establishment of specialized mechanisms in Liberia, Côte d'Ivoire, and elsewhere in Africa marks a major development in the response to VAW across the continent. In this book I have shown that there is variation in how these mechanisms are established and in how they perform. I argue that while international pressure drove the creation of the mechanisms in both countries, domestic pressure and dynamics played a more critical role in their institutionalization. I also argue that greater degree of institutionalization of Liberia's WACPS led to the norm becoming more salient in the country's specialized unit, in comparison to Côte d'Ivoire, where police officers and gendarmes still reported that they withdrew rape cases. These conclusions offer key insights into the implementation not only of the international women's justice norm, but of women's rights norms more broadly.

In this concluding chapter, I discuss the theoretical and policy implications of these findings. I begin with a discussion of the book's contribution to the literature. I explain that the findings advance the IR literature by identifying when and how international actors and domestic actors and conditions are most impactful on the domestic implementation of an international norm at multiple levels. I then focus on the policy implications of establishing specialized mechanisms. I ask the question: what do specialized mechanisms mean for women's access to justice and for the campaigns to end VAW in Africa? I argue that while specialized mechanisms can play an important role in both endeavors, they need to be adapted to the local setting and have strong and sustained domestic input into their establishment and operation, especially from civil society organizations. I further underline the need to adopt a holistic approach to addressing VAW because of how social, cultural, and economic factors impact survivors' engagement with the criminal justice system and their ability to get justice.

Global Norms and Local Action. Peace A. Medie, Oxford University Press (2020). © Oxford University Press.
DOI: 10.1093/oso/9780190922962.001.0001

The Domestic in the Implementation of International Norms

The findings of this study are relevant for theoretical debates in IR, gender and politics, and African studies. There is growing attention to implementation in the IR literature. The literature has explored how international pressure and domestic dynamics interact to influence norm implementation (Acharya, 2004; Avdeyeya, 2015; Betts and Orchard, 2014; Deere, 2009; Montoya, 2013). This book makes several contributions to this literature. First, it advances how we conceptualize and study implementation by disaggregating the implementation process into three stages: creation, institutionalization, and street level. By disaggregating, we are able to show that an international actor like the UN is not equally influential across the implementation process. This is to say that the international pressure that leads to the creation of a specialized mechanism is not guaranteed to lead to its rapid institutionalization. We are also able to specify when and how domestic actors and conditions make the most impact on the implementation process. Without this disaggregation, we risk underestimating or overestimating the influence of international and domestic factors, as well as the degree to which states are implementing a norm. For example, if we conceptualized implementation as only the creation of a specialized mechanism, we would conclude that both Liberia and Cote d'Ivoire performed similarly. However, when the implementation process is disaggregated, we are then able to demonstrate that these countries diverged in their implementation of the norm.

A second and related contribution that this study makes to the IR literature is to specify the conditions under which international and domestic actors and conditions influence the implementation process. The literature has underlined how international and domestic factors interact to affect implementation. Indeed, the scholarship has emphasized that the local context cannot be overlooked (Acharya, 2004; Merry, 2006; Zwingel, 2011). Domestic actors translate, reconstruct, appropriate, and adapt international norms to local settings and sometimes even reject them. This book builds on this literature by showing how domestic actors and conditions can affect the pace of institutionalization of a norm. It also sheds light on the strategies that domestic actors employ.

It offers other insights into international actors and their influence in the domestic implementation of international norms. The peacebuilding literature has debated the influence of international actors in post-conflict states and the agency of post-conflict states more broadly. Tholens and Groß (2015) have argued that norm diffusion in post-conflict states is distinct from diffusion in other contexts:

> [Post-war states] are under significant pressure to reform by very powerful international actors. The situation may be described partly as one of "limited statehood" in some states. This implies that the voluntary nature of the norm process is disputed, and that norms spread through a wide array of mechanisms, ranging from persuasion to coercion. Peacebuilding contexts, therefore, differ somewhat from "regular" norm diffusion taking place under conditions of voluntary selection, inasmuch as peacebuilding tends to take on a more intrusive and "direct" character and, consequently, often appears more like policy transfer. (p. 255)

This intrusiveness of liberal peacebuilding and its attempt to advance a particular agenda in post-conflict states has been critiqued (Mac Ginty & Richmond, 2013). This study, adds to the literature by showing that while post-conflict states are subject to persuasion, they negotiate if and how implementation occurs and are not simply passive recipients of international norms. In Liberia, the government wanted to build capacity to hold perpetrators of sexual violence accountable (partly because of domestic pressure), such that the idea of a specialized unit aligned with its priorities. In Côte d'Ivoire, the police and gendarmerie agreed to create a specialized unit, even though it did not align with their priorities, but did not prioritize its formalization and installation across the country, such that institutionalization moved at a slower pace. Both cases demonstrate that the interests and preferences of the government, and of key gatekeepers, cannot be dismissed when trying to understand how international norms are implemented at the domestic level. This finding illustrates how post-conflict states can exhibit agency, even when it appears that they are under the thumb of the UN and other powerful international actors. This knowledge should inform how we analyze norm diffusion, international interventions, and politics in areas of limited statehood.

The arguments presented in this book also advance the gender and politics literature. This literature has shown that women's movements play a central role in states' adoption of progressive women's rights laws and policies (Adomako Ampofo, 2008; Anyidoho, Crawford, & Medie, 2020; Crawford & Anyidoho, 2013; Htun & Weldon, 2010; Kang, 2015; Kang & Tripp, 2018;

Tripp, Casimiro, Kwesiga, & Mungwa, 2009; Tsikata 2009). This study builds on this scholarship by demonstrating that women's movements also play a key role in the implementation process. Member organizations employ several strategies, including protests, to pressure states and IOs to prioritize implementation. However, just as the strength of the movement matters for setting the agenda and changing policy, it also matters for implementation. Thus a strong movement is more likely to have an impact on the institutionalization of a specialized mechanism. This book demonstrates that the influence of women's movements extends beyond policy adoption to encompass implementation and offers new avenues to understanding how they are able to advance women's rights.

These findings on IOs and women's movements are also important for the African studies literature. It provides critical insights into how international and domestic actors affect implementation in the security sector. The ability of international actors involved in reforming security sector agencies to make substantial and sustainable changes in the police and other agencies can be called into question due to the persistent deficiencies within these institutions (see Hills, 2008). Indeed, the reform efforts in Liberia and Côte d'Ivoire are far from being described as successful. However, significant headway was made in rapidly institutionalizing Liberia's WACPS. Côte d'Ivoire also made some progress, though at a slower pace. This study has shed some light on when and how substantial and sustainable change in the security sector is more likely to occur.

Specialized Units and the Campaigns to End Violence against Women in Africa

The findings of this book show that specialized units have the potential to increase girls and women's access to justice and to reduce revictimization by law enforcement officers. However, they have also shown that more work needs to be done to improve these units. VAW is one of the greatest threats to women in Africa. While it is a global problem rooted in patriarchal gender norms that foster gender inequality, Africa is particularly affected. Conflict has exacerbated certain forms of this violence, including domestic violence and non-partner sexual violence, and the effects have been devastating for its victims, their family, and the society. Specialized units are one of many tools that have been introduced to address this problem. It is expected that they will do a better job of investigating, arresting, and prosecuting perpetrators and with treating victims with sensitivity, as compared to regular units within the criminal justice sector.

Indeed, across the continent, more stringent laws and enhanced law enforcement are being embraced as key measures for addressing VAW. In evaluating the progress that has been made by states, researchers in academia and in the policy arena look at the laws passed within countries. In Africa, the policy arena has also begun to pay attention to the establishment of specialized mechanisms. Thus, where they exist, states are judged to be making good progress. When enforced, the laws have the potential to send a strong message about the non-tolerance of VAW and could also deter offenders. However, this and other studies have made clear that enforcement often does not happen, and when it does, it often does not match the gender-responsive model that we seek. Weaknesses within the police force and gendarmerie, even a reformed and specialized one, mean that many survivors who seek it will not get justice from the formal criminal justice system. This clearly demonstrates that much work needs to go into strengthening specialized mechanisms. There is a need for domestic ownership of these institutions on the part of the government and civil society and a willingness to devote resources to them. Even in Liberia, where domestic pressure and government support were strong, resources devoted to the WACPS by the government were highly insufficient. This issue is especially pressing as the UN and other international agencies draw down their missions. Without a strong domestic buy-in and sense of ownership, there is a risk of relapsing into business as usual, even in specialized mechanisms.

However, even in their present state, it is clear that the specialized units have contributed to an increase in the referral of rape and domestic violence cases in both countries, although the referral of rape cases is higher. This differs from what pertained before and during the conflict in both countries, when these offenses were often trivialized and the decision on how to proceed lay with the victim's relatives or the perpetrator. Indeed, this study demonstrates that although many offenders continue to act with impunity, the likelihood that they will be held accountable for their actions has increased with the creation of the gender desk and the WACPS. These mechanisms send a signal to offenders that the state no longer condones such violence. Indeed, officers in Côte d'Ivoire reported a decrease in the number of cases reported since the war ended. While this could be a result of the deterrence effect, it is also possible that this reduction is because girls and women face more dire consequences for reporting rape and domestic violence. For example, perpetrators who now know that they will be arrested and prosecuted might be saying and doing things to frighten survivors and their relatives from reporting this violence. Similarly, a wife who knows that her husband could be prosecuted might be less likely to ask the police to counsel him out of fear that he would be arrested and prosecuted. More research is needed to better understand how these mechanisms affect the behavior of both offenders and victims.

However, the increase in case referral (when these referrals end in prosecution) is also important as it temporarily separates the survivor from her abuser. In the case of domestic violence, it gives her a reprieve and the time needed to re-establish herself. The incarceration of the offender also temporarily prevents him from victimizing other women. However, the police are only able to investigate and refer cases; the decision to prosecute rests with the office of the prosecutor. Thus, even when the police perform effectively, deficiencies in the courts can stall cases. For example, Monrovia's Criminal Court E had a huge backlog of cases that had been referred by the WACPS but were left sitting on the docket because there was only one judge in the court (Moore, 2010). The problem was also attributed to the weakness of the evidence collected by the WACPS. Thus, police officers did have some impact on whether an offender was prosecuted, but the evidence collected was only one of several factors affecting the outcome of cases in the justice system. In settings where the justice system, for reasons including the lack of trained personnel, stymies prosecutions, strong evidence will not prevent an offender from escaping justice. The police are only one in a chain of actors who determine if offenders will be held accountable and if it will be easier for girls and women to access justice. This underscores the need for reform across the security sector. These institutions are closely interlinked and cannot function effectively if their personnel are not equally capable.

This study has further shown that the discussion about access to justice cannot occur without a consideration of the health, social, and economic well-being of the survivor. As explained in Chapter 1 and illustrated in the background chapters on Liberia and Côte d'Ivoire, VAW impacts all areas of women's lives and their well-being. Thus, arrest and prosecution of the offender is only one concern for most women. For victims of rape and domestic violence, there are concerns about health care, basic needs, and retaliation from the offender. Rape survivors also face stigmatization, while domestic violence survivors risk losing their homes and the financial support of their partner. Poverty prevents survivors from reporting and from following through after they have reported; stigmatization causes many to conceal the violence they have suffered; pressure and threats from relatives and the perpetrator frighten others away from reporting their abusers and cause some to try to withdraw their case from the police or gendarmerie. These dynamics are present in many countries across the continent and have prevented the specialized mechanisms from functioning effectively. Thus, law enforcement officers often find that the rules of their unit are at odds with the preferences of the complainant. While increased reporting and the increase in case referral suggests that the specialized units served to overcome some of these challenges and thus have an important role to play in enhancing women's access to justice, this clash between the procedures of the criminal justice system and the preferences of the complainant persists. This demonstrates that in addition to devoting resources to these units, maintaining pressure on them, and monitoring their performance, stakeholders have to pay close attention to the social, cultural, and economic barriers to women's access to justice. In other words, reforming the criminal justice system cannot happen in isolation but needs to be closely linked to addressing the social, cultural, and financial barriers that many survivors face. It requires states to adopt a holistic approach to addressing VAW.

A holistic approach recognizes the entirety of the challenges that confront the survivors of these and other forms of VAW. A holistic approach to addressing VAW would include medical care and socioeconomic support. Free or heavily subsidized medical care is very important due to the high level of female poverty in these and many other countries in Africa. The social and economic ramifications of leaving a violent relationship and of disclosing it to the police also need to be addressed. There is a need for shelters that can protect women and their children from retaliation, and economic programs that will support them in getting back on their feet and will prepare them to earn a living. There is also a need for a strong social support network—that should include counselors—into which survivors can be absorbed, to assist them in weathering the social backlash that results from seeking help from the police.

While states have emphasized the criminal justice response, the medical and socioeconomic components remain weak. Both Liberia and Côte d'Ivoire had only a handful of shelters, which were mostly underfunded. In Liberia, NGOs paid for victims' medical care, and the same was done in Côte d'Ivoire, but this free service could not meet the needs of the entire population of survivors and many did not know it existed. Social and economic support were highly inadequate in both countries so that most survivors, after reporting to the police or gendarmerie, found themselves bereft of relatives and friends and of a home and money. These conditions discouraged reporting and caused women to try to withdraw their cases. Any effort to increase women's access to justice cannot occur in isolation; specialized agencies should aim to provide a holistic response to the problem.

The approach should not be to compel women to report violence and to cooperate with law enforcement officers. Instead, the focus should be on creating the conditions that make cooperation favorable. Indeed, evidence from Liberia shows that compelling women to cooperate in the absence of a strong support structure can constitute another source of pressure on them. A holistic approach would make reporting and cooperating with the police easier for survivors of violence. This does not mean that a police station has to provide all of these services, but that it should be connected to other service providers and work with them every step of the way to protect and support survivors. Liberia's MoGD has tried to coordinate this through the GBV Taskforce and has had some success, but the support provided is insufficient. Furthermore, while the police tries to work with members of the taskforce, including safe homes, it is not clear that they recognize that these organizations are integral to the enforcement of the law. In other words, not only are safe homes, health centers, and other related service providers essential for women's rights and wellbeing, but they are also essential for the enforcement of the law. It is therefore critical that specialized units are part of a vital and cohesive network of actors who provide support to survivors of sexual and physical violence. Rwanda's One-Stop Centres appear to be a step in this direction. However, it is clear that there is much more work to be done by law enforcement and other government agencies, IOs, and NGO in Liberia, Côte d'ivoire, and many other countries, to provide a holistic response to VAW. Specialized mechanisms in the police force and gendarmerie are not a panacea for VAW. However, when they are adequately resourced and are combined with social and economic support services for survivors, they can encourage women to report violence and mitigate the problems that often arise from this action.

APPENDIX

Data Collected and the Data Collection Process

Fieldwork for this book was conducted between 2010 and 2017; I collected data in Liberia in 2010 and 2011 and in Côte d'Ivoire from 2014 to 2017 on how the police in both countries, and the gendarmerie in Côte d'Ivoire, responded to violence against women (VAW) before, during, and after the conflict in both countries. Because a range of state and non-state actors played a role in how these security sector agencies responded to VAW, data were collected from several groups of individuals and institutions in both countries. Based on desktop research, I built a list of interviewees in state agencies, international organizations, and civil society working on the issue of VAW and added to this list when fieldwork began and as it progressed. The objective of the data collection process was to understand how the police and gendarmerie had responded to VAW over three time periods (pre-conflict, conflict, and post-conflict) and how international organizations and women's organizations had impacted this response. This objective informed the research design, the kind of data collected, and the interview questions.

In Liberia, data were collected in Monrovia in Montserrado County and Gbarnga in Bong County in the form of semi-structured interviews, observation sessions, newspapers articles published before and after the conflict, police records, as well as documents produced by the UN Mission in Liberia (UNMIL), local and international nongovernmental organizations (NGOs), the Ministry of Gender and Development, the Ministry of Justice, and other government agencies. I conducted a total of 154 interviews in three phases. The first set of interviews, totaling 134, was conducted in Monrovia from June to October 2010.[1] Another 16 interviews were conducted in May and June 2011, 10 in Monrovia and 6 in Gbarnga. The third phase was between 2015 and 2016 and involved data collection outside of Liberia. In 2012 I conducted a phone interview with an officer who had served before the conflict. In 2015 in Ghana, I interviewed one individual who had served in a senior capacity in UNMIL during the establishment of the Women and Children Protection Section (WACPS) and I conducted a phone interview with another in 2016. I also conducted a phone interview with a senior police officer in the Liberian National Police (LNP) force in 2016. All interviewees gave verbal consent to participation in the study.

Interviewees included 18 survivors of rape and intimate partner violence; 51 police officers; 10 United Nations personnel; 25 staff members of the Ministry of Gender and Development, Ministry of Justice, and Ministry of Interior; 10 staff members of international organizations; and founders and staff members of 15 local NGOs, 12 of which were women's organizations.[2] I also observed police officers, staff members of government agencies, and representatives of local and international organizations in Liberia with their consent. At police stations that I visited, I observed and took notes of police officers' interactions with complainants, victims, and the accused, when cases were reported. I also observed and took notes at two meetings of the National GBV Taskforce in Monrovia, which were attended by stakeholders from the government and by representatives of local and international organizations. I did not work with a research assistant in Liberia.

I made three visits to Côte d'Ivoire for this study. The first was from June to August 2014, the second in July 2015, and the third in September 2017. The data collected were in the form of semi-structured interviews; focus group discussions; police and gendarmerie records; newspaper articles published before, during, and after the conflict; and documents produced by the UN Operation in Côte d'Ivoire (UNOCI), the Ministry of Interior and Security, and other relevant government agencies, and by local and international NGOs. I conducted a total of 180 interviews in-country over the three years; 170 of these interviews were conducted in 2014 and 2015. I also conducted one interview in Ghana, and four interviews by phone.[3] Twenty-three of the in-country interviews were conducted in Bouaké, and the majority of the interviews were in French.[4] I conducted interviews with a range of actors, including two officials from the Ministry of Justice and two senior officials in the Ministry of Interior and Security; interviews with 12 officials of the UN peacekeeping mission, one director of an international NGO; and interviews with staff of 17 NGOs, of which seven were women's organizations. I also interviewed 56 police officers and gendarmes and 63 survivors of intimate partner violence and rape. I also conducted five focus group discussions; three were all-female groups and two were all-male. Two of the focus groups were in Abidjan and three were in Bouaké. Each group had 8–10 participants and the discussions, which were recorded, averaged 97 minutes. I spoke French at an upper-intermediate level and conducted all in-country interviews alongside a research assistant who clarified my questions to interviewees when necessary and translated slang and other terminologies with which I was unfamiliar. In 2014 and 2015, I worked with a female Ivoirian research assistant, and in 2017 I worked with a male Ivoirian research assistant.[5]

I arrived in Liberia with a list of individuals to interview, but also employed a snowball sampling technique to identify key individuals within the government, the UN, and NGOs to interview. I visited every police station in Monrovia and the sole police station in Gbarnga. I attempted to (but did not) speak to every police officer in each police station I visited and made multiple visits when an officer was not available. I sometimes had to pause an interview and continue on another day when an officer had to attend to a case. I followed the same format in including police officers and gendarmes in the study in Côte d'Ivoire.

Similar to Liberia, I went to Côte d'Ivoire with the names of individuals I sought to interview within the UN mission, international and local NGOs, and government agencies, based on their work on the issue of VAW. I also employed a snowball sampling technique to identify many others to interview in these sectors. To speak with street-level bureaucrats, I then visited nine police stations in Abidjan and two in Bouaké. I also visited three gendarmeries in Abidjan and two in Bouaké. I spoke with the commissioner and commandant, respectively, of each police station and gendarmerie where they were available and then to gender focal points and personnel of the gender desks, where these desks had been installed. I also spoke to officers who were not assigned to a gender desk and were not focal points. In both countries I received formal permission from the relevant authorities to conduct interviews with the law enforcement officers.

Data collection and analyses were guided by a feminist research ethic. This ethic can be defined as a "methodological commitment to any set of research practices that reflect on the power of epistemology, boundaries, relationships, and the multiple dimensions of the researcher's location throughout the entirety of the research process . . ." (Ackerly & True, 2010, p. 2). This approach also seeks to promote gender justice. I sought to ensure that my research did not cause harm to participants and that it would produce knowledge that informs efforts to increase women's access to justice. These points guided the project design and my engagements with all participants, including survivors of violence.

I was a doctoral student during the period of data collection in Liberia. I was born in Liberia and lived there until the outbreak of the conflict, so I knew the country and spoke English with a Liberian accent. This rendered me an insider in some respects, even as my Ghanaian nationality and training in the United States marked me as an outsider. I had ties that facilitated the process of contacting interviewees in government ministries, NGOs, and within international organizations. I had completed my PhD when I began data collection in Côte d'Ivoire. In contrast to my experience in Liberia, I had no personal ties in Côte d'Ivoire, which I visited for the first time in 2014. This was also the first Francophone country I had visited as an adult and my first time working in French. Thus, while my identity as an African woman made me an insider in some respects, I was also an outsider. My links (and the lack thereof) affected my ability to gain access to institutions and to individuals. However, in both countries, I found that most NGOs were eager to discuss their work and to connect me to others with whom I could speak.

I worked closely with NGOs to identify survivors of violence with whom I could speak about their decision to report or not report rape and intimate partner violence and their experiences with the criminal justice system. I interviewed survivors of intimate partner and non-partner sexual violence, many of whom were poor and still recovering from the trauma they had overcome. I therefore worked with counselors employed by NGOs (three in Côte d'Ivoire and one in Liberia) to contact survivors to participate in the study.[6] I explained the research objectives to the counselors and discussed with them the questions that I would ask survivors. Counselors then contacted survivors they had previously worked with and assessed to be able to participate in the study.[7] Those who were willing to participate in the study were invited for the interview. All interviews were conducted on the premises of the NGOs where psychosocial counselors were present. In two of the NGOs in Côte d'Ivoire, the counselors were in the room for the entirety of the interviews. The counselors and I prioritized the well-being of the survivors and worked to ensure their comfort and prevent emotional distress, beginning with the location selected for the interviews. The decision to interview survivors on the premises of NGOs that provided a range of services (and thus did not only serve victims of violence), and which was often in a different neighborhood than theirs, was to ensure the confidentiality of the interviews. It was important that their participation in the study not be known to others. Indeed, some interviewees, particularly survivors of rape, had not disclosed their victimization to relatives or friends.

I made sure to identify myself as a researcher who did not have a connection to the government. This is partly because agents of the security sector, including gendarmes, had been implicated in the rape of civilians. I therefore sought to dispel any fears that the interviewees might have that they were interacting with an agent of the security sector. It was also important that interviewees be able to speak freely about their experiences with the police and gendarmerie and know that there would be no repercussions for doing so. I also explained to them that I had no connection to the UN or other international organizations or to an NGO. This was important so as not to raise false hope among survivors that I would be able to offer the kinds of assistance these actors sometimes provide. However, I informed interviewees of relevant organizations that offered a variety of services to survivors, where they were not aware of these organizations. Where I determined that there was a need, I connected them to particular individuals within these organizations who could offer them assistance.

I explained the research project to survivors and described its objectives as well as the kind of questions that would be asked. I then asked for their permission to conduct the interviews and to record the interviews. Interviewees gave verbal consent and where they agreed, the interview was recorded. Where they objected to a recording, I only took notes. Each survivor was given the equivalent of between US$5 and US$10 to cover lunch and their transportation fare to and from the NGO premises where the interview was conducted. The amount received by each individual was determined by their fare.

Issues of power also affected my interaction with other groups of interviewees, particularly police officer and gendarmes. Scholars have noted that the researcher's positionality impacts access to research sites and to certain kinds of knowledge (Bouka, 2015; Henry, Higate, & Sanghera, 2009; Yacob-Haliso, 2018). While I was in a relative position of power when interviewing survivors of violence, the balance often shifted when I interviewed law enforcement officers. The security sector in both countries remains heavily male dominated, more so in Côte d'Ivoire than in Liberia. Indeed, the Gendarmerie Nationale de Côte d'Ivoire was an all-male institution until 2015. While I was able to access these spaces after receiving the written permission from the police and gendarmerie, there were still challenges to getting information. Indeed, in a few brigades and police stations, I found the reception to be less than welcoming until I presented this piece of paper. On several occasions, officers where hostile until they realized that I was a researcher. Even after it became clear that I was a researcher authorized to conduct interviews, some interviewees asked questions about my age, credentials, and marital status, presumably to confirm that I was qualified to be conducting the study. There were several takeaways from these experiences, one of them being the insights I gained into the treatment received by the female survivors of violence when they interact with law police officers and gendarmes.

With the exception of the commanding officer of the WACPS and women's rights advocates who asked that their identity be disclosed, I have maintained the confidentiality of police officers in both countries and gendarmes in Côte d'Ivoire and for all other groups of interviewees. This was important to protect interviewees from any backlash that could ensue from their participation in the study. All interviewees were asked to discuss their experiences and to assess the performance of state agencies. Many interviewees, including police officers and gendarmes, revealed information that was critical of the government. This was a sensitive matter, particularly in Côte d'Ivoire where the security sector was politicized. I therefore wanted everyone to be able to speak freely and to avoid any repercussions from participating in this study. Thus, I have assigned a number to each police officer and gendarme in the text and have used a combination of alphabets to create initials when referencing other groups of interviewees.

I am grateful to all participants in this study who were generous with their time. I am especially grateful to the survivors of violence who travelled from their homes to meet me and shared their very difficult stories with me. This book would not have been possible without them.

Notes

Introduction

1. Street-level describes the point at which the law is enforced. It is where law enforcement officers and citizens interface.
2. A few African countries established specialized mechanisms before this time.
3. See R. Charli Carptenter (2006) for a discussion of gender-based violence against boys and men in conflict.
4. Domestic violence/IPV also encompasses psychological abuse (Jewkes, 2002), but interviews with police officers focused on their response to physical and sexual violence.
5. My definition of practice draws on the discussion of norm operationalization by Huelss (2017) and on the definition of "best practice" by Davis-Roberts and Carroll (2010).

Chapter 1

1. This attention has not been translated into adequate action. Keck and Sikkink (1998) discuss the growth in attention to VAW, which began in the 1980s.
2. UC Berkeley School of Law (2015, p. 29) suggests that children are less stigmatized than adults.
3. See Committee on the Status of Women reports.
4. States that have amended the rape law: Benin, Botswana, Burundi, Botswana, Comoros, Democratic Republic of Congo, Eritrea, Ghana, Liberia, Madagascar, Niger, Rwanda, Senegal, Seychelles, South Africa, Sudan, Tanzania, Uganda, Zambia, and Zimbabwe.
5. States that have passed a marital rape law: Angola, Benin, Burundi, Cabo Verde, Comoros, Ghana, Guinea Bissau, Lesotho, Mauritius, Mozambique, Namibia, Nigeria, Rwanda, Sao Tome and Principe, Seychelles, Sierra Leone, South Africa, Tanzania, Togo, Tunisia, Uganda, Zimbabwe.
6. Post-conflict: Angola, Burundi, Chad, Côte d'Ivoire, Democratic Republic of Congo, Eritrea, Ethiopia, Liberia, Rwanda, Sierra Leone, South Sudan, Sudan, and Uganda.
7. Ghana (1998), Mauritius (1994), Namibia (1993), Nigeria (1958 and 1986), Uganda (1998), Seychelles (1998), and Zimbabwe (1995 and 1997).

Chapter 3

1. I use "intimate partner violence" and "domestic violence" interchangeably. Although intimate partner violence is only one form of domestic violence, the latter term is used in policy documents and by personnel of Liberia's criminal justice sector.
2. Men and boys were also victims of sexual violence.
3. This is not unique to Liberia or to GBV. A 2005 study revealed that Africans turned to customary courts to address about 80 percent of all disputes. See Laure-Hélène Piron (2005), *Donor Assistance to Justice Sector Reform in Africa: Living Up to the New Agenda?* Open Society Justice Initiative. The Ministry of Justice's 1973 Annual Report noted that on issues of marital relations, customary law was more firmly rooted than statutory law.
4. The common law definition of the term "rape," in the absence of a special statute defining the crime, prevailed in Liberia by force of the Act of 1869, adopting the common law of England and America, see Coleman v. RL, http://www.liberlii.org/lr/cases/LRSC/1898/1.html (accessed March 7, 2019).
5. Ibid.
6. The newspapers analyzed spanned October 1981–March 1990. However, due to the destruction of the newspaper archives, all newspapers published during these dates were not available. It is, therefore, possible that other stories of rape were published that I could not include in my analyses.
7. Not all women were forced to fight.
8. This recognition has not, however, necessarily translated into state funding of the initiatives proposed in policy documents.
9. Horn et al. (2015) state that women said they would only report to the police after all else had failed (p. 7).
10. It is possible that younger people are more likely to report than adults.

Chapter 4

1. The common law definition of the term "rape," in the absence of a special statute defining the crime, prevailed in Liberia by force of the Act of 1869, adopting the common law of England and America;
2. The reports were housed at the University of Liberia, but most of them were destroyed during the civil war. The ones that survived the war and that I analyzed covered the following time periods: October 1, 1958–September 30, 1959; October 1, 1962–September 30, 1963; October 1965–September 1966; October 1, 1967–September 30, 1968; October 1, 1968–September 30, 1969; October 1, 1971–September 30, 1972; October 1, 1972–December 31, 1972; January 1, 1973–November 30, 1973; January 1, 1976–December 31, 1976; January 1, 1977–December 31, 1977; January 1, 1979–December 31, 1979; January 1, 1980–January 31, 1980.
3. Both of these concerns were raised in the draft resolutions that were co-sponsored by the state's delegation at the Nairobi Conference in 1985.

4. Ruth Caesar was also the head of the Committee on Gender Equity, Women, and Child Development in the National Transitional Legislative Assembly from 2003 to 2005.

Chapter 5

1. The report does not specify if this is non-partner-perpetrated violence.

Chapter 6

1. Ministère de la Femme, de la Famille, et de l'Enfant (MFFE).
2. Ministère de la Solidarité, de la Famille, de la Femme et de l'Enfant (MSFFE).

Chapter 7

1. Ministère de la Famille, de la Femme et des Affaires Sociales (MFFAS).

Appendix

1. One of these was a telephone interview with an individual who had served on the police force before the conflict.
2. I visted every police station in Monrovia and the sole police station in Gbarnga. There was an estimated 80 police officers stationed in Monrovia in 2010 and 2011.
3. Two of these were with individuals I had previously interviewed in-country.
4. A few survivors of intimate partner violence spoke a mixture of French and Dioula. My research assistant translated in these cases. Some UN personnel also spoke English or a mix of English and French.
5. Interviews with survivors of violence were in 2015; the male research assistant did not participate in any interviews with survivors of violence.
6. In one of the NGOs in Côte d'Ivoire, my contact was a medical doctor. In Abidjan, I met one survivor when she came to a police station, where I was conducting interviews, to report a rape. She was the only survivor not contacted through a counselor. She asked to speak with me mainly to voice her dissatisfaction with the police handling of her complaint.
7. I also relied on counselors and staff of these NGOs to contact focus group participants within the communities in which they worked, including some who had participated in the organizations' programs.

References

Abidjan.net. 2016, January 2. Message à la Nation de SEM Alassane Ouattara, Président de la République. Retrieved from http://news.abidjan.net/h/578320.html

Aboa, Ange. 2017, October 9. Aide to Ivory Coast Parliament Speaker Arrested over Arms Cache. Reuters. Retrieved from https://www.reuters.com/article/us-ivorycoast-arms/aide-to-ivory-coast-parliament-speaker-arrested-over-arms-cache-idUSKBN1CE2GI

Abrahams, Naeemah, Rachel Jewkes, Lorna J. Martin, Shanaaz Mathews, Lisa Vetten, & Carl Lombard. 2009. Mortality of Women from Intimate Partner Violence in South Africa: A National Epidemiological Study. *Violence and Victims*, 24(4), 546–556.

Acharya, Amitav. 2004. How Ideas Spread: Whose Norms Matter? Norm Localization and Institutional Change in Asian Regionalism. *International Organization*, 58(2), 239–275.

Ackerly, Brooke, & Jacqui True. 2010. *Doing Feminist Research in Political and Social Science*. New York: Palgrave Macmillan.

Adams, Monni. 2006. Inherited Rules and New Procedures in Three Trials in Canton Bo, Southwestern Côte d'Ivoire. *Anthropos*, 101(1), 9–19.

Adinkrah, Mensah 2011. Criminalizing Rape within Marriage: Perspectives of Ghanaian University Students. *International Journal of Offender Therapy and Comparative Criminology*, 55(6), 982–1010.

Adinkrah, Mensah. 2014. Intimate Partner Femicide-Suicides in Ghana: Victims, Offenders, and Incident Characteristics. *Violence against Women*, 20(9), 1078–1096.

Adjei, Stephen Baffour. 2016a. "Correcting an Erring Wife Is Normal": Moral Discourses of Spousal Violence in Ghana. *Journal of Interpersonal Violence*, 33(12), 1–22, doi: 10.1177/0886260515619751

Adjei, Stephen Baffour. 2016b. Masculinity and Spousal Violence: Discursive Accounts of Husbands Who Abuse Their Wives in Ghana. *Journal of Family Violence*, 31(4), 411–422.

Adomako Ampofo, Akosua. 2008. Collective Activism: The Domestic Violence Bill Becoming Law in Ghana. *African and Asian Studies Review*, 7, 395–421. doi: 10.1163/156921008X359597.

Adomako Ampofo, Akosua, & John Boateng. 2007. Multiple Meanings of Manhood among Boys in Ghana. In T. Shefer, K. Rataele, A. Strebel, N. Shabalala, & R. Buikema (Eds.), *From Boys to Men*, (50–74). Lansdowne: UCT Press.

Adomako Ampofo, Akosua, & Mansah Prah. 2009. "You may beat your wife, but not too much": The Cultural Context of Violence against Women in Ghana. In Kathy Cusack & Takyiwaa Manuh (Eds.), *The Architecture for Violence Against Women in Ghana* (93–128). Accra: Gender Research and Human Rights Documentation Centre.

Africa News. 2009, January 26. President Sirleaf's Annual Message Part 2. Retrieved from http://www.africanews.com/site/list_messages/22858

African Women and Peace Support Group. 2004. *Liberian Women Fighting for the Right to Be Seen, Heard and Counted*. Trenton, NJ: Africa World Press.

REFERENCES

Akpan, M. B. 1973. Black Imperialism: Americo-Liberian Rule over the African Peoples of Liberia, 1841–1964. *Canadian Journal of African Studies*, 7(2), 217–236.

Alemika, Etannibi E. O. 2009. Police Practice and Police Research in Africa. *Police Practice and Research*, 10(5–6), 483–502.

allAfrica. 2002. Female Lawyers Get Patent to Prosecute Rape Cases. Retreived from https://allafrica.com/stories/200011160027.html

allAfrica. 2006. Text of Inaugaural Address by President Ellen Johnson of Liberia. Retrieved from https://allafrica.com/stories/200601170106.html

Amoakohene, Margaret Ivy. 2004. Violence against Women in Ghana: A Look at Women's Perceptions and Review of Policy and Social Responses. *Social Science & Medicine*, 59, 2373–2385.

Amnesty International. 2004. Liberia Recommendations to the International Reconstruction Conference, New York, February 5–6, 2004.

Amnesty International. 2010. *"I Can't Afford Justice": Violence against Women in Uganda Continues Unchecked and Unpunished*. London: Amnesty International.

Amnesty International. 2013. *Côte d'Ivoire: The Victor's Law*. London: Amnesty International.

Anderson, E. R. 1952. *Liberia: America's African Friend*. Chapel Hill: University of North Carolina Press.

Anderson, Dacvid M., & Julianne Weis. 2018. The Prosecution of Rape in Wartime: Evidence from the Mau Mau Rebellion, Kenya 1952–50. *Law and History Review*, 36(2), 267–294.

Annan, Jeannie, & Moriah Brier. 2010. The Risk of Return: Intimate Partner Violence in Northern Uganda's Armed Conflict. *Social Science & Medicine*, 70, 152–159.

Anyidoho, Nana Akua, & Gordon Crawford. 2013. Ghana: Struggles for Rights in a Democratizing Context. In Bard A. Andreassen, & Gordon Crawford (Eds.), *Human Rights, Power and Civic Action: Comparative Analyses of Struggles for Rights in Developing Societies* (88–119). London: Routledge.

Anyidoho, Nana Akua, Gordon Crawford, & Peace A. Medie. 2020. The Role of Women's Movements in the Implementation of Gender-Based Violence Laws. *Politics & Gender*, early view.

Armah-Attoh, Daniel, E. Gyimah-Boadi, & Annie Barbara Chikwanha. 2007. Corruption and Institutional Trust in Africa: Implications for Democratic Development. Afrobarometer Working Paper No. 81.

Assepo, Eugène Assi. 2000. Les modes extrajudiciaires de règlement des litiges en Côte d'Ivoire. *Law and Politics in Africa, Asia and Latin America*, 33(3), 304–332.

Avdeyeva, Olga A. 2015. *Defending Women's Rights in Europe: Gender Equality and EU Enlargement*. Albany: State University of New York Press.

Ayeni, Victor Oluwasina. 2016. Introduction and Preliminary Interview. In V. Ayeni (Ed.), *The Impact of the African Charter and the Maputo Protocol in Selected African States* (1–16). Pretoria: Pretoria University Press.

Bacon, Laura. 2012. Building an Inclusive, Responsive, National Police Service: Gender-sensitive Reform in Liberia, 2005–2011. *Innovations for Successful Societies*. http://successfulsocieties.princeton.edu/sites/successfulsocieties/files/Policy_Note_ID19 1.pdf

Badmus, Isiaka Alani. 2009. Explaining Women's Roles in the West African Tragic Triplet: Sierra Leone, Liberia, and Cote d'Ivoire in Comparative Perspective. *Journal of Alternative Perspectives in the Social Sciences*, 1(3), 808–839.

REFERENCES 211

Bah, Abu Bakarr. 2010. Democracy and Civil War: Citizenship and Peacemaking in Côte d'Ivoire. *African Affairs, 109*, 437.

Banda, Fareda. 2006. Blazing a Trail: The African Protocol on Women's Rights Comes into Force. *Journal of African Law, 50*(1), 72–84.

Barnett, Jessica Penwell, Eleanor Maticka-Tyndale, & Trocaire Kenya. 2016. Stigma as Social Control: Gender-Based Violence Stigma, Life Chances, and Moral Order in Kenya. *Social Problems, 0*, 1–16. doi: 10.1093/socpro/spw012

Basu, Soumita. 2016. The Global South Writes 1325 (too). *International Political Science Review, 37*(3), 362–374.

Bavier, Joe. 2017. Army Mutiny Exposes Cracks in Ivory Coast Success Story. Reuters. Retrieved from https://www.reuters.com/article/us-ivorycoast-military-analysis/army-mutiny-exposes-cracks-in-ivory-coast-success-story-idUSKBN15326E

Berkeley Human Rights Center. 2015. *The Long Road: Accountability for Sexual Violence in Conflict and Post-Conflict Settings*. Berkeley, CA: Berkeley Human Rights Center.

Betts, Alexander, & Phil Richard. 2014. *Implementation and World Politics: How International Norms Change Practice*. Oxford: Oxford University Press.

Bevacqua, Maria. 2000. *Rape on the Public Agenda: Feminism and the Politics of Sexual Assault*. Evanston: Northeastern University Press.

Björkdahl, Annika. 2002. Norms in International Relations: Some Conceptual and Methodological Reflections. *Cambridge Review of International Affairs, 15*(1), 9–23.

Blay-Tofey, Morkeh, & Bandy X. Lee. 2015. Preventing Gender-Based Violence Engendered by Conflict: The Case of Cote d'Ivoire. *Social Science & Medicine, 146*, 341–347.

Bledsoe, Caroline. 1976. Women's Marital Strategies among the Kpelle of Liberia. *Journal of Anthropological Research, 32*(4), 372–389.

Bledsoe, Caroline. 1984. The Political Use of Sande Ideology and Symbolism. *American Ethnologist, 11*(3), 455–472.

Boakye, Kofi E. 2009. Culture and Nondisclosure of Child Sexual Abuse in Ghana: A Theoretical and Empirical Exploration. *Law & Social Inquiry, 34*(4), 951–979.

Bond, Johanna E. 2014. CEDAW in Sub-Saharan Africa: Lessons in Implementation. *Michigan State Law Review, 2*, 241–263.

Boneparth, Ellen, & Emily Stoper. 1988. *Women, Power and Policy: Toward the Year 2000* (2nd ed.). New York: Pergamon Press.

Boutellis, Arthur. 2011. *The Security Sector in Côte d'Ivoire: A Source of Conflict and a Key to Peace*. New York: International Peace Institute.

Bovcon, Maja. 2014. The Progress in Establishing the Rule of Law in Côte d'Ivoire under Ouattara's Presidency. *Canadian Journal of African Studies, 48*(2), 185–202.

Brehm, John, & Scott Gates. 1997. *Working, Shirking, and Sabotage: Bureaucratic Response to a Democratic Public*. Ann Arbor: University of Michigan Press.

Brewer, Gene A. 2005. In the Eye of the Storm: Frontline Supervisors and Federal Agency Performance. *Journal of Public Administration Research and Theory, 15*(4), 505–527.

British Broadcasting Corporation (BBC). 2011. Cote d'Ivoire: Pro-Gbagbo Women Group Stage Sit In at UN Military Base. Retrieved from lexisnexis.com.

Brown, G. W. 2014. Norm Diffusion and Health System Strengthening: The Persistent Relevance of National Leadership in Global Health Governance. *Review of International Studies, 40*(5), 877–896.

Buchanan, Allen, & Robert O. Keohane. 2006. The Legitimacy of Global Governance Institutions. *Ethics & International Affairs, 20*(4), 405–437.

Busby, Joshua William. 2007. Bono Made Jesse Helms Cry: Jubilee 2000, Debt Relief, and Moral Action in International Politics. *International Studies Quarterly, 51*, 247–275.

Cardenas, Sonia. 2007. *Conflict and Compliance: State Responses to International Human Rights Pressure.* Philadelphia: University of Pennsylvania Press.

Cardoso, L. F., J. Gupta, S. Shuman, H. Cole, D. Kpebo, & K. L. Falb. 2016. What Factors Contribute to Intimate Partner Violence against Women in Urban, Conflict-Affected Settings? Qualitative Findings from Abidjan, Côte d'Ivoire. *Journal of Urban Health: Bulletin of the New York Academy of Medicine, 93*(2), 364–378.

Carlson, Sharon. 2005. *Contesting and Reinforcing Patriarchy: An Analysis of Domestic Violence in the Dzaleka Refugee Camp.* Oxford: Refugee Studies Centre.

Carpenter, Charli R. 2006. Recognizing Gender-Based Violence against Civilian Men and Boys in Conflict Situations. *Security Dialogue, 37*(1), 83–103.

De Carvalho, Benjamin, & Schia Niels Negelhus. 2009. *The Protection of Women and Children in Liberia.* NUPI Policy Brief. Retrieved from https://www.files.ethz.ch/isn/117409/PB-01-09-de%20Carvalho-Schia-1.pdf

Cohen, Dara Kay. 2013. Explaining Rape during Civil War: Cross-National Evidence (1980–2009). *American Political Science Review, 107*(3), 461–477.

Cohen, Dara Kay, & Ragnhild Nordås. 2014. Sexual Violence in Armed Conflict: Introducing the SVAC Dataset, 1989–2009. *Journal of Peace Research, 51*(3), 418–428.

Cohn, Carol. 2003. Mainstreaming Gender in UN Security Policy: A Path to Political Transformation? Working Paper no. 204, Boston Consortium on Gender, Security and Human Rights.

Committee on the Elimination of Violence against Women. 1992. General Recommendation 19. Retrieved from https://tbinternet.ohchr.org/Treaties/CEDAW/Shared%20Documents/1_Global/INT_CEDAW_GEC_3731_E.pdf

Commonwealth of Liberia. 1824. Statute of Laws of the Commonwealth of Liberia, and Plan of Civil Government. Retrieved from http://hydrastg.library.cornell.edu/fedora/objects/liber:007/datastreams/pdf/content

Cortell, Andrew P., & James W Davis. 2000. Understanding the Domestic Impact of International Norms: A Research Agenda. *International Studies Review, 2*(1), 65–87.

Committee on the Elimination of Discrimination against Women. 2010. Consideration of reports submitted by States Parties under Article 18 of the Convention on the Elimination of All Forms of Discrimination against Women. Combined initial to third periodic reports of States Parties: Côte d'Ivoire. Retrieved from https://undocs.org/en/CEDAW/C/CIV/1-3

Crafty, K. F. T. 2011. Da Love There. On *Da Love There* [CD]. Monrovia, Liberia: H Avenue Records.

Crawford, Gordon, & Nana Akua Anyidoho. 2013. Ghana: Struggles for Rights in a Democratizing Context. In Bard A. Andreassen & Gordon Crawford (Eds.), *Human Rights, Power and Civic Action: Comparative Analyses of Struggles for Rights in Developing Societies* (88–119). London: Routledge.

Crook, Richard C. 1997. Winning Coalitions and Ethno-Regional Politics: The Failure of the Opposition in the 1990 and 1995 Elections in Côte d'Ivoire. *African Affairs, 96*(383), 215–242.

Daddieh, Cyril K. 2001. Elections and Ethnic Violence in Côte d'Ivoire: The Unfinished Business of Succession and Democratic Transition. *African Issues, 49*(1–2), 14–19.

Davies, Sara E., & Jacqui True. 2015. Reframing Conflict-Related Sexual and Gender-Based Violence: Bringing Gender Analysis Back in. *Security Dialogue*, 46(6), 495–512.

Davis-Roberts, Avery, & David J. Carroll. 2010. Using International Law to Assess Elections. *Democratization*, 17(3), 416–441.

Diabete, Henriette. 1975. *La Marche des Femmes sur Grand Bassam*. Abidjan.

Debusscher, Petra, & Maria Martin de Almagro. 2016. Post-Conflict Women's Movements in Turmoil: The Challenges of Success in Liberia in the 2005-aftermath. *The Journal of Modern African Studies*, 54(2), 293–316.

Deere, Carolyn. 2009. *The Implementation Game: The TRIPS Agreement and the Global Politics of Intellectual Property Reform in Developing Countries*. New York: Oxford University Press.

Doku, Teye David, & Kwaku Oppong Asante. 2015. Women's Approval of Domestic Physical Violence against Wives: Analysis of the Ghana Demographic and Health Survey. *BMC Women's Health*, 15(120), 1–8.

Dube, Jim. 2008. Resurrecting the Rule of Law in Liberia. *Maine Law Review*, 60(2), 575–586.

Dunkle, Kristin L., Rachel K. Jewkes, Heather C. Brown, Glenda E. Gray, James A. McIntryre, & Siobán D. Harlow. 2004. Gender-Based Violence, Relationship Power, and Risk of HIV Infection in Women Attending Antenatal Clinics in South Africa. *Lancet*, 363, 1415–1421.

Durevall, Dick, & Annika Lindskog. 2015. Intimate partner violence and HIV in Ten Sub-Saharan African Countries: What do the Demographic and Health Surveys Tell Us? *The Lancet Global Health*, 3(1), e34–e43.

Ellovich, Risa S. 1985. The Law and Ivoirian Women. *Anthropos*, 80(1–3), 185–197.

Emenike, E., S. Lawoko, & K. Dalal. 2008. Intimate Partner Violence and Reproductive Health of Women in Kenya. *International Nursing Review*, 55(1), 97–102.

Engwicht, Nina. 2018. The Local Translation of Global Norms: The Sierra Leonean Diamond Market. *Conflict, Security & Development*, 18(6), 463–492.

Falb, Kathryn L., Jeannie Annan, Denise Kpebo, & Jhumka Gupta. 2015. Reproductive Coercion and Intimate Partner Violence among Rural Women in Côte d'Ivoire: A Cross-Sectional Study. *African Journal of Reproductive Health*, 18(4), 61.

Fayemi, Kayode J. 2004. Governing Insecurity in Post-Conflict States: the Case of Sierra Leone and Liberia. In Alan Bryden & Heiner Hänggi (Eds.), *Reform and Reconstruction of the Security Sector*. London: Transaction Publishers.

FIND On New Code For Gang Rape. 2005, 14 September. *The Analyst*. Retrieved from https://allafrica.com/stories/200509140360.html

Fisher, B. S., L. E. Daigle, F. T. Cullen, & M. G. Turner. 2003. Reporting Sexual Victimization to the Police and Others: Results from a National-Level Study of College Women. *Criminal Justice and Behavior*, 30(1), 6–38.

Fleischman, J. 1993. An Uncivil War. *Africa Report*, 38(3), 56.

Fuest, V. 2008a. Liberia's Women Acting for Peace: Collective Action in a War-Affected Country. In Ellis Stephen & Ineke van Kessel (Eds.), *Movers and Shakers: Social Movements in Africa*. Boston: Brill.

Fuest, Veronika. 2008b. This Is the Time to Get in Front: Changing Roles and Opportunities for Women in Liberia. *African Affairs*, 107(427), 201–224.

Gawaya, Rose, & Rosemary Semafumu Mukasa. 2005. The African Women's Protocol: A New Dimension for Women's Rights in Africa. *Gender and Development*, 13(3), 42–50.

Geneva Centre for the Democratic Control of Armed Forces. 2011. *Côte d'Ivoire*. Geneva: Geneva Centre for the Democratic Control of Armed Forces.

George, Alexander, & Andrew Bennett. 2005. *Case Studies and Theory Development in the Social Sciences*. Cambridge, MA: MIT Press.

Gibbs, James L. 1960. *Some Judicial Implications of Marital Instability among the Kpelle*. Unpublished doctoral dissertation, Harvard University.

Gifford, Paul. 1993. *Christianity and Politics in Doe's Liberia*. New York: Cambridge University Press.

Ginty, Roger Mac, & Oliver P. Richmond. 2013. The Local Turn in Peace Building: A Critical Agenda for Peace. *Third World Quarterly, 34*(5), 763–783.

Global News Network: Liberia. 2016, July 28. Secret Societies Implicated as Liberia Passes Domestic Violence Bill without FGM Ban. Retrieved from http://gnnliberia.com/2016/07/28/secret-societies-implicated-liberia-passes-domestic-violence-bill-without-fgm-ban/

Global News Network. 2016a, July 28. Lack of FGM Ban in Domestic Violence Law Fails Liberia's Girls, Activists Say. Retrieved from http://gnnliberia.com/2016/07/28/lack-fgm-ban-domestic-violence-law-fails-liberias-girls-activists-say/

Government, Women's Groups Decry Post-War Sexual Violence. 2007, January 15. Africa News. Retrieved from www.lexisnexis.com.

Green, December. 1999. *Gender Violence in Africa: African Women's Responses*. New York: St. Martin's Press.

Grimm, Sonja, & Brigitte Weiffen. 2018. Domestic Elites and External Actors in Post-Conflict Democratisation: Mapping Interactions and their Impact. *Conflict, Security & Development, 18*(4), 257–282.

Gqola, Pumla Dineo. 2007. How the 'Cult of Femininity' and Violent Masculinities Support Endemic Gender Based Violence in Contemporary South Africa. *African Identities, 5*(1), 111–124.

Hautzinger, Sarah. 2002. Criminalising Male Violence in Brazil's Women's Police Stations: From Flawed Essentialism to Imagined Communities. *Journal of Gender Studies, 11*(3), 243–251.

Henries, Banks A. D. 1974. *Women and Girls in Higher Education in Liberia*. Monrovia: Ministry of Education.

Hillebrecht, Courtney. 2012. Implementing International Human Rights Law at Home: Domestic Politics and the European Court of Human Rights. *Human Rights Review, 13*, 279–301

Hills, Alice. 2016. Does Police Work Need a Police Institution? The Evidence from Mogadishu. *Policing and Society: An International Journal of Research and Policy, 26*(4), 393–410.

Hills, Alice. 2008. The Dialetic of Police Reform in Nigeria. *The Journal of Modern African Studies, 46*(2), 215–234.

Horn, Rebecca, Eve S. Puffer, Elisabeth Roesch, & Heidi Lehmann. 2014. Women's Perceptions of Effects of War on Intimate Partner Violence and Gender Roles in Two Post-Conflict West African Countries: Consequences and Unexpected Opportunities. *Conflict and Health, 8*(12). 1–14.

Horn, Rebecca, Eve S. Puffer, Elisabeth Roesch, & Heidi Lehmann. 2015. 'I don't Need an Eye for an Eye': Women's Responses to Intimate Partner Violence in Sierra Leone and Liberia. *Global Public Health: An International Journal for Research, Policy and Practice, 11*(1–2), 108–121.

Hossain, Mazeda, Cathy Zimmerman, Ligia Kiss, Drissa Kone, Monika Bakayoko-Topolska, David K. A. Manan, Heidi Lehmann, & Charlotte Watts. 2014. Men's and Women's Experiences of Violence and Traumatic Events in Rural Côte d'Ivoire before, during and after a Period of Armed Conflict. *BMJ Open, 4,* 1–9.

Hudson, Heidi. 2009. Peacebuilding Through a Gender Lens and the Challenges of Implementation in Rwanda and Côte d'Ivoire. *Security Studies, 18*(2), 287–318.

Huelss, Hendrick. 2017. After Decision-Making: The Operationalization of Norms in International Relations. *International Theory, 9*(3), 381–409.

Human Rights Watch. 2010. Afraid and Forgotten Lawlessness, Rape, and Impunity in Western Côte d'Ivoire. Retrieved from https://www.hrw.org/report/2010/10/22/afraid-and-forgotten/lawlessness-rape-and-impunity-western-cote-divoire

Human Rights Watch. 2011. *"They Killed Them Like It Was Nothing": The Need for Justice for Côte d'Ivoire's Post-Election Crimes.* Human Rights Watch. Retrieved from https://www.hrw.org/report/2011/10/05/they-killed-them-it-was-nothing/need-justice-cote-divoires-post-election-crimes

Human Rights Watch. 2013. *"No Money, No Justice": Police Corruption and Abuse in Liberia.* Human Rights Watch. Retrieved from https://www.hrw.org/report/2013/08/22/no-money-no-justice/police-corruption-and-abuse-liberia

Htun, Mala, & Laurel Weldon. 2012. The Civic Origins of Progressive Policy Change: Combating Violence against Women in Global Perspective, 1975–2005. *American Political Science Review, 106*(3), 548–569.

Innovation for Successful Societies Oral History Program. 2008a. Joseph Kekula. Innovation for Successful Societies, Princeton University.

Innovation for Successful Societies Oral History Program. 2008b. Kaki Fakondo. Innovation for Successful Societies, Princeton University.

Innovation for Successful Societies Oral History Program. 2008c. Mohamed Idris. Innovation for Successful Societies, Princeton University.

Innovation for Successful Societies Oral History Program. 2008d. Paavani Reddy. Innovation for Successful Societies, Princeton University.

Institut National de la Statistique (INS) & ICF International. 2012. Enquête Démographique et de Santé et à Indicateurs Multiples de Côte d'Ivoire 2011–2012. Maryland: INS and ICF International.

Interpeace. 2015. *Obstacles à la Cohésion Sociale et Dynamiques de Violence Impliquant les Jeunes dans l'Espace Urbain.* Abidjan: Interpeace.

International Crisis Group. 2006. *Liberia: Resurrecting the Justice System.* Crisis Group Africa Report No. 107.

International Rescue Committee. 2011. *International Rescue Committee Côte d'Ivoire Program: Emergency Response.* International Rescue Committee.

Interview, Joseph Kekula, Monrovia, May 14, 2008, Innovations for Successful Societies.

Interview, Paavani Reddy, Monrovia, May 17, 2008, Innovations for Successful Societies.

Interview, Peter F. Zaizay, Monrovia, May 12, 2008, Innovations for Successful Societies.

IRIN. 2012. Fighting gender-based violence in Sierra Leone. Retrieved from https://www.refworld.org/docid/527ce18d4.html

IRIN. 1999. Liberia: Special Report on the Challenges Ahead. Retrieved from http://www.africa.upenn.edu/Newsletters/irinw_9999c.html

IRIN. 2008. Special Court for Sexual Violence Underway. Retrieved from http://www.thenewhumanitarian.org/report/77406/liberia-special-court-sexual-violence-underway

Isser, Deborah H., Stephen C. Lubkemann, & Saah N'Tow. 2009. Looking for Justice: Liberian Experiences with and perceptions of Local Justice Options. *Peaceworks*, 63. Washington, DC: US Institute of Peace.

It Is Time for Peace. 1990, June 8. *Daily Observer*, pp. 1, 6. Copy in possession of author.

Ivković, Sanja Kutnjak, & Adri Sauerman. 2015. Threading the Thin Blue Line: Transition Towards Democratic Policing and the Integrity of the South African Police Service. *Policing and Society: An International Journal of Research and Policy*, 25(1), 25–52.

Jeune Afrique. 2017, October 3. Côte d'Ivoire: Nouvelles manifestations d'anciens rebelles démobilisés à Man et Bouaké. Retrieved from https://www.jeuneafrique.com/479799/politique/cote-divoire-nouvelles-manifestations-danciens-rebelles-demobilises-a-man-et-bouake/

Jewkes, Rachel, Loveday Penn-Kekana, & Hetty Rose-Junius. 2005. "If They Rape Me, I Can't Blame Them": Reflections on Gender in the Social Context of Child Rape in South Africa and Namibia. *Social Science & Medicine*, 61, 1809–1820.

Jewkes, Rachel. 2002. Intimate Partner Violence: Causes and prevention. *The Lancet*, 359(9315), 1423–1429.

Joachim, Jutta M. 2007. *Agenda Setting, the UN, and NGOs: Gender Violence and Reproductive Rights*. Washington, DC: Georgetown University Press.

Johnson, Bettie. 2015, April 12. Liberian Police Chief Stresses Zero Tolerance for Rape. *Front Page Africa*. Retrieved from https://allafrica.com/stories/201504021498.html

Johnson, Kirsten, Jana Asher, Stephanie Rosborough, et al. 2008. Association of Combatant Status and Sexual Violence with Health and Mental Health Outcomes in Postconflict Liberia. *300* (6), 676–690.

Kang, Alice J. 2015. *Bargaining for Women's Rights: Activism in an Aspiring Muslim Democracy*. University of Minnesota Press.

Kang, Alice J., & Aili Mari Tripp. 2018. Coalitions Matter: Citizenship, Women, and Quota Adoption in Africa. *Perspectives on Politics*, 16(1), 73–91.

Kaye, Dan K., Florence M. Mirembe, Grace Bantebya, Annika Johansson, & Anna Mia Ekstrom. 2006. Domestic Violence as Risk Factor for Unwanted Pregnancy and Induced Abortion in Mulago Hospital, Kampala, Uganda. *Tropical Medicine and International Health*, 11(1), 90–101.

Kofi Annan Institute for Conflict Transformation. 2011. *FAQs on Rape and the Revised Rape Law*. Monrovia, Liberia.

Keck, Margeret, & Kathryn Sikkink. 1998. *Activists beyond Borders: Advocacy Networks in International Politics*. Ithaca, NY: Cornell University Press.

Keiser, Lael R. 1999. State Bureaucratic Discretion and the Administration of Social Welfare Programs: The Case of Social Security Disability. *Journal of Public Administration Research and Theory*, 9(1), 87–106.

Keiser, Lael R., & Joe Soss. 1998. With Good Cause: Bureaucratic Discretion and the Politics of Child Support Enforcement. *American Journal of Political Science*, 42(4), 1133–1156.

Kposowa, Augustine J., & Dina Aly Ezzat. 2016. Religiosity, Conservatism, and Acceptability of Anti-Female Spousal Violence in Egypt. *Journal of Interpersonal Violence*, 34(12), 2525–2550.

Kumar, Krishna. (Ed.). 2001. *Women and Civil War: Impact, Organizations, and Action*. London: Lynne Rienner.

Leboeuf, Aline. 2016. *La Réforme du Secteur de Sécurité à l'Ivoirienne*. Institut Francais de Relations Internationales.

Liberia Institute of Statistics and Geo-Information Services (LISGIS) [Liberia], Ministry of Health and Social Welfare [Liberia], National AIDS Control Program [Liberia], and Macro International Inc. 2008. *Liberia Demographic and Health Survey 2007.* Monrovia: Liberia Institute of Statistics and Geo-Information Services (LISGIS) and Macro International Inc.

Liberia's Judiciary must be Strengthened to Stamp Out Rape and Other Crimes: UN Expert. 2006. States News Service. Retrieved from lexisnexis.com.

Liberian Women Recommend Severe Punishment for Rapists. 2004, May 21. The Inquirer Newspaper. Retrieved from https://allafrica.com/stories/200405210637.html

Lin, Ann Chih. 2000. *Reform in the Making: The Making of Social Policy in Prison.* Princeton, NJ: Princeton University Press.

Mahoney, James. 2007. Qualitative Methodology and Comparative Politics. *Comparative Political Studies, 40*(2), 122–144.

Malan, M. 2008. *Security Sector Reform in Liberia: Mixed Results from Humble Beginnings.* Strategic Studies Institute. Retrieved from http://www.strategicstudiesinstitute.army.mil/pdffiles/pub855.pdf

Mama, Amina. 1995. Feminism or Femocracy: State Feminism and Democratisation in Nigeria. *Africa Development, 20*(1), 37–58.

Martin, Patricia Yancey. 2005. *Rape Work: Victims, Gender, and Emotions in Organization and Community Context.* New York: Routledge.

Massaquoi, Williams N. 2007. Women and Post-Conflict Development. A Case Study on Liberia. Unpublished masters thesis, Massuchusetts Institutte of Technology.

Mathews, Shanaaz, Rachel Jewkes, & Naeemah Abrahams. 2014. 'So I'm Now the Man': Intimate Partner Femicide and its Interconnections with Expressions of Masculinities in South Africa. *British Journal of Criminology, 55*(1), 107–124.

Mayamba, Thierry Nlandu. 2013. Building a Police Force "for the Good" in DR Congo: Questions That Still Haunt Reformers and Reform Beneficiaries. The Nordic Africa Institute. Retrieved from http://www.diva-portal.org/smash/get/diva2:689701/FULLTEXT01.pdf

Maynard-Moody, Steven, & Michael Musheno. 2003. *Cops, Teachers and Counselors: Narratives of Street-Level Judgment.* Ann Arbor: University of Michigan Press.

McAllister, A. 1896. *A Lone Woman in Africa: Six Years on the Kru Coast.* New York: Eaton & Mains.

Medie, Peace A. 2013. Fighting Gender-Based Violence: The Women's Movement and the Enforcement of Rape Law in Liberia. *African Affairs, 112*(448), 377–397.

Medie, Peace A. 2012. *Police Behavior in Post-Conflict States: Explaining Variation in Police Responses to Domestic Violence, Internal Human Trafficking, and Rape.* Unpublished dissertation, University of Pittsburgh.

Medie, Peace A. 2017. Rape Reporting in Post-Conflict Côte d'Ivoire: Accessing Justice and Ending Impunity. *African Affairs, 116*(464), 414–434.

Medie, Peace A. 2015. Women and Postconflict Security: A Study of Police Response to Domestic Violence in Liberia. *Politics & Gender, 11* (3), 478–498.

Medie, Peace A. 2019. Women and Violence in Africa. *Oxford Research Encyclopedia of African History, pp. 1–21.* Oxford: Oxford University Press.

Medie, Peace A., & Alice J. Kang. 2018. Power, Knowledge and the Politics of Gender in the Global South. *European Journal of Politics and Gender, 1*(1–2), 37–53.

Medie, Peace A., & Shannon Drysdale Walsh. 2019. International Organizations, Nongovernmental Organizations, and Police Implementation of Domestic Violence Policies in Liberia and Nicaragua. *Politics & Gender*, early view.

Meger, Sara. 2016. *Rape Loot Pillage: The Political Economy of Sexual Violence in Armed Conflict*. New York: Oxford University Press.

Merry, Sally Engle. 2006. *Human Rights and Gender Violence: Translating International Law into Local Justice*. Chicago: University of Chicago Press.

Meyers, Marcia K., & Susan Vorsanger. 2007. Street-Level Bureaucrats and the Implementation of Public Policy. In B. Guy Peters and Jon Pierre (Eds.), *Handbook of Public Administration* (153–163). London: Sage Publications.

Mills, D. 1926. *Through Liberia, by Lady Dorothy Mills*. London: Duckworth.

Mills, E. J., S. Singh, B. Nelson, & J. B. Nachega. 2006. The Impact of Conflict on HIV/AIDS in Sub-Saharan Africa. *International Journal of STD & AIDS*, 17(11), 713–717.

Ministere de la Famille, de la Femma, et de l'Enfant [MSFFE]. 2005. *Beijing + 5*. Abidjan: Ministere de la Famille, de la Femma, et de l'Enfant.

Ministere de la Famille, de la Femma, et de l'Enfant [MSFFE]. 2014. *National Strategy to Combat Gender-Based Violence*. Abidjan: Ministere de la Famille, de la Femma, et de l'Enfant.

Moffett, Helen. 2006. "These Women, They Force Us to Rape Them": Rape as Narrative of Social Control in Post-Apartheid South Africa. *Journal of Southern African Studies*, 1, 129–144.

Montoya, Celeste. 2009. International Initiative and Domestic Reforms: European Union Efforts to Combat Violence against Women. *Politics & Gender*, 5(3), 325–348.

Montoya, Celeste 2013. *From Global to Grassroots: The European Union, Transnational Advocacy, and Combating Violence against Women*. New York: Oxford University Press.

Moore, Gina. 2010, October 10. Liberia's "Rape Court": Progress for Women and Girls Delayed? *The Christian Science Monitor*. https://www.csmonitor.com/World/Africa/Africa-Monitor/2010/1010/Liberia-s-Rape-Court-Progress-for-women-and-girls-delayed

Moran, Mary H. 1990. *Civilized Women: Gender and Prestige in Southeastern Liberia*. Ithaca, NY: Cornell University Press.

More Liberians Cross Borders. 1990, June 12. *Daily Observer*, p. x. Copy in possession of author.

Morris, J. B. 2005. *The Establishment of the Ministry of Gender and Development: A Case Study of the Changing Role of Women in Liberia*. Master's thesis. Retrieved from ProQuest Dissertations and Theses (1428541).

Morrison, Andrew, Mary Ellsberg, & Sarah Bott. 2007. Addressing Gender-Based Violence: A Critical Review of Interventions. *The World Bank Research Observer*, 22(1), 25–51.

Moussa, Sangaré. 2016. Genre et Reconstruction du Lien Social dans un Contexte Post-Crise: Une Illustration des Organisations Feminines dans des Milieux Ruraux de l'Ouest de la Côte d'Ivoire. *European Journal of Business and Social Sciences*, 5(1), 11–32.

Msibi, Thabo. 2009. Not Crossing the Line: Masculinities and Homophobic Violence in South Africa. *Agenda*, 23(80), 50–54.

Muganyizi, Projestine S., Charles Kilewo, & Candida Moshiro. 2004. Rape against Women: The Magnitude, Perpetrators and Patterns of Disclosure of Events in Dar es Salaam, Tanzania. *Africa Journal of Reproductive Health*, 8(3), 137–146.

Muhanguzi, Florence Kyoheirwe. 2011. Gender and Sexual Vulnerability of Young Women in Africa: Experiences of Young Girls in Secondary Schools in Uganda. *Culture, Health & Sexuality: An International Journal for Research, Intervention and Care*, 13(6), 713–725.

National Population Commission. 1988. *The National Policy on Population for Social and Economic Development, the Republic of Liberia*. Monrovia, Liberia: National Population Council.

National Transitional Government of Liberia. 2004. Joint Needs Assessment. Retrieved from http://www.cifor.org/publications/pdf_files/reports/assessment.pdf

NTLA Passes Rape Bill. 2005. *The Inquirer Newspaper*. Retrieved from https://allafrica.com/stories/200512020748.html

Nelson, Sarah. 1996. Constructing and Negotiating Gender in Women's Police Stations in Brazil. *Latin American Perspectives*, 23, 131–148.

Nobel Prize, The. 2011. *Leymah Gbowee Facts*. Retrieved from https://www.nobelprize.org/prizes/peace/2011/gbowee/facts/

Nwabunike, Collins, & Eric Y. Tenkorang. 2017. Domestic and Marital Violence among Three Ethnic Groups in Nigeria. *Journal of Interpersonal Violence*, 32(18), 2751–2776.

Okello, Moses Chrispus, & Lucy Hovil. 2007. Confronting the Reality of Gender-Based Violence in Northern Uganda. *International Journal of Transitional Justice*, 1(3), 433–443.

Okenwa, Leah, Stephen Lawoko, & Bjarne Jansson. 2011. Contraception, Reproductive Health and Pregnancy Outcomes among Women Exposed to Intimate Partner Violence in Nigeria. *The European Journal of Contraception and Reproductive Health Care*, 16(1), 18–25.

Olonisakin, 'Funmi. 2008. *Lessons Learned from an Assessment of Peacekeeping and Peace Support Operations in West Africa*. Accra, Ghana: Kofi Annan International Peacekeeping Training Center.

Olonisakin, 'Funmi & Cheryl Hendricks. 2013. Engaging (In)security as an Entry Point for Seeking Redress in Gender Inequality in Africa. *Africa Peace and Conflict Journal*, 6(1), 1–14.

Omanyondo, Marie-Claire O. 2004. *Sexual Gender-Based Violence and Health Facility Needs Assessment*. World Health Organization. Retrieved from https://www.who.int/hac/crises/lbr/Liberia_GBV_2004_FINAL.pdf

Orchard, Phil. 2014. Implementing a Global Internally Displaced Persons Protection Regime. In Alexander Betts & Phil Orchard (Eds.) *Implementation and World Politics: How International Norms Change Practice*. Oxford: Oxford University Press.

Oumar, Coulibaly Z. 2014, December 19. *Cote d'Ivoire: Police nationale—Des Organismes des Nations—Unies Aident à la Promotion du Genre*. Retrieved from https://fr.allafrica.com/stories/201412222385.html

Pailey, Robtel. 2014. Patriarchy, Power Distance and Female Presidency in Liberia. In B. Jallow (Ed.), *Leadership in Postcolonial Africa: Trends Transformed by Independence*, (169–188). New York: Palgrave Macmillan.

Paye-Layleh, Jonathan. 2002, May 9. Panicked, Wounded Civilians Flee as Fighting Surges in Liberia's 3-Year-Old Insurrection. *Associated Press*. Retrieved from lexisnexis.com.

Paye-Layleh, Jonathan. 2003, November 20. Women March to Demand Disarmament, End to Crimes against Women. *Associated Press International*. Retrieved from www.lexisnexis.com

Piccolino, Giulia. 2018. Peacebuilding and Statebuilding in Post – 2011 Cote d'Ivoire: A Victor's Peace? *African Affairs*, 117(468), 485–508.

Piron, Laure-Hélène. 2005. *Donor Assistance to Justice Sector Reform in Africa: Living Up to the New Agenda?* Open Society Justice Initiative.

Porter, Holly E. 2015. Mango Trees, Offices and Altars: The Role of Relatives, Non-governmental Organisations and Churches after Rape in Northern Uganda. *International Journal on Minority and Group Rights*, 22(3), 309–334.

Prah, Mansah. 2003. Chasing Illusions and Realising Visions: Reflections on Ghana's Feminist Experience. In Signe Arnfred, Babere Kerata Chacha, Amanda Gouws, Josephine Ahikire, Ayodele Ogundipe, Charmaine Pereira, Mansah Prah, Charles Ukeje, Felicia Arudo Yieke (Eds.), *Gender Studies and Activism in Africa*. Dakar: Council for the Development of Social Science Research in Africa.

Prügl, Elisabeth, & J. Ann Tickner. 2018. Feminist International Relations: Some Research Agendas for a World in Transition. *European Journal of Politics and Gender*, 1(1–2), 75–91.

Punish Rape, Sodomy Suspects—NACROG Executive. 2005, June 8. The Analyst. Retrieved from lexisnexis.com.

Rape Cases Must Claim the Attention of All. 2006, December 13. The Inquirer. Retrieved from www.lexisnexis.com.

Rape, Sexual Violence in Check. 2005, July 28. The Analyst. Retrieved from lexisnexis.com.

Raustiala, Kal. 2000. Compliance and Effectiveness in International Regulatory Cooperation. *Case Western Reserve Journal of International Law*, 32(3), 387–440.

Raustiala, Kal & Anne-Marie Slaughter. 2002. International Law, International Relations and Compliance. In W. Carlsnaes, T. Risse-Kappen, & B. Simmons (Eds.), *Handbook of International Relations* (538–558). London: Sage Publications.

Reliefweb. 2005, July 6. *Liberia: 6 July Press Brief*. The United Nations Mission in Liberia. Retrieved from https://reliefweb.int/report/liberia/liberia-6-july-press-brief-ms-joana-foster-unmil-senior-gender-adviser-hon-vaba

Reliefweb. 2006, March 8. *Liberia: When Sexual Violence Is a "Normal" Way of Life—Helping Victims, Educating Communities*. International Rescue Committee. Retrieved from https://reliefweb.int/report/liberia/liberia-when-sexual-violence-normal-way-life-helping-victims-educating-communities

Republic of Liberia. 1949. *Revised Laws and Administrative Regulations for Governing the Hinterland*. Copy in possession of author.

Risse, Thomas, & Stephen C. Ropp. 2013. Introduction and Overview. In T. Risse, S. Ropp, & K. Sikkink (Eds.), *The Persistent Power of Human Rights: From Commitment to Compliance* (3–25). New York: Cambridge University Press.

Roggeband, Conny. 2016. Ending Violence against Women in Latin America: Feminist Norm Setting in a Multilevel Context. *Politics & Gender*, 12(1), 143–167.

Salacuse, Jeswald J. 1969. *An Introduction to Law in French-Speaking Africa. Volume 1: Africa South of the Sahara*. Charlottesville: The Michie Company.

Santos, Cecilia MacDowell. 2004. En-gendering the Police: Women's Police Stations and Feminism in Sao Paolo. *Latin American Research Review*, 39(3), 29–55.

Santos, Cecilia MacDowell. 2005. *Women's Police Stations: Gender, Violence, and Justice in Brazil*. Basingstoke, UK: Palgrave Macmillan.

Schneider, Elizabeth M. 1991. The Violence of Privacy. *Connecticut Law Review*, 23, 973–999.

Schwab, G. (with G. W. Harley). 1947. *Tribes of the Liberian Hinterland: Report of the Peabody Museum Expedition to Liberia*. Cambridge, MA: Peabody Museum.

Sekre, Alphonse Gbodie. 2008. La Justice Indigene et la Consolidation de l'Autorite Coloniale en Cote d'Ivôire. *Rivista Trimestrale di Studie Documentazione dell'Istituto Italiano per l'Africa e l'Oriente*, 63(4), 638–657.

Senah, Gbatemah. 2016, July 15. President Sirleaf Threatens to Issue Executive Order on Domestic Violence Act. *The Bush Chicken*. Retrieved from https://www.bushchicken.com/president-sirleaf-threatens-to-issue-executive-order-on-domestic-violence-act/

Senah, Gbatemah. 2016a, July 25. Representatives Pass Domestic Violence Bill; FGM Ban Excluded. *The Bush Chicken*. Retrieved from https://www.bushchicken.com/representatives-pass-domestic-violence-bill-fgm-ban-excluded/

Sibley, J. L., & D. Westermann. 1928. *Liberia—Old and New: A Study of Its Social and Economic Background with Possibilities of Development*. London: James Clarke.

Simmons, Beth A. 2009. *Mobilizing for Human Rights: International Law in Domestic Politics*. New York: Cambridge University Press.

Solanke, Lukman Bola. 2016. Spousal Violence and Pregnancy Termination among Married Women in Nigeria. *African Health Sciences*, 16(2), 429–440.

Speed Up the Rape Bill. 2005, 18 November. *The Inquirer Newspaper*. Retrieved from https://allafrica.com/stories/200511200079.html

Stafford, Nancy Kaymar. 2007. Permission for Domestic Violence: Marital Rape in Ghanaian Marriages. *Women's Rights Law Reporter*, 29(2–3), 63–75.

Stark, Lindsay, Ann Warner, Heidi Lehmann1, Neil Boothby, & Alastair Ager. 2013. Measuring the Incidence and Reporting of Violence against Women and Girls in Liberia Using the "Neighborhood Method." *Conflict and Health*, 7(20), 1–9.

Steady, Filomina Chioma. 2011. *Women and Leadership in West Africa: Mothering the Nation and Humanizing the State*. New York: Palgrave Macmillan.

Stewart, T. M. 1886. *Liberia: The Americo-African Republic*. New York: E. O. Jenkins' Son.

Strong, R. P. (Ed.). 1930. *The African Republic of Liberia and the Belgian Congo. Based on the Observations Made and the Material Collected during the Harvard African Expedition 1926–1927*. Cambridge, MA: Harvard University Press.

Swiss, S., P. J. Jennings, G. V. Aryee, G. H. Brown, R. M. Jappah-Samukai, M. S. Kamara, R. D. Schaak, & R. S. Turay-Kanneh. 1998. Violence against Women during the Liberian Civil Conflict. *Journal of the American Medical Association*, 279(8), 625–629.

Tamale, Sylvia. 2001. Think Globally, Act Locally: Using International Treaties for Women's Empowerment in East Africa. *Agenda*, 50, 97–104.

Tankebe, Justice. 2008. Colonialism, Legitimation and Policing in Ghana. *International Journal of Law, Crime & Justice* 36(1), 67–84.

Tankebe, Justice. 2013. In Search of Moral Recognition? Policing and Eudemonic Legitimacy in Ghana. *Law & Social Enquiry*, 38(3), 576–597.

Tauxier, Louis. 1932. *Réligion, Moeurs, et Coutumes des Agnis de la Côte-d'Ivoire (Indenié et Sanwi)*. Paris: Paul Geuthner.

Tenkorang, Eric Y., Adobea Y. Owusu, Eric H. Yeboah, & Richard Bannerman. 2013. Factors Influencing Domestic and Marital Violence against Women in Ghana. *Journal of Family Violence*, 281, 771–781.

Tholens, S., & L. Groß. 2015. Diffusion, Contestation and Localisation in Post-War States: 20 Years of Western Balkans Reconstruction. *Journal of International Relations and Development, 18*, 249–264.

Toby, Peter M. 2010, August 31. Liberia: Lawyers Denounce Rape Laws as Unjust. *New Democrat*. Retrieved from https://allafrica.com/stories/201008310721.html

Toungara, Jeanne Maddox. 1994. Inventing the African Family: Gender and Family Law Reform in Cote d'Ivoire. *Journal of Social History, 28*(1), 37–61.

Treib, Oiliver. 2014. Implementing and Complying with EU Governance Output. *Living Reviews in European Governance, 9*(1), 1–47.

Tripp, Aili Mari. 2001. The Politics of Autonomy and Cooptation in Africa: The Case of the Ugandan Women's Movement. *Journal of Modern African Studies, 39*(1), 101–128.

Tripp, Aili Mari. 2010. Legislating Gender-Based Violence in Post-Conflict Africa. *Journal of Peacebuilding and Development, 3*(5), 7–20.

Tripp, Aili Mari. 2015. *Women and Power in Post-Ponflict Africa*. New York: Cambridge University Press.

Tripp, Aili Mari, Isabel Casimiro, Joy Kwesiga, & Alice Mungwa. 2009. *African Women's Movements: Transforming Political Landscapes*. New York: Cambridge University Press.

Tseblis, George. 2002. *Veto Players: How Political Institutions Work*. Princeton, NJ: Princeton University Press.

Tsikata, Dzodzi. 2009. Women's Organizing in Ghana since the 1990s: From Individual Organizations to Three Coalitions. *Development, 52*, 185–192. doi: 10.1057/dev.2009.8

Turshen, Meredeth, & Clotilde Twagiramariya (eds.). 1998. *What Women do in Wartime: Gender and Conflict in Africa*. London: Zed Books.

UC Berkeley School of Law. 2015. The Long Road: Accountability for Sexual Violence in Conflict and Post-Conflict Settings. Human Rights Center. Retrieved from https://www.law.berkeley.edu/wp-content/uploads/2015/04/The-Long-Road-August-2015.pdf

Umubyeyi, Aline, Margareta Persson, Ingrid Mogren, & Gunilla Krantz. 2016. Gender Inequality Prevents Abused Women from Seeking Care Despite Protection Given in Gender-Based Violence Legislation: A Qualitative Study from Rwanda. *PLOS* https://doi.org/10.1371/journal.pone.0154540

United Nations (UN). 1986. *Report of the World Conference to Review and Appraise the Achievements of the United Nations Decade for Women: Equality, Development and Peace*. United Nations Publication A/Conf. 116/28/Rev.1.

United Nations (UN). 2012. Statement by the Special Representative of the Secretary-General on Sexual Violence in Conflict Margot Wallström, https://www.un.org/sexualviolenceinconflict/wp-content/uploads/2012/07/Statement-by-SRSG-on-Côte-dIvoire-26-January-2011.pdf.

United Nations Economic and Social Council (UNESC). 1995. *Monitoring the Implementation of the Nairobi Forward Looking Strategies for the Advancement of Women*. E/CN.6/1995/3/Add.4.

United Nations General Assembly. 1993. Declaration on the Elimination of Violence against Women. Retrieved from https://www.un.org/en/genocideprevention/documents/atrocity-crimes/Doc.21_declaration%20elimination%20vaw.pdf

United Nations High Commissioner for Refugees (UNHCR). 2001. *How to Guide: Sexual and Gender Based Violence Program in Liberia*. Retrieved from https://www.unhcr.org/3c4d6af24.pdf

United Nations Mission in Liberia (UNMIL). 2008. *Research on Prevalence and Attitudes to Rape in Liberia*. United Nations Mission in Liberia Legal and Judicial Support Division.

United Nations Mission in Liberia (UNMIL). n.d. Office of the Senior Gender Advisor. Retrieved from https://unmil.unmissions.org/office-senior-gender-adviser

United Nations News. 2014, January 27. *Security Sector Reform, National Reconciliation Needed in Côte d'Ivoire Ahead of 2015 Polls, UN Says*. Retrieved from https://news.un.org/en/story/2014/01/460582-security-sector-reform-national-reconciliation-needed-cote-divoire-ahead-2015#.WgWchracZ1P

United Nations News. 2016, May 31. *Côte d'Ivoire: UN Envoy Welcomes Progress Made in Addressing Sexual Violence Crimes*. Retrieved from https://news.un.org/en/story/2016/05/530852-cote-divoire-un-envoy-welcomes-progress-made-addressing-sexual-violence-crimes#.Wf7jszOcZ1O

United Nations Office on Drugs and Crime (UNODC). (2010). *Handbook on Effective Police Responses to Violence against Women*. New York: United Nations.

United Nations Office on Drugs and Crime (UNODC). 2018. *Global Study on Homicide: Gender-Related Killings of Girls and Women*. Vienna: UNODC.

United Nations Operation in Cote d'Ivoire (UNOCI). 2016, July 15. *Counselling Offices for Victims of Gender-Based Violence to be Opened Very Soon*. Retrieved from https://onuci.unmissions.org/en/counseling-offices-victims-gender-based-violence-be-opened-very-soon

United Nations Operation in Cote d'Ivoire (UNOCI). n.d. *Réforme du Secteur de la Sécurité (RSS)*. Retrieved from https://onuci.unmissions.org/réforme-du-secteur-de-la-sécurité-rss-0

United Nations Police (UNPOL). 2015. *Gender Toolkit: Standardized Best Practices on Gender Mainstreaming in Peacekeeping*. New York: United Nations.

United Nations Security Council (UNSC). 2000. Resolution 1325 (2000). Retrieved from http://unscr.com/en/resolutions/doc/1325

United Nations Security Council (UNSC). 2003a. *Report of the Secretary-General on the Situation in Liberia, Pursuant to the Letter Dated 29 November 2002 (S/2002/1305) from the President of the Security Council*. S/2003/227. Retrieved from http://www.un.org/ga/search/view_doc.asp?symbol=S/2003/227

United Nations Security Council (UNSC). 2003b. *Report of the Secretary-General to the Security Council on Liberia, September 11, 2003*. S/2003/875. Retrieved from http://www.un.org/ga/search/view_doc.asp?symbol=S/2003/875

United Nations Security Council (UNSC). 2003c. Resolution 1509 (2003). Retrieved from http://unscr.com/en/resolutions/doc/1509

United Nations Security Council (UNSC). 2005. Sixth progress report of the Secretary-General on the United Nations Mission in Liberia. Retrieved from http://www.un.org/en/ga/search/view_doc.asp?symbol=S/2005/177.

United Nations Security Council (UNSC). 2006. Thirteenth Progress Report of the Secretary-General on the United Nations Mission in Liberia. Retrieved from https://undocs.org/S/2006/958

United Nations Security Council (UNSC). 2012. Thirtieth progress report of the Secretary-General on the United Nations Operation in Côte d'Ivoire. Retrieved from https://www.securitycouncilreport.org/atf/cf/%7B65BFCF9B-6D27-4E9C-8CD3-CF6E4FF96FF9%7D/s_2012_506.pdf

United Nations Women. 2011. *2011–2012 Progress of the World's Women*. New York: United Nations Women.

United Nations Women. 2012. *Handbook for Legislation on Violence against Women*. New York: United Nations Women.

United Nations Women. 2015. *A Framework to Underpin Action to Prevent Violence against Women*. New York: United Nations Women.

UNMIL Raises Concerns About Judicial System. 2006, October 19. The Inquirer. Retrieved from www.lexisnexis.com.

Uthman, Olalekan, Stephen Lawoko, & Tahereh Moradi. 2010. Sex Disparities in Attitudes towards Intimate Partner Violence against Women in Sub-Saharan Africa: Socio-Ecological Analysis. *BMC Public Health, 10*, 223.

Visal, Claudine. 1977. Guerre des sexes à Abidjan: Masculin, féminin, CFA. *Cahiers d'Études Africaines, 17*(65), 121–153.

Vinck, Patrick, & Phuong N. Pham. 2013. Association of Exposure to Intimate-Partner Physical Violence and Potentially Traumatic War-Related Events with Mental Health in Liberia. *Social Science & Medicine, 77*(1), 4–49.

Walsh, Shannon Drysdale. 2015. *Transnational Advocacy Networks and Institution-Building: The Emergence of Women-Focused Policing Units*. Paper Presented at the Latin American Studies Association Conference.

Wambua, Pauline M. 2015. Police Corruption in Africa Undermines Trust, but Support for Law Enforcement Remains Strong. *Afrobarometer Dispatch* No. 56.

Waylen, Georgina. 2007. Women's Mobilization and Gender Outcomes in Transitions to Democracy: The Case of South Africa. *Comparative Political Studies, 40*(5), 521–546.

Weldon, Laurel. 2002. *Protest, Policy and the Problem of Violence against Women: A Cross-National Comparison*. Pittsburgh: University of Pittsburgh Press.

Wills, K. J. 1986, November 16. Rights Groups Depicts Army Abuses in Liberia. *New York Times*, p. 1.

Winter, Søren. (1990). Integrating implementation research. In Dennis J. Palumbo & Donald J. Calista (Eds.), *Implementation and the Policy Process*. New York: Greenwood Press.

Women and Children Protection Section. 2011. *Liberia National Police: Background*. Copy in possession of author.

Women and Children Protection Section. n.d.a *Women and Children Protector*. Copy in possession of author.

Women and Children Protection Unit. n.d.b *Training Manual: Investigation of Sexual Abuse and Exploitation in Liberia*. Copy in possession of author.

Women Decry Criminal Activities. 2004, January 20. The Inquirer Newspaper. Retrieved from https://allafrica.com/stories/200501200731.html

Wood, Jean Elisabeth. 2009. Armed Groups and Sexual Violence: When Is Wartime Rape Rare? *Politics & Society, 17*(1), 131–162.

World Health Organization. 2013. *Global and Regional Estimates of Violence against Women: Prevalence and Health Effects of Intimate Partner Violence and Non-Partner Sexual Violence*. Geneva: World Health Organization.

World Health Organization. 2009. Gender-based Violence, Health, and the Role of the Health Sector. Retrieved from http://siteresources.worldbank.org/INTPHAAG/Resources/AAGGBVHealth.pdf

Worzi, Alvin. 2017, August 15. Liberia: FGM Excluded from Domestic Violence Act. *Daily Observer*. Retrieved from https://allafrica.com/stories/201708190035.html

Zannettino, Lana. 2012. "... There is No War Here; It Is Only the Relationship That Makes Us Scared": Factors Having an Impact on Domestic Violence in Liberian Refugee Communities in South Australia. *Violence Against Women, 18*(7), 807–828.

Zavis, A. 1993, July 21. Day-Old Ceasefire Ends in Liberia. *Associated Press.* Retrieved from www.lexisnexis.com.

Zimmermann, Lisbeth. 2016. Same Same or Different? Norm Diffusion between Resistance, Compliance, and Localization in Post-conflict States. *International Studies Perspectives, 17*(1), 98–115.

Zimmermann, Lisbeth. 2017. More for Less: The Interactive Translation of Global Norms in Postconflict Guatemala. *International Studies Quarterly, 61*(4), 774–785.

Zwingel, Susanne. 2011. How Do Norms Travel? Theorizing International Women's Rights in Transnational Perspective. *International Studies Quarterly, 56*(1), 115–129.

Index

Note: Page numbers followed by *f* indicate a figure on the corresponding page. Page numbers followed by *t* indicate a table on the corresponding page.

For the benefit of digital users, indexed terms that span two pages (e.g., 52–53) may, on occasion, appear on only one of those pages.

Abaka, Charlotte, 149
Abidjan, 3–4, 9–10, 91, 93, 94–95, 96–97, 100, 103–6, 107, 116–18, 138–39, 180, 186
Abobo neighbourhood, 96–97, 100, 114–15, 141–42, 182
Abused Women and Girls Project in Monrovia, 60, 82
Accra III Peace Agreement (2004), 94
activism by women's movements. *See also* women's movements/organizations
criticism of, 112
government response to, 118–19
policy adoption and, 5–6, 26–27
in post-conflict countries, 31
specialized mechanisms and, 39
advocates for women's rights, 45–46, 61–62, 152
African Charter on Human and People's Rights on the Rights of Women in Africa (Maputo Protocol), 27–28
African Union (AU), 17–18
African Women Peace and Support Group (AWPSG), 79–80
aggravated assault. *See also* sexual violence
in marriage, 54–55
referral to court, 177–79
training of officers, 164–65, 172, 180, 184
Akan ethnic groups, 93
alcohol abuse and VAW, 22, 101
American Colonization Society, 54
America specialized policing, 6–7
Americo-Liberian rights, 54, 56–57, 58–59
Angola, patriarchal gender norms, 20–21
anti-democratic female power structure, 112
anti-GBV policy documents, 86
anti-VAW programs, 82–83, 153

Association of Female Lawyers of Côte d'Ivoire (AFJCI), 113, 115–16, 158
Association of Female Lawyers of Liberia (AFELL), 80–81, 84, 85, 86, 131, 153
Association of Ivoirian Women (AFI), 112
autonomous women's movements, 45–46, 129–30, 132–33, 143–44
awareness-raising of sexual violence
in post-conflict campaigns, 106
by United Nations, 126, 127, 139–40, 148–49, 156–57
by women's movements/organizations, 70, 82, 130, 141–42

Bah-Kenneh, Assatu, 133–34, 153
Bakayoko, Hamed, 140–41
Banks, Philip, 154
Bernard, Zeor, 85
bilateral trade and investment deals, 43–44
blacklisting of Côte d'Ivoire, 140–41, 144
Boryenneh, Elizabeth, 80–81
Bouaké, 3–4, 9–10, 91, 104–5, 106–8, 182, 186
Brazilian police force, 28–29
Brazil specialized policing, 6–7
breadwinner women, 60–61, 62
British colonial law, 30–31
Brownell, Mary, 79
Brutus, Lois Lewis, 131
Bryant, Charles Gyude, 61–62, 125–26, 128, 130–31, 133–34
Bureau d'Accueil Genre, 2–3

Caesar, Ruth, 82, 84, 130–31
capacity building by United Nations, 128, 157–58, 160–61

228 INDEX

Centre for Prevention and Assistance for Victims of Sexual Violence, 114
Christianity, 55, 110
Civil Code, Côte d'Ivoire (1964), 110
civil remedies, 25, 90–91
civil society organizations, 26–27, 44–45, 114, 115, 152, 192
civil wars
  defined, 11, 13
  domestic violence and, 92, 100
  First Ivoirian Civil War (2002-2004), 11, 91
  First Liberian Civil War (1989-1997), 11
  international pressure over, 139, 141, 142
  rape and, 170
  Second Ivoirian Civil War (2011), 11, 91
  Second Liberian Civil War (1999-2003), 11
  sexual violence and, 53, 60–61, 104, 152–53
  SSR strategy after, 138–39
  VAW before and after, 73, 78, 94–99, 109, 112–13
  women's movement during, 130
Clemens, Hawa, 79
coercion, 10, 43–44, 62–63, 98–99, 194
Coleman, Felicia, 86
Coleman v. Republic of Liberia (1898), 57–58
Committee on Gender Equity, Women, and Child Development, 84
common rape, 76
Comprehensive Peace Agreement (2003), 53, 134–35
conflict, defined, 11
conflict-recruitment mechanisms, 21–22
conflict-resolution process, 83
Convention on the Elimination of all Forms of Discrimination against Women (CEDAW), 25, 26–27
corrective rape practices, 19–20
Côte d'Ivoire's National Action Plan for the Implementation of UNSC Resolution 1325 on Women, Peace, and Security, 113
Côte d'Ivoire VAW. *See also* violence against women
  after Ivoirian conflict, 99
  blacklisting of Côte d'Ivoire, 140–41, 144
  domestic violence, 98–99, 100, 111
  gender desks, 124, 138, 156, 159–60, 180
  introduction to, 89–90
  before Ivoirian conflict, 91
  during Ivoirian conflict, 94
  legal systems and authority, 90
  Resolution 1325 action plan, 27
  sexual violence, 104
  summary of, 108
Côte d'Ivoire VAW and justice norms
  fieldwork conducted on, 9
  institutionalization impact on, 4–5
  overview of, 12–13
  patriarchal gender norms, 20–21
  peacekeeping presence in, 8
  political dynamics, 5, 45, 94, 159
  street-level officers, 13
  violence against women, 2–4
Côte d'Ivoire VAW response
  after Ivoirian conflict, 117
  domestic pressure from women's organizations, 112, 114
  international pressure, 112, 116
  introduction to, 109
  before Ivoirian conflict, 109
  during Ivoirian conflict, 113
  legal and institutional reforms, 117
  summary of, 118
creation of specialized police units, 125
Criminal Court E, 32–33, 71, 86, 136–37, 197
criminalization of FGM, 112–13
criminalization of marital rape, 84–85
criminal justice system
  community relations and, 69, 71
  distrust of, 24
  formal criminal justice system, 64, 108
  gaps in, 63–64
  lack of confidence in, 92–93
  lack of formal justice, 17–18
  non-tolerance of VAW, 196
  penalties, 26
  progress in addressing VAWs, 83
  response to women, 48–49
  sectors of, 6–7, 10–11
  women-friendly measures in, 110–11
criminal remedies, 90–91
customary authority, 55, 90–91
customary courts, 6, 54, 56, 59, 72, 89, 90–91, 206n3
customary justice for women, 56–57, 90
Cuttington College, 56–57

INDEX

Daily Observer, 58, 79
Danish International Development Agency (DANIDA), 86
death from VAW, 22–23, 76–77, 85, 100, 109–10, 179
death penalty, 84
Democratic Party of Côte d'Ivoire (PDCI), 112
Demographic and Health Survey (Côte d'Ivoire), 100, 104
Demographic and Health Survey (Ghana), 62, 63
Demographic and Health Survey (Liberia), 18–19, 67, 74–75
Detective Division of the LNP, 76
Devolution of Estates Act, 32–33
Disarmament, Demobilization, and Reintegration program, 104
discretionary decision-making, 168–69, 172, 175–76, 183
dispute-resolution systems, 59, 72, 90–91, 106
divorce, 54–55, 56–57, 59, 84, 91, 110
Doe, Samuel, 54, 59–60, 77, 79
domestic pressure from women's organizations
 Côte d'Ivoire VAW response, 112, 114
 Liberian VAW response, 77, 79, 130
 specialized police units, 125*t*, 129, 141, 150, 158
domestic violence. *See also* marital rape
 civil remedies, 25, 27
 civil wars and, 92, 100
 in Côte d'Ivoire, 98–99, 100, 111
 criminal justice problems, 24–25
 defined, 10, 18–19, 205n2, 206n1
 intimate partner violence, 10, 98–99, 206n1
 laws against, 30–31, 109–10, 112–13
 in Liberia, 62
 before Liberian conflict, 55
 partner-perpetrated sexual violence, 18–19, 22
 performance of officers, 188
 rates of, 19, 20–21
 referral of cases, 3
 reporting statistics, 23, 65–66, 199
 rules guiding responses to, 168
 survivor interviews, 9–10
 women's movement advocates, 48–49

Domestic Violence against Women at the Nairobi Conference, 74–75
Doss, Alan, 149
drug abuse and VAW, 22
dual legal systems, 54, 89–90

Economic Community of West African States (ECOWAS), 28, 79–80, 82, 83, 134–35, 144
Economic Community of West African States Monitoring Group (ECOMOG), 82
Ecumenical Women's Organization, 79
emancipation of women, 101
embedded units, 18, 32–34
emergence vision in Côte d'Ivoire, 159
emotional violence, 62, 100
ethnic differences, 90–91
European Union (EU), 43–44, 138–39, 158
ever-partnered women, 60–61
extrajudicial adjudication, 76–77

Fakondo, Kaki, 150
Family Law within the Civil Code, 110
family pressures, 91–92
Family Support Unit (Sierra Leone), 150
fear of domestic violence, 102
Federation of Women's Organizations in Côte d'Ivoire, 114–15
female chiefs, 93
female college enrollment rate, 56–57
female genital mutilation (FGM), 18–19, 29–30, 85, 109–10, 112–13
female traditional councils, 56
feminism/feminists, 28–29, 112
femocracy, 112
First Ivoirian Civil War (2002-2004), 11, 91
First Liberian Civil War (1989-1997), 11
forced marriage, 18–19, 29–30
formal criminal justice system, 64, 108
French Metropolitan Law, 90

gang rape, 83–84, 95–96
Gbagbo, Laurent, 94–95, 96–97, 115–16, 145
Gbarnga, 3–4, 9–10, 167–68, 173
Gbowee, Leymah, 132–33
gender-based violence (GBV)
 anti-GBV policy documents, 86
 against boys/men, 21
 defined, 10

230 INDEX

gender-based violence (GBV) (*cont*.)
  introduction to, 1–2, 3
  lack of reporting on, 17–18
  lack of training and expertise on, 82
  new focus on, 183
  officer training, 181
  rates of, 21
  specialized criminal justice system mechanisms, 18, 32
  specific resources for, 28–29, 117–18
gender desks in Côte d'Ivoire, 124, 138, 156, 159–60, 180
gendered violence, 72, 101, 108
gender inequality, 19–20, 30–31
gender power relations, 31
gender reform, 144, 160–61
gender-responsive policing, 5
gender status quo, 60–61, 62
General Recommendation 19 of DEVAW, 26–28, 29–30
German Corporation for International Cooperation (GIZ), 144
Gierycz, Dorota, 149
Global Summit to End Sexual Violence in Conflict (2014), 140–41
government ministries, 157–58
Government's Adoption of Rule of Law Agenda, 133, 144
Guatemala, 43–44
gynecological care, 60

handbooks for training, 28, 150, 164–65, 170–71
HIV/AIDS testing, 60
HIV infection, 22–23, 104–5
holistic approach to addressing VAW, 192, 197–99
Houphouët-Boigny, Felix, 93, 94, 110
humanitarian aid/assistance, 72, 78–83
human rights, 84, 113, 114, 128, 133, 134–35, 139–40, 141, 149, 180–81
Human Rights Division of UNOCI, 104
Human Rights Watch, 95–96, 114–15
human trafficking, 18–19, 168
Hunt Alternatives Fund, 153

Idris, Mohamed, 154
"Improvement of the Role and Status of Women in Liberia" workshop, 75
impunity and sexual violence, 6–7
independent units, 18, 32–34

infertility trauma, 175
informal criminal justice system, 108
informal justice mechanisms, 64, 97–98
infrastructural and resource constraints, 165, 182
inspector general of police (IGP), 153
institutional capacity, 43–44
institutional context of specialized police units, 135, 145, 154, 160
institutionalization
  defined, 3
  impact of, 4–5
  of Liberian dual legal system, 54
  specialized criminal justice system mechanisms, 192
  of special police units, 123–25, 146, 147*t*, 162
  of women and children protection section, 147
institutionalization of specialized police units, 123–25, 146, 147*t*, 162
institutional reforms in post-conflict Côte d'Ivoire, 117
institutional reforms in post-conflict Liberia, 83
Inter-Faith Mediation Council, 79–80
Internally Displaced People's (IDP) camps, 80–81
International Criminal Court, 94–95
International Crisis Group (ICG), 54
international NGOs, 9, 78
international norms
  criminal justice system, 24–25
  domestic implementation of, 41, 43, 47*f*
  implementation strategies, 49, 176–77, 193
  influence of, 48
  introduction to, 1, 2*f*, 7–8
  women's rights laws and, 31
international organizations (IOs), 1, 5–6, 78, 82, 83, 118–19, 124
international pressure, 4–5, 116, 126, 139, 148, 156
international relations (IR), 42, 43, 46
International Rescue Committee (IRC), 82–83, 85, 95, 97, 116
international women's justice norm
  adoption of international policies, 30
  central argument, 4
  confluence of international and domestic factors, 43
  implementation of, 6

introduction to, 1–4, 2f, 41–42, 47f
key terms defined, 10
methods and sources, 9
overview of, 12
political dynamics, 5
scope of, 8
specialized police units, 129, 141, 150, 158
street-level implementation, 48
summary of, 49, 193
theory of, 42
violence against women in Africa, 25
international women's rights norms
access to justice, 5
advocates for, 45–46, 61–62, 152
informal justice system, 64
institutionalizing of, 81–82
laws governing, 31, 48–49, 56–57
NGOs for, 9–10, 55–56, 65, 109
socioeconomic empowerment, 77
interviews, survivors, 9–10
intimate partner violence (IPV), 10, 98–99, 206n1. *See also* domestic violence
Ivoirian Association for the Defence of Women's Rights (AIDF), 112–13
Ivoirian conflict (2002-2011)
activism by women's movement, 31
institutional reforms after, 117
introduction to, 89
legal reforms after, 117
VAW after, 99, 117
VAW before, 91, 109
VAW during, 94, 113

Ja'neh, Kabineh, 130–31, 133–34
Johnson Sirleaf, Ellen, 61–62, 85, 87–88, 132, 150–51, 152
Joint Needs Assessment (2004), 127, 133

Karman, Tawakkol, 132
kidnapping of girls, 59–60
Klein, Jacques Paul, 128
Kpelle peoples, 56
Kvinna till Kvinna, 85

law enforcement. *See also* specialized criminal justice system mechanisms; specialized police units
domestic violence, 30–31, 109–10, 112–13
embedded units, 18, 32–34
governing women's rights, 31, 48–49, 56–57

male-run police stations, 32
rape, 106
reforms, 31–32
statutory law, 54–55
Law of Repression of some Forms of Violence against Women, 109–10
Law on Equality Between Couples, 110
learning visits, 141, 150
legal reforms in post-conflict Côte d'Ivoire, 117
legal reforms in post-conflict Liberia, 83
legal systems and authority in Côte d'Ivoire, 90
legal systems and authority in Liberia, 54
Leigh-Sherman, Theresa, 79–80
Lewis, Johnnie, 136–37
LGBT issues, 19–20
Liberation Tigers of Tamil Eelam of Sri Lanka, 21–22
Liberia National Police (LNP), 73, 149, 154–55
Liberian Conflict (1989-2003)
activism by women's movement, 31
domestic violence before, 55
institutional reforms after, 83
non-partner rape before, 55
non-partner rape during, 59
VAW after, 61
VAW before, 55, 73
VAW during, 59, 78
Liberian Frontier Force, 58–60
Liberian Women's Initiative (LWI), 79–80
Liberia VAW. *See also* violence against women
Criminal Court E, 32–33
domestic violence, 62
introduction to, 53
legal systems and authority, 54
before Liberian conflict, 55
during Liberian conflict, 59
police force units, 32–33
response to, 73
sexual violence, 67
summary of, 72
Liberia VAW and justice norms
fieldwork conducted in, 9–10
institutionalization impact on, 4–5
overview of, 12–13
patriarchal gender norms, 20–21
peacekeeping presence in, 8
street-level officers, 13
violence against women, 2–4

Liberia VAW response
  after Liberian Conflict, 83
  domestic pressure, 77, 79
  international pressure, 78, 82
  introduction to, 73
  legal and institutional reforms, 83
  before Liberian Conflict, 73
  during Liberian Conflict, 78
  summary of, 87
lobbying efforts by United Nations, 149–50, 157–58
low-income communities, 100. *See also* poverty and VAW

male-dominated legislature, 84
male hierarchy, 56
male-led nuclear family, 110
male power/superiority beliefs, 19–20
male-run police stations, 32
Maputo Protocol. *See* African Charter on Human and People's Rights on the Rights of Women in Africa
marital disputes, 59
marital rape. *See also* domestic violence
  criminalization of, 84–85
  exemptions for, 30–31
  informal resolution of, 106–7
  in Liberia, 67–68
matrilineal inheritance, 93
media presence of women's organizations, 150–51
medical care to survivors, 79, 82–83
methods and sources, 9
Ministry for Family and Promotion of Women (1993), (Côte d'Ivoire), 110
Ministry for the Condition of Women (1976), (Côte d'Ivoire), 110
Ministry of Family, Women, and Social Affairs (MFFAS), (Côte d'Ivoire), 138
Ministry of Gender and Development (MoGD) (Liberia), 9–10, 61–62, 75, 76, 81, 85, 151–52, 155, 199
Ministry of Interior and Security (Côte d'Ivoire), 9–10
Ministry of Justice (MoJ) (Liberia), 75, 80–81
Ministry of Solidarity, Family, Women, and Children (2011), (Côte d'Ivoire), 110
Ministry of Solidarity, Family, Women, and Children (MSFFE), (Côte d'Ivoire), 114, 115–16, 118–19

Ministry of Solidarity and Women (2000), (Côte d'Ivoire), 110
Ministry of Women, Family, and Children (Côte d'Ivoire), 9–10
Ministry of Women Affairs and Family, (Côte d'Ivoire), 112
Monrovia, 3–4
multiethnic coalition of women, 93
Muslim leaders, 55
My Sister's Place, 80–81

Namibia, 26–27
narrative accounts of women's movement, 131–32, 142–43, 151
National Action Plan for the Implementation of Resolution 1325, 86, 115–16
National Assembly, 159–60
National Committee to Fight Violence against Women and Children, 114
National GBV Platform, 114
National Gendarmerie, 117–18, 123, 138, 146–47
National Gender Policy, 86
National Human Rights Commission of Côte d'Ivoire, 114
National Patriotic Front of Liberia (NPFL), 54
National Policy on Population for Social and Economic Development (1988), 74–75
National School of the Gendarmerie, 117–18
National Security Council, 138
National Strategy to Combat Gender-Based Violence, 117
National Transitional Government of Liberia (NTGL), 61–62, 123, 128–29, 130–31, 132–33, 134–35, 136, 145–46
National Transitional Legislative Assembly (NTLA), 84, 135
National Women's Commission of Liberia, 80
negative reproductive health outcomes, 22–23
Nepalese implementation challenges, 45
New Penal Code, 83–84
Nicaragua, 43–44, 45–46
Nobel Peace Prize, 132, 142–43
"non-bailable" offense, 174
non-governmental organisations (NGOs)
  introduction to, 9–10
  reporting mechanisms for domestic violence, 103

SGBV Crimes Unit, 86
socioeconomic factors, 65
United Nations collaboration, 107–8, 179
Women's NGO Secretariat of Liberia, 85
non-partner rape, 18–19, 55
non-partner sexual violence, 20, 22
non-specialized agencies, 32
non-tolerance of VAW, 196
non-withdrawal policy, 169–70, 175
norm diffusion, 5, 8, 193–94
norm implementation, 4, 6, 9, 42, 49–50, 193
norm localization, 5
Norwegian Refugee Council (NRC), 167–68

Office of Training, Projects, and Evaluation, 118
One-Stop Centre in Kigali, 28–29
Organization for Children, Women, and Family (ONEF), 118, 138
Organization of Africa Unity (OAU), 79
Ouattara, Alassane, 94–95, 96, 140–41, 144–45, 159
Ouattara, Dominique, 143–44

partner-perpetrated sexual violence, 18–19, 22. *See also* marital rape
patriarchal gender norms, 20–21, 60–61, 92–93
peace-building, 28–29, 125–26, 128, 132, 136, 142–43, 152, 159, 162, 193–94
peacekeeping presence, 8, 125–26, 127–28, 136, 160–61
physical violence, 10, 62, 100
police corruption, 106–7
police reform, 125–26, 136, 155, 161–62
political context of specialized police units, 133, 144, 152, 159
political opportunism, 28–29
political stability, 44–45, 92–93, 159
politicization of women's organizations, 159
poverty and VAW, 22, 100, 101, 172–73, 177–78, 197–98
pro-prosecution policy, 169–70
prosecution approaches, 6–7, 66–67
protests by women's organizations, 6, 113, 142, 151, 159
Protocol on Gender and Development (2008), 28

psychological trauma of survivors, 22–23, 97, 175
psychosocial care to survivors, 79, 82–83, 115–16

rape. *See also* marital rape; sexual violence
 amendments to laws, 30–31
 civil wars and, 170
 common rape, 76
 corrective rape practices, 19–20
 criminal justice system problems, 24–25
 defined, 10, 206n1, 206n4
 gang rape, 83–84, 95–96
 laws against, 106
 non-partner rape, 18–19
 performance of officers, 173, 186
 rates of, 19
 referral of cases, 3
 reporting statistics, 23, 92–93, 107
 rules guiding responses to, 168
 survivor interviews, 9–10
 virginity and, 104–5
 wartime rape, 21–22
 women's movement advocates, 48–49
rebel threat to political stability, 159
record-keeping problems, 167–68
re-democratization, 28–29
regional organizations, 17–18, 27
Registration of Customary Marriage and Divorce Act, 32–33
religious organizations, 48–49
reporting VAW, 17–18, 23, 65–66, 199
Republican Forces of Côte d'Ivoire (FRCI), 96–97, 139–40
research design-case selection, 2–3
re-victimization of survivors
 criminalization issues, 74
 decreases in, 28–30
 help for, 24, 76, 111, 123
 introduction to, 3
 summary of, 163–64, 165–66, 181, 183, 186, 190
Revised Laws and Administrative Regulations for Governing the Hinterland (1949), 54, 56–57
Rule of Law Agenda, 133, 144, 161–62
Rule of Law Committee, 136–37
rules guiding street-level responses, 168, 183
rural-urban migration, 54
Rwanda, 28–29, 138–39, 141

Sande secret society, 56, 57
Saturday Courts, Sierra Leone, 32
Save the Children workshop, 82
Scarborough, Ellen Mills, 56-57
secondary victimization, 19, 73, 76
Second Ivoirian Civil War (2011), 11, 91
Second Liberian Civil War (1999-2003), 11
security sector politicization, 144
security sector reform, 145
self-blame, 67-68
Sexual Assault and Abuse Police Handbook (2009), 150, 164-65, 170-71
Sexual Assault Squad, 170
sexually transmitted diseases, 22-23, 175
sexual violence. *See also* aggravated assault; awareness-raising of sexual violence; rape
  civil wars and, 53, 60-61, 104, 152-53
  in Côte d'Ivoire, 104
  criminal justice system problems, 24-25
  defined, 10
  impunity and, 6-7
  in Liberia, 67
  non-partner, 20, 22
  partner-perpetrated, 18-19, 22
  rates of, 19
  wartime sexual violence, 21-22
Sexual Violence against Women and Children resolution, 74
SGBV Crimes Unit, 86, 167, 176-77
SGBV Joint Program, 85-86
Sieh, Beatrice Munah, 153
Sierra Leone, 20-21, 32-33, 63-64, 150
simple assault, 65-66, 111, 171, 177
social expectations, 91-92, 102-3
social harmony, 58, 59
socioeconomic factors
  empowerment of women, 77
  NGOs and, 65
  officers' perception of offense, 174
  support for survivors, 25, 168-69, 198-99
Soro, Guillaume, 159-60
South Africa
  death from VAW, 22-23
Southern African Development Community (SADC), 28
specialized courts, 34-39
specialized criminal justice system mechanisms, 3-4, 18, 32, 35t, 41
  domestic implementation of, 46
  gender-based violence, 18, 32
  introduction to, 3-4, 18, 192
  United Nations promotion of, 49-50
specialized mechanisms, 18
specialized police units
  advocates for women's rights, 152
  aggravated assault training, 164-65, 172, 180
  Brazilian police force, 28-29
  creation of, 125
  domestic pressure, 125t, 129, 141, 150, 158
  gender desks in Côte d'Ivoire, 124, 138, 156, 159-60
  Government's Adoption of Rule of Law Agenda, 133, 144
  institutional context, 135, 145, 154, 160
  institutionalization of, 123-25, 146, 147t, 162
  international pressure, 126, 139, 148, 156
  introduction to, 123-25
  political context, 133, 144, 152, 159
  political stability, threats to, 159
  reforms led by UN, 136, 155
  reforms not led by UN, 160
  security sector politicization, 144
  security sector reform, 145
  summary of, 161, 195
  Women and Children Protection Section, 125, 125t
statutory law, 54-55
street-level implementation of international women's justice norm
  aggravated assault officer training, 164-65, 172, 180, 184
  bureaucratic behavior, 61-62, 173
  defined, 205n1
  gender desks in Côte d'Ivoire, 124, 138, 156, 159-60, 180
  infrastructural and resource constraints, 165, 182
  introduction to, 48, 163-64
  in Liberia, 164
  performance of officers, 173-77, 186-88
  rules guiding responses, 168, 183
  summary of, 189
Suakoko, Queen, 56
survivor interviews, 9-10
survivors of domestic violence and rape. *See also* re-victimization of survivors; victims of domestic violence and rape
  criminal justice sector agencies, 17-18
  introduction to, 9-10

legal aid to, 79
medical/psychosocial care to, 79, 82–83
psychological trauma of, 22–23, 97, 175
psychosocial care, 79, 82–83, 115–16
retaliation fears, 97–98
re-victimization of, 3, 24, 32, 111
socioeconomic support for, 25, 168–69, 198–99
stigmatization of, 19, 23, 175

Taylor, Charles, 49–50, 54, 75, 79, 132–33
That Is Love (song), 63–64
Third World Conference on Women, 74
Trade-Related Aspects of Intellectual Property Rights (TRIPS), 43–44, 45
trade sanctions, 43–44
training
 aggravated assault officer training, 164–65, 172, 180, 184
 handbooks for, 28
 inadequacies of, 168
 lack of on GBV, 82
 police and gendarmerie training by UN, 117–18
transnational activism, 25
transnational advocacy networks, 11, 43–44

Uganda, 20–21, 45, 60–61
UN Conference on Women, 74
UN Country Team, 127
UN Declaration on the Elimination of all Forms of Violence against Women (DEVAW), 26–28, 29–30
UN General Assembly (UNGA), 127
United Nations (UN)
 aggravated assault prosecution, 179
 awareness-raising by, 126, 127, 139–40, 148–49, 156–57
 capacity building by, 128, 157–58, 160–61
 gender programming, 116
 ideational tools, 126
 international pressure from, 4–5, 116
 introduction to, 1, 2–3
 learning visits, 141, 150
 lobbying efforts by, 149–50, 157–58
 Peacebuilding Fund, 86–87, 123, 138–39, 158
 police and gendarmerie training by, 117–18
 reforms led by, 136, 155

reforms not led by, 160
 specialized criminal justice system mechanisms, 49–50
 specialized police units, 136, 141
United Nations Children's Fund (UNICEF), 80, 82, 116, 125–26
United Nations Development Programme (UNDP), 75, 116, 140–41, 155, 160–61
United Nations Division for the Advancement of Women, 6–7
United Nations Economic and Social Council, 78
United Nations High Commissioner for Refugees, 80–81
United Nations Mission in Liberia (UNMIL), 67–69, 86–87, 125–28, 135–36
United Nations Office on Drugs and Crime, 6–7
United Nations Operations in Côte d'Ivoire (UNOCI), 94, 104, 118, 139–40, 145–46, 157
United Nations Police (UNPOL), 155, 167, 170–71
United Nations Population Fund (UNFPA), 85–86, 116
United Nations Secretary General, 136–37
United Nations Security Council (UNSC), 6–7, 11, 125–26
UN Model Strategies and Practical Measures on the Elimination of Violence against Women in the Field of Crime Prevention and Criminal Justice (1997), 28
UN Office on Drug and Crime's (UNODC) Handbook on Effective Responses to Violence against Women, 28
UN Security Council, 26–27, 83, 127
UN Security Council Resolution 1325 (2000) on Women, Peace, and Security, 26–27
unwanted pregnancies, 22–23, 97
urban poverty, 101

victims of domestic violence and rape. *See also* survivors of domestic violence and rape
 blaming of, 67–68, 103, 104–5
 negative treatment of, 48–49
 secondary victimization, 19, 73, 76
 stigmatization of, 92–93, 106–7
 treating with sensitivity, 184–86

violence against women (VAW). *See also* Côte d'Ivoire VAW; Liberia VAW; women's movements/organizations
  in Africa, 18
  alcohol abuse and, 22, 101
  America specialized policing, 6-7
  anti-VAW programs, 82-83, 153
  Brazil specialized policing, 6-7
  death from, 22-23, 76-77, 85, 100, 109-10, 179
  domestic adoption of international policies, 30
  emotional violence, 62, 100
  female genital mutilation, 18-19, 29-30, 85, 109-10, 112-13
  holistic approach to addressing, 192, 197-99
  human trafficking, 18-19, 168
  international women's rights norms, 1-4, 2f, 6, 25
  introduction to, 17-18
  key terms defined, 10
  overview of, 12
  physical violence, 10, 62, 100
  poverty and, 22, 100, 101, 172-73, 177-78, 197-98
  reporting of, 17-18, 23, 65-66, 199
  simple assault, 65-66, 111, 171, 177
  specialized criminal justice system mechanisms, 3-4, 18, 32, 35t, 41
  summary of, 40
  unwanted pregnancies from, 22-23, 97
  war-related violence, 21-22, 60, 62-63, 108
virginity and rape, 104-5

Wallström, Margot, 140
Warner, Bennetta Holder, 57-58, 86-87
war-related violence, 21-22, 60, 62-63, 108
Women and Children Protection Section (WACPS)
  establishment of, 164-65
  informal rules of, 173
  infrastructural and resource constraints, 165
  introduction to, 2-3, 4-5
  overview of, 32-34, 123, 147
  rape and, 57-58
  rules guiding responses to, 168
  specialized police units, 125-29, 125t, 146-47, 154-33, 161-62
  VAW and, 73, 86-87, 118-19
Women in Development approach, 78
Women in Peacebuilding Network (WIPNET), 80, 85, 114-15
women-only institutions, 56
women's access to justice, 89
women's ministry, 49-50
women's movements/organizations. *See also* activism by women's movements; domestic pressure from women's organizations
  African studies literature, 195
  autonomous women's movements, 45-46, 129-30, 132-33, 143-44
  awareness-raising, 70, 82, 130, 141-42
  civil war and, 130
  media presence of, 150-51
  narrative accounts of, 131-32, 142-43, 151
  pressure from, 158
  protests by, 6, 113, 142, 151, 159
  regional organizations, 17-18, 27
Women's NGO Secretariat of Liberia (WONGOSOL), 85
women's rights. *See* international women's rights norms
World Bank, 127, 133
World Health Organization (WHO), 20, 62-63, 127

Yopougon neighbourhood, 96-97, 118